KANGAROOS,
KIWIS
and
ROUGHYEDS

Michael Turner
(with introductions by Brian Walker)

Contents:

© Oldham Rugby League Heritage Trust: 2007

Published by the Oldham Rugby League Heritage Trust: 2007

The moral rights of the author have been asserted.
All rights reserved. No part of this publication may be reproduced, stored in a retrieval system, or transmitted, in any form or by any means, electronic, mechanical, photocopying, recording or otherwise without the prior written permission of the copyright owner, nor be otherwise circulated in any form of binding or cover other than that in which it is published and without a similar condition being imposed on the subsequent purchaser.

ISBN 978-0-9546393-1-0

Printed by
Oldham Colourprint Ltd
Gravel Walks, Cross Street, Mumps, Oldham, OL1 3HH.

ACKNOWLEDGEMENTS:

I would like to give special thanks to the following individuals who have been most helpful in providing images or information during the preparation of this work over the many years of planning and research, with sincere apologies to anyone inadvertently overlooked:

Most notably:
Brian Walker: Without doubt the driving force who has brought this work to completion. Brian's input in all facets of the production of this book has been immense. Suffice to say that without his contribution, "Kangaroos, Kiwis and Roughyeds" would be a much less significant volume.
Mick Harrop: The chairman of the Oldham Rugby League Heritage Trust. A tireless worker in the quest to retain the and preserve everything connected with the history of Oldham RLFC.
Robert Gate: Rugby League historian. His encyclopaedic knowledge of our game is truly amazing.
Sean Fagan: An Australian rugby league connoisseur whose website "rl1908.com", and the information contained therein, has been a godsend in the preparation of this book.
Steve Brown: Lifelong Roughyed supporter whose technical expertise combined with a genuine and comprehensive knowledge of the subject matter has proved invaluable.
Sarah Turner: For countless hours spent on the design features that so enhance this publication.

Fellow trustees: **Tim Hughes and Dave Whitehead.**

Geoff Cooke - Ian Wilson - Roger Halstead.

Jean Brooks - Joe Warham - Tony Collins - Jeff Quigley (Aus.) - Bud Lisle (N.Z.) - Edna Stansfield - Allan Read - Trevor Simms - Harry Edgar - Sid Little - Vince Nestor - David Middleton (Aus.) - Andrew Cudbertson - Tom Wadsworth - Pat Walsh (Aus.) - John Donovan - Graham Bannerman - Terry Williams (Aus.) - John Etty - Stephen Bennett - Dave Parker - Joe Collins - Dave Blackburn - Brian Holland - Jim Rochford - Bernie Wood (N.Z.) - Tom Parkinson - Dennis Cooper - Alan Stacey - Jennifer Turner - John Blair - Frank Stirrup - Peter Fox - Andy Howard.

The staff at the Oldham M.B.C. Local Interest Centre for their kind assistance and cooperation.

Mary Turner and Ann Walker for genuine help and extreme patience.

During the period of preparation the Oldham rugby league fraternity has lost some of its greatest servants who also contributed to the publication: Alan Kellett – Fred Laughton – Don Yates.

The research of other rugby league historians has also been a major help and special mention should be given to the work of Raymond Fletcher, David Howes and Irvin Saxton.

The photographs used in this publication have come from many sources and time periods. They are therefore of varying quality. We have decided to include some of the more "faint and grainy" images because they are the only copies available for the match or individual involved. They are all relevant to this work and if not shown here it is unlikely they will ever be seen elsewhere. Most of these are from old newspapers salvaged from scrapbooks. If the original was available every effort has been made to obtain it. I'm sure one would have to agree that the quality of the publication has been enhanced rather than compromised by these images.

This work is indebted to the photographic archive maintained by the *Oldham Evening Chronicle* and it is to the continuing credit of the subsequent administrations that this wonderful collection of imagery has survived throughout the years.

Special thanks to all our advertisers whose funding has made this publication possible.

Cover and chapter leader pages designed by Sarah Turner.

THE OLDHAM RUGBY LEAGUE HERITAGE TRUST:

The Trust was formed by a group of Oldham RLFC supporters who first met back in 1995 to discuss the formation of the club's Hall of Fame.

At that time it was realised that in and around the town there were a number of people who owned representative caps, medals and other awards won by Oldham players from bygone eras, some of whom wished to donate those items to the Hall of Fame.

To protect the ownership of this collection and at the same time ensure it was kept available for generations of Oldhamers to come, the Trust, under the guidance of OMBC Museum, the Charity Commission and a local firm of solicitors, was formed.

Many of the items in the collection have been donated but from time to time the Trust bids for Oldham rugby- related items at auction, again in an attempt to either keep them in the Borough, or bring them back to the town. For instance, a deal has recently been negotiated to secure the future of a collection of medals and caps awarded to Sid Rix, one of the sport's greatest players. Rix, a three-quarter who played for Great Britain and who was selected to tour Australia and New Zealand, also represented the Oldham club in each of four consecutive Challenge Cup finals played during the 1920s. The medals which he was awarded for playing in each of those four finals are included in the collection.

As a result of the Trust's endeavours the people of Oldham now have access to one of the best rugby club collections of important memorabilia in the world.

In recent years, amongst other activities, the Trust has organised:
Exhibitions – a record attendance for OMBC's flagship "Gallery Oldham" - when its collection was displayed there.
Film shows - rugby enthusiasts attended the sell-out showing of the Mitchell & Kenyon collection of Edwardian rugby films in conjunction with the British Film Institute.
Books – Kiwis, Kangaroos and Roughyeds is the third from the Trust's presses.

Should you visit the Trust's website www.orl-heritagetrust.org.uk ,besides uncovering a mine of information surrounding the Oldham club's rich history and its players, you will find details of many books and publications that have connections with the club.

Foreword:

Extract from OLDHAM RLFC - The Complete History

In the early days of the Northern Union there was no greater attraction on the fixture list than a visit from one of the overseas touring teams. This, of course, meant the "Kangaroos" of Australia or the "Kiwis" of New Zealand.

In a future publication I hope to give a comprehensive account of all the Oldham games against our Antipodean rivals, but here I will just list the results with a brief résumé of the first encounters.

The text above was taken from my first book covering the history of Oldham RLFC which was published in 1997. It has taken some time but I finally got around to the task and a most fascinating project it has proved to be. When one looks at the interest level generated in the tour matches over the years, it is a reflection of the state of Rugby League in general. In the early days of the game, when 12,000 miles was truly a long, long way, there was considerable curiosity from the public to come and see these athletes who had travelled so far to demonstrate their skills. The "hype" factor was quite evident, even back in the Edwardian days, and the arrival of the tourists was always heralded with grand proclamations of their deeds and prowess on the rugby field. Sometimes these plaudits were well deserved, on other occasions less so.

The first official tour under the rules of the Northern Union - later to become the Rugby League - was a tremendous success. The team that would come to be known as "The All Golds" from New Zealand created great interest and played to big crowds. They won the Test series and their playing personnel so impressed Northern Union club officials that some were enticed to stay in England at the conclusion of the tour. Indeed two of the star players, the legendary Lance Todd and the great all-round athlete G.W. Smith, made their debuts against each other for Wigan and Oldham respectively on February 19th 1908, when two goals from Joe Ferguson and a try from Welshman Tom Llewellyn gave Oldham a seven points to five victory before an attendance of 25,000 at Central Park. This was immediate proof that acquiring these men from down under could be a sound investment. In contrast, the visit of the first Kangaroos in 1908 was something of a financial disaster. The Test series was lost and for the most part the attendances were disappointing. Nevertheless, the Australians persevered with the tours, although it is interesting to note that for the next two trips to the U.K. the visit was billed as being by an Australasian tour party. In truth there were only four New Zealanders in the 1911 squad and just one for the 1921 trip. After that first excursion the attendance figures for the Aussies got better until for many spectators the tour match on the fixture list became the "must see" game of the season.

Oldhamers were no exception. From the moment when Joe Ferguson kicked those first points in 1907 right up until Des Foy's last minute score in 1986 these fixtures provided everything that makes Rugby League the great team sport that it is. That is not to say that on some occasions the games did not quite live up to the anticipation. However, there were enough thrills, spills, genuine excitement and drama to make for fond memories of these encounters for those of us fortunate enough to witness them first hand.

Still, it is now over twenty years since the last visit of the Kangaroos, when on a bitterly cold night in 1986 the "no-hope" Roughyeds gave the Australians a mighty fright at

Watersheddings. It is forty-six years since John Noon's heroics with the boot gave the combined Oldham and Rochdale side a narrow victory over the 1961 Kiwis. And it is over fifty, yes fifty years from the time when the 1956 Kangaroos were demolished by the Oldham team that would be crowned worthy league champions later that season. Now, in these days of summer rugby, when the playing seasons both north and south of the equator are concurrent, it is hard to imagine that these grand events will ever resurface. Indeed by the time of the latter winter tours the itineraries were but a fraction of the original sorties when well over thirty matches would be played (45 on the first Kangaroo tour) and the tourists would still be in the UK over the Christmas and New Year period.

So, if it is confined to history books such as this that it has to be, then let the following pages delve deep into the rich vein of sporting folklore that encompassed the matches that Oldham played against the national teams of Australia and New Zealand. When what mattered most to the workers in the cotton mills, engineering works and other places of toil in the east Lancashire borough was the anticipation of what delights would ensue in the coming treat. Being able to cheer on their heroes - the likes of Joe Ferguson, Alf Wood, Bob Sloman, Jack Stephens, Frank Stirrup, Alan Davies, Bob Irving, Martin Murphy and Terry Flanagan - against the best the Kangaroos and Kiwis had to offer. Knowing that these wonder men, from the other side of the world - G.W. Smith, "Dally" Messenger, Duncan Thompson, Frank Burge, Dave Brown, Maurice Robertson, Clive Churchill, George Menzies, Reg Gasnier, Johnny Raper, Henry Tatana, Graeme Langlands and Mal Meninga - would emerge from the Watersheddings tunnel intent on lowering the Oldham colours and relishing the prospect.

Not so much "happy days", more ecstasy.

Here it is then, a comprehensive look at the tour games with additional features for the matches against the French, recollections from Roger Halstead (the rugby league reporter for the *Oldham Evening Chronicle* for over forty years), the World Club Championship and moving into the twenty first century with the couple of pre-season "warm-up" games by the new Oldham club against Australian "District" opposition.

Once again, special thanks to **Brian Walker** for his introductory narrative, not only to the whole book which follows, but also all the individual chapters.

For the main tour matches I have used the old fashioned "press-style" of scorers in CAPITAL letters. This is how the reports appeared as I researched them and I thought it appropriate to reproduce it here. Also the first time a player is featured in a match report, I have tried to include the forename and then just the surname for consequent mentions.
Some of the attendances in the match reports vary from those in the tour fixture list at the end of each section. The figure in the match report was usually taken from the local press coverage whereas the tour lists have been gathered from various sources.

Michael Turner - October 2007.

Introduction:

My earliest recollection of Oldham playing against a touring side was formed fifty years ago. It was the 1956-57 season when the club both topped the league and won the championship and the fixture planners had scheduled the side to play a mid-week match against the Australians. Nothing wrong

The 1956-57 Champions and impressive conquerors of the 1956 Kangaroos.
Back row: G. Jenkins (Coach), D. Vines, D. Turner, C. Winslade, K. Jackson, S. Little, J. Keith,
W. Howard (President).
Middle row: R. Cracknell, A. Davies, W.B. Ganley, D. Ayres, J. Etty.
Front row: F. Daley, Mascot, F. Pitchford.

with that, you might say, except the kick-off time for the big game was 3pm on a November Wednesday! There were no floodlights in rugby league back then.

I didn't watch much of the match. I just heard it. I was ten years old and a pupil at Watersheddings junior school. I remember during afternoon break being in the schoolyard - just a punt of a rugby ball away from the ground - watching the football specials unloading hundreds of supporters. It was a grey, damp, autumn day and the Ripponden Road area was packed with Oldhamers, collars up, heading for the turnstiles. For us it was begrudgingly back to the classroom trying to keep tally of the score as the cheers went up. The 4 o'clock bell had hardly stopped signalling the end of the school day before a bunch of us were scooting over to the ground only to find that the gates hadn't yet re-opened and it would be a frustrating wait until 10 minutes before full-time before we'd eventually be let in.

I didn't know too much about the Aussies – I don't think I even knew they played in green and gold - but I did know they were something special and that they hadn't come from the other side of the world to lie down. Three weeks earlier packers had squeezed 21,500 into the Watersheddings ground for a league match against Halifax and the atmosphere was pulsating. But, whilst the mid-week afternoon kick-off had ensured that the attendance for the Australian game was cut to half that of the Halifax match, when Derek Turner scored Oldham's third and final try the atmosphere was so electrifying it was as though the ground had been plugged-in to the national grid. Winning against Halifax, Huddersfield or Hull was one thing but beating the Kangaroos 21-2 was something else. I was hooked.

I haven't missed any of Oldham's matches against touring sides since. That's why I'm so pleased to be able to write this introduction to Michael's new book although George Orwell might have been a better choice. He wrote, "Serious sport has nothing to do with fair play. It is bound up with hatred, jealousy, boastfulness, disregard of all rules and sadistic pleasure in witnessing violence. In other words, it is war without the shooting." Words that could have helped form the opening paragraphs of many a journalist's report on a club vs. tourist encounter. But the ferocity was only one face of these often magnificent matches, the other being the fine players, wonderful football, sheer excitement, moments of drama and fabulous tries.

I'm a dyed-in-the-wool Roughyed and the gate-money would have to be prised out of my pocket to pay to watch a Wigan vs. St. Helens or Leeds vs. Bradford match, but wild horses wouldn't have kept me from Central Park to watch Wigan play the Kiwis or from Headingley to see Leeds take on the Australians. But, sadly, because the playing seasons both here and in Australia and New Zealand now run simultaneously, extensive tours are almost impossible to organise despite having both produced some of the most exciting rugby league ever seen which had an immense impact on the sport.

Here's a book that is equally important to the history of the development of rugby league down-under as it is to that of the Oldham club. It is a joint history because without clubs like Oldham acting as beacons to the early rugby-playing colonials the only code played in the antipodes today would be union. So, what happened all those years ago that would make such an impact on the evolution of rugby league both here and on the other side of the world?

The first ever rugby tour to these shores - in the days when union was the only rugby code - was  made by the New Zealand Native Football Team (the Maoris), who, during the 1888-89 season, played a massive 74 matches against sides spread throughout the length and breadth of the British Isles, including Oldham, to whom they lost on March 4th 1889, in one of the last games played at the old Clarksfield ground. The players were claimed by some as being both too controversial (three players walked off during a Test match against England in protest at refereeing decisions and it is said they also lost one match after drinking too much champagne!) and of being

The New Zealand Native Football Team of 1888-89.

professionals playing within an amateur code. By others they were recognised as a very serious squad who developed a combination of fast, attacking, running, open rugby and tough forward play, setting a style expected from all future New Zealand touring sides, whether union or league.

One thing is for sure - they played much tougher opposition than the 1905 All Blacks who were the next side to tour. By that time there were two different ways of playing rugby in the United Kingdom. There was the old style still played by many of the clubs that had opposed the Maoris 16 years earlier and the more crowd-pleasing, lineout-free style, played by those northern clubs who had since broken away from the grip of the Rugby Football Union to form their own Northern Union (later to become the Rugby Football League). Whilst the All Blacks returned to New Zealand winning 31 of their 32 matches, because of this split they avoided the might of clubs such as Hull, Bradford, Wakefield Trinity, Dewsbury, Halifax, Leeds, Swinton, St Helens, Widnes, Wigan and Oldham.

George (G.W.) Smith during his Oldham playing days.

Nevertheless, it was while the 1905 tourists journeyed home that the seeds for the first antipodean tour to the Northern Union were sown. Perhaps the main protagonist was Auckland's star back George (GW) Smith, who was also a successful hurdler and track runner and had been to England three years earlier when he'd competed in the Amateur Athletic Association championships. He'd been impressed then by what he'd seen of Northern Union rugby and the crowds that it attracted, and when he'd returned with the All Blacks it had developed to become even more of a crowd-puller. He must have impressed them too, having been approached to sign for one of the northern clubs - believed to be Oldham – which he eventually joined in 1908.

Each of the New Zealand players had been allowed just 3 shillings (15p) a day expenses and was paid no wages. Many would arrive home penniless and some jobless. Even then there had been cries of professionalism by some. The tour had generated a fortune for the NZRU, which unwisely voted its secretary and treasurer bonuses of 75 and 35 guineas respectively! This just spurred on the players to spread the news about the huge gate-paying crowds attending matches in northern England and the benefits Northern Union players enjoyed, as opposed to the pittance received by the tourists. Later that year Smith was in Sydney with the visiting Auckland team and met with several influential individuals including both James Giltinan, a well known figure in Sydney sporting circles, and Test cricketer and rugby enthusiast Victor Trumper. The financial success of the All Blacks' tour to the United Kingdom had been well publicised in the Australian press but had only succeeded in creating unrest amongst many of the country's leading players as the All Blacks

Side by side, the two most famous names from the early days of rugby league in Australasia.

Albert Baskerville and H.H. (Dally) Messenger, pictured in the 1907 New Zealand team group.

were now due to play in Australia. The recent New South Wales vs. Queensland game had attracted 32,000 gate-paying customers and the players had got nothing, an experience they didn't want repeating, should they be selected to face the New Zealanders.

Like the majority of revolutions it was no single issue that brought about change but Smith's discussions in Sydney coupled with the success of the professional game in England encouraged not just the first tour of the Northern Union by a New Zealand side in 1907 but the setting-up the following year of the New South Wales Rugby League in Australia and with it a second tour of the Northern Union - this time by an Australasian side.

Albert Henry Baskerville, a 24 year-old postal employee and a noted player for the Oriental club in Wellington, was also an enthusiastic visionary of the game. Spurred on by Smith, he became obsessed with the idea of forming a tour to the Northern Union. Early in 1907 he posted his proposals to the Oldham offices of Joseph Platt, treasurer to the Northern Union, and, by the end of March, Platt had cabled back saying that, with the proviso that the visiting team must be up to the promised strength, his proposition had been accepted. More than three-quarters of the 200 first-class players in New Zealand were believed to have applied to be included on the tour.

The outbound squad played three games against New South Wales and persuaded Australia's greatest star, Dally Messenger, to join them. None of the 26 selected players had ever played under Northern Union rules but, nevertheless, they won 19 and drew two of their 35 matches, including winning the Test series 2-1. A powerful Oldham side beat them 8-7, the first of many Watersheddings tussles against Kiwi and Kangaroo. Ten of the tourists either stayed or returned to play for Northern Union clubs, thus starting the introduction of overseas stars into the English game.

Sadly, Baskerville contracted pneumonia *en route* home and died whilst in Brisbane. Without both his and Smith's input the expansion of the game into the southern hemisphere would have been in serious doubt and as a consequence the history of the game here would have been quite different too.

Nowadays, the demands of satellite TV have curtailed, probably forever, the anticipation, excitement, and sheer enjoyment that many of us experienced from watching our clubs battle it out with those men from many thousands of miles away. Those of us who have grown up with the tours will enjoy this book immensely. Those who didn't will hopefully enjoy reading about what we enjoyed!

Brian Walker

OLDHAM R.L.F.C

NEW ZEALAND

1907 1907
1907 1907

OLDHAM R.L.F.C

AUSTRALIA RUGBY LEAGUE TOUR

NEW ZEALAND RUGBY LEAGUE

November 23rd 1907.
OLDHAM 8   NEW ZEALAND 7

Back Row.—W. Trevarthen, H. R. Wright, W. Johnston, T. Cross, A. Lile, C. J. Pearce, D. G. Fraser.
Third Row.—Harold Rowe, G. B. Smith, W. Mackrell, E. Wrigley, J. A. Lavery, C. A. Byrne, D. Gilchrist, E. L. Watkins, W. T. Tyler.
Second Row.—J. B. Wynyard, C. Dunning, L. B. Todd, D. McGregor, H. G. Palmer, H. S. Turtill, J. C. Gleeson, W. T. Wynyard.
Front Row.—A. Callam, Heni Tyne, A. H. Baskerville, H. H. Messenger, A. F. Kelly.

NORTHERN UNION.

A Mud Struggle.

SNOW, HAIL AND RAIN AT WATERSHEDDINGS.

All Blacks Lose Again.

THE PACIFIC STEAM NAVIGATION Co. *R M S*

Souvenir of the

NEW ZEALAND

RUGBY

12

Postal worker Albert Baskerville's letter, seeking approval for a tour of the Northern Union by a group of New Zealand rugby union players, had dropped through the Oldham letterbox of its treasurer, Joseph Platt, in the early weeks of 1907. Now, Baskerville and his trail-blazing Kiwis arrived in town having already played 13 matches against English and Welsh club sides. At Watersheddings they were to face their biggest test of the tour so far. They were here to play a star-spangled Oldham team that had won all 12 of its matches played during the season to date and which had already booked a place in the Lancashire Cup final. Come the end of the campaign they would top the league - consisting of 27 clubs - seven points ahead of their nearest rivals.

A line-up of notables from the first New Zealand tour: left to right.
J.C. Gleeson *(Treasurer),* **J.H. Smith** *(Referee - Widnes),* **H.H. Messenger,**
H.R. Wright, **G.W. Smith**.

Photograph courtesy of Sean Fagan.

(Opposite) Perhaps the finest tour souvenir of all time.
A photograph of the 1907-08 New Zealand touring team, the "All Golds", signed by all the squad.
Included are such legendary names as **George (G.W.) Smith, Lance Todd, "Dally" Messenger,**
"Bumper" Wright *and* **Albert Baskerville.**
Back Row*: W. Trevarthen, H.R. Wright, W. Johnston, T. Cross, A. Lile, C.J. Pearce, D.G. Fraser.*
Third Row*: H. Rowe, G.W. Smith, W.Mackrell, E. Wrigley, J. Lavery, C.Byrne, D. Gilchrist,*
E. Watkins, W. Tyler.
Second Row*: J.R. Wynyard, C. Dunning, L.B. Todd, D. McGregor, H.J. Palmer (manager),*
H.S. Turtill, J.C. Gleeson, W.T. Wynyard.
Front Row*: A. Callam, H. Tyne, A.H. Baskerville, H.H. Messenger, A.F. Kelly.*

November 23rd 1907.
OLDHAM 8   NEW ZEALAND 7

The match at Watersheddings was *"keenly anticipated from the day the fixtures were released."* Snow, hail and rain! These were the conditions that greeted the teams, but a good sized crowd turned up nonetheless. Oldham took the field looking "*spic and span*" in their new shirts and the crowd gave a mighty cheer for the home team, which was echoed as Baskerville's Kiwis, under the captaincy of Hercules Richard "Bumper" Wright, followed them out on to the pitch. Prior to the kick-off, brought forward to 2.45 pm because of fears over poor light, the tourists performed the Maori war chant, the "haka".

Albert Baskerville

The heavy condition of the playing surface made open play difficult and was probably responsible for two early failed penalty attempts, one from each team, when the normally reliable Joe Ferguson and "Dally" Messenger each missed the opportunity to open the scoring.

Oldham were having the best of the early exchanges and looked certain to score after a good break by centre Tom Llewellyn, only for his winger Arthur Oldershaw to drop the final pass. However, the Roughyeds eventually took the lead thanks to a FERGUSON penalty goal. The lead was increased soon afterwards by the opening try. Half-back Tom White fielded a kick from Hubert Turtill, the Kiwi full-back, and replied with a kick towards the left wing. Messenger half charged down the ball which then bounced awkwardly deceiving both himself and half-back Edgar Wrigley. OLDERSHAW capitalised on the indecision of the two Kiwi defenders to pounce on the ball and, using centre Llewellyn as a foil, he made to pass to the Welshman before racing over to score. Although unconverted, the try atoned for Oldershaw's earlier error and gave Oldham a five point advantage in what always looked like being a closely fought match. The last score of the half came after an infringement by Billy Dixon gave a penalty chance to New Zealand which was converted by MESSENGER. Half-time followed with Oldham leading 5 - 2.

The second period opened with the snow coming down thicker than ever. Oldham again took the game to the visitors with some vigorous play from the forwards in which Bert Avery and Billy Longworth were particularly outstanding aided by the ever consistent Ferguson. A scrum near the Kiwi try line set the scene for the next score when scrum-half Dai BEYNON took the ball from the scrum and *"dodged over in the twinkling of an eye".* The conversion was missed but the six point advantage meant that the tourists now needed to score twice to overhaul the Roughyeds' total.

In the failing winter light New Zealand set about the task with an extended spell of pressure on the Oldham line. However, the Oldham defence, defending the Penny Rush stand end of the ground with the snow and hail blowing into their faces, held firm. That is, until the very last minute of the game when George Smith broke out from his own half, kicked ahead and dribbled the ball to the try line. Joseph LAVERY was up to support the breakaway by his centre and duly beat the Oldham cover to dive on the ball and score the first ever try by a touring team at Watersheddings. MESSENGER converted superbly from the touchline, an effort that, notwithstanding the closeness of the score, was met with generous applause from the Oldham spectators. There was just enough time to restart the match and for Oldham to contain the Kiwis' last attack before the final whistle sounded. The teams thus retired with Oldham the victors by eight points to seven.

OLDHAM:
R.L. Thomas; G. Tyson, W. Dixon, T. Llewellyn, A. Oldershaw; T. White, D. Beynon; J. Ferguson, J. Wilkinson, A. Smith, H. Topham, A. Avery, W. Longworth.

NEW ZEALAND:
H. Turtill; J. Lavery, G.W. Smith, W.T. Tyler, H.H. Messenger; E. Wrigley, A. Kelly; C.J. Pearce, T.W. Cross, W. Johnston, H.R. Wright, W.M. Trevarthen, D. Gilchrist.

Attendance: 12,000

*The Oldham captain **Joe Ferguson** who scored the first points in a match against a touring team with opposite (above) **Hercules Richard "Bumper" Wright**, the New Zealand skipper and **Joe Lavery** the first Kiwi to score a try at Watersheddings.*

The tourists had arrived in Oldham by train on the Friday evening of November 22nd. They were initially conveyed to the Red Lion Hotel, Cross Street, where a banner was on display with the message, *"Oldham F.C. H.Q. welcomes the New Zealanders"*. After refreshments the party was then taken to the "second house" at the Theatre Royal in the town centre where the variety bill included such luminaries as; Agnes and Julius Zanzig, Madeline Rossiter, The Miners Quartet, Chanti and the Sutcliffe Troupe!

On the day of the match the New Zealanders were the guests of the Mayor, Dr. Robert Gourlay (also the club's physician) for lunch at the Town Hall, before being transported up to Watersheddings.

After the game the players and officials of both teams returned to the Town Hall for an *excellent dinner* provided by the Oldham Catering Co., with wines supplied by Mr. H. Rowley. Amongst the invited guests were Mr. T. Bolton and Mr. J. Grime, president and chairman respectively of Oldham Athletic A.F.C. Former Oldham players John Armstrong, Philip Sydney Stott and John Rye were also in attendance. It emerged that the new shirts worn by the Oldham players were subsequently presented to their opponents after the match, with a jersey also given to the non-playing members of the squad.

His worship the Mayor opened the after-dinner speeches making a point to thank Mr. Joseph Platt, treasurer of the Northern Union, for his endeavours in making the tour possible. Hercules "Bumper" Wright, the New Zealand captain, responded by saying that this was his first game played in snow! He went on to thank the referee and touch judges for their excellent and impartial service and also Joe Ferguson and his team for the able manner in which they played. He then proposed a toast to Oldham Football Club, after which the New Zealand contingent sang "For he's a jolly good fellow" in the Maori language! The proceedings were brought to a conclusion with a rendition of "Auld Lang Syne" followed by the Maori war cry.

Above: **The S.S. Ortona which brought the New Zealanders to England.**
The Ortona was built in 1899. She was used for the Australia service of the Orient Line - Pacific Steam Navigation Company until 1906, and then transferred to the Royal Mail Steam Packet Company. Later she was renamed the Arcadian and ended up being torpedoed in the Eastern Mediterranean during the First World War.

1907-08			
NEW ZEALAND	TOUR		
OPPONENTS	RESULT	SCORE	ATTENDANCE
Bramley	won	25 - 6	6,000
Huddersfield	won	19 - 8	9,000
Widnes	won	26 - 11	7,000
Broughton Rangers	won	20 - 14	24,000
Wakefield Trinity	drew	5 - 5	5,800
Leeds	won	8 - 2	12,231
St. Helens	won	24 - 5	4,500
Merthyr Tydfil	won	27 - 9	7,000
Keighley	won	9 - 7	8,000
Wigan	lost	8 - 12	30,000
Barrow	lost	3 - 6	7,500
Hull	won	18 - 13	12,000
Leigh	lost	9 - 15	8,000
Oldham	lost	7 - 8	12,000
Runcorn	lost	0 - 9	4,500
Dewsbury & Batley	won	18 - 8	7,000
Swinton	won	11 - 2	4.000
Rochdale Hornets	won	19 - 0	8,000
Bradford Northern	lost	2 - 7	2,000
Halifax	lost	4 - 9	11,000
Yorkshire	won	23 - 4	3,000
Warrington	lost	7 - 8	8,000
Hunslet	drew	11 - 11	19,000
Salford	won	9 - 2	12,000
Wales	lost	8 - 9	15,000
Hull Kingston Rovers	won	6 - 3	10,000
Cumberland	lost	9 - 21	4,000
England	lost	16 - 18	10,000
Lancashire	lost	4 - 20	6,500
GREAT BRITAIN at Leeds	lost	6 - 14	8,000
York	lost	3 - 5	4.500
Ebbw Vale	won	3 - 2	8,000
GREAT BRITAIN At Chelsea	won	18 - 6	14,000
GREAT BRITAIN At Cheltenham	won	8 - 5	4,000
St. Helens	won	21 - 10	4,000

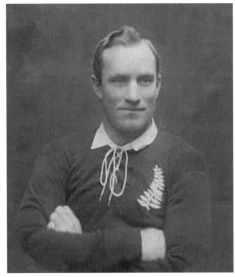

*The incomparable **Herbert Henry "Dally" Messenger**. Seen here in the New Zealand kit for the 1907-08 tour.*
The Australian three-quarter was the first international Rugby League superstar. A crowd puller and pleaser for both the "All Golds" and the first Kangaroos.

<u>Above</u>: Brochure to promote the 1907-08 New Zealand tour.
*<u>Right:</u> **George (G.W.) Smith**, the famous all- round sportsman who signed for Oldham at the conclusion of the tour.*

The 1907-08 tour was indeed a financial success. The players were well rewarded for their initial outlay of £50 each to take part. The attendances were good enough to see the touring party make a handsome profit for their investment, although the deciding Test played at Cheltenham was a notable exception. Dick (J.R.) Wynyard was top try scorer with 15 and Dally Messenger kicked 60 goals and added seven tries. Most appearances went to Hubert "Jum" Turtill who played in an incredible 33 of the 35 games.

December 26th 1908.
OLDHAM 11 AUSTRALIA 5

It was as if the New Zealanders had departed the revolving door in one direction as the Australians entered from another! The Australian Rugby Union had refused to accept payment to its players in compensation for time lost at work due to injuries incurred on the field so a breakaway eight club New South Wales Rugby League was formed in 1908. In an effort to quickly improve its status the fledgling league arranged to send a tour party to Great Britain to play matches during the 1908-09 season. A 34-player-strong-squad, which included a splattering of Kiwis, arrived at Tilbury on 27th September 1908. Vice-captain "Dally" Messenger returned for his second tour within months.

As the Wallabies (Australian Rugby Union team) were also touring in Britain the NSWRL squad soon became known as the Kangaroos which happily has remained the dominant marsupial down-under ever since!

By the time the Kangaroos arrived in Oldham they had played 23 matches, 14 of which had been won and three drawn. The first Test had already been played in London, ending in a 22-22 stalemate. Oldham had three players in the British side, forwards Billy Longworth and Arthur Smith and winger George Tyson. The Australians had also beaten a strong Lancashire County side that had included Oldham forwards Longworth and Smith and three-quarter George Smith, who had remained to play for Oldham when the New Zealand tourists departed for home, by 20 points to 6. Oldham forwards Bill Nanson and Joe Ferguson and three-quarter Billy Dixon had played against the Aussies in a Cumberland County side that had been whacked 52-10 and finally Billy Longworth had been included in a Northern League side that lost 10-9 at Everton's Goodison Park.

Oldham had lost just two of its 19 matches so far that season, were again riding high in the league and had reached the final of the Lancashire Cup.

A John Bull type figure waits for the incoming tourists.

Souvenir brochure for the first Australian tour centring on a photograph of the legendary H.H. "Dally" Messenger.

December 26th 1908.
OLDHAM 11   AUSTRALIA 5

Just eleven months after the New Zealand touring team it was the turn of the first *Kangaroos* to visit Oldham. The match was played on Boxing Day in bright sunshine, albeit still a frosty, cold, Watersheddings afternoon. To ensure the match went ahead the pitch had been covered with straw to protect the surface.

H.H. (Dally) Messenger

There was some discontent amongst the Oldham supporters in the run-up to the game as the admission price had been increased to one shilling (5p). However, the Oldham committee were quick to point out that this was a stipulation made by the league for all of the tour matches and the decision was out of their hands.

Oldham had played Hull K.R. the previous day with the outcome that Joe Ferguson, Billy Dixon and Bert Avery were unfit. Their places were taken by Billy Longworth, Dai Beynon and Tom White. In contrast Australia, who had been without star man "Dally" Messenger for their Christmas Day encounter at Leeds, now included him for the match at Watersheddings. Oldham were first to take the field and there was a special cheer for the classy half-back Beynon who was making his first appearance of the season. The applause was repeated when the tourists entered the arena, to be followed   by a chorus of jeers when referee Frank Renton took to the field.

The Australians opened with *great dash* in their play. The first action of the match saw full-back Charlie Hedley follow up his own kick and tackle George Smith (now in the Oldham ranks) as he fielded the ball. After only two minutes Oldham were penalised at a scrum. MESSENGER, now wearing the colours of his own country, opened the scoring with a penalty goal. Oldham replied and good running by Tom Llewellyn and "Birdie" Dixon got George Tyson away. He attempted to kick over his opposing winger Mick Bolewski to no avail, as the Aussie jumped up and blocked the effort. Alf Wood tried a shot at goal after a mark but was off target.

The play was end-to-end and after Smith had made a good break into the Australian half the tourists returned the compliment when Bill Heidke broke clear to give Jim Abercrombie a scoring chance but a great tackle by Wood saved the day for the Roughyeds. After this Oldham gradually began to take control of the game. Billy Jardine, the Oldham forward, was unlucky when a penalty attempt came back off the upright and then Longworth had a try

***George Tyson** scored Oldham's first ever points against Australia. He was also the hero of the Test series scoring a try in all three matches.*

disallowed after following up a kick by Dixon. Mr Renton's decision to annul the score, presumably for off-side, brought howls of derision from the spectators. Eventually the Oldham pressure paid off and slick handling from all of the home three-quarter line culminated with winger TYSON scoring a try.

Although Wood missed the conversion attempt, Oldham now had a deserved lead. The first half ended with the tourists on the offensive. The last action of the half saw Dixon save the Oldham line in the face of an Australian forward dribble.

Early in the second half Messenger fumbled the ball with the line at his mercy. Nevertheless, Australia tried hard to recapture the lead but a number of both drop goal attempts and penalties all proved fruitless. Oldham increased their lead after more fine handling by the back division. First Beynon and White moved the ball to the right from where Tyson set off on a cross-field run. Thereafter, both the home centres, Smith and Llewellyn, linked up with him to send DIXON over for a fine try. Again, Wood was off target with the conversion attempt. In contrast, Oldham's final try was a scrappy affair. Beynon dribbled the ball forward direct from a scrum where it rested over the visitors' try line. A mass of players hurled themselves at the ball with the result that a try was awarded to LONGWORTH. This time the conversion was entrusted to WHITE who made no mistake.

Five minutes from time Australia rallied and this time a spell of pressure by the forwards produced a try for Jim ABERCROMBIE. Messenger missed the goal. This was the last score of the match which ended in an Oldham victory by eleven points to five.

The press of the day gave special mention to Beynon, Longworth and Wood (kicking apart) for Oldham and stated that the tourists were best served by Hedley, Deane, Holloway and Abercrombie.

OLDHAM: A. Wood; G. Tyson, G.W. Smith, T. Llewellyn, 'B'. Dixon; T. White, D. Beynon; J. Wright, J. Wilkinson, H. Topham, W. Jardine, W. Longworth, W. Nansen.

AUSTRALIA: C. Hedley; H. Messenger, S. Deane, W. Heidke, M. Bolewski; A. Butler, A. Holloway; L. O'Malley, A. Burdon, S. Pearce, E. Courtney, J. Abercrombie, P. Walsh.

Attendance: 15,000   Referee: Mr. F. Renton - Hunslet

After the match both sets of players and officials, along with a number of "enthusiasts",

were taken in three wagonettes, via Ripponden Road and Huddersfield Road, to the Reform Club in the town centre, where Mr. H. Rowley of the Elevenways Inn, had provided a "thick tea"! A convivial atmosphere permeated the proceedings, which were punctuated by speeches from Mr. Joseph Platt on behalf of the Oldham club and Mr. James Giltinan, the manager of the tourists, who endeared himself to the gathering by pouring praise on to the renowned Oldham half-back of yesteryear, Arthur Lees. At the conclusion of the festivities the tourists departed for the return journey to their tour HQ in Southport.

> *Sandy Pearce; The Australian forward in the 1908 team who returned to play for the Kangaroos at Watersheddings in 1921. Notice the irregular hooped jersey. The light blue and maroon colours represented (as they still do) New South Wales and Queensland.*

1908-09 Australian Tour			
Opponents	**Result**	**Score**	**Att**
Mid-Rhondda	Won	20 - 6	7,500
Bradford Northern	Won	12 - 11	4,000
Rochdale Hornets	Won	5 - 0	3,000
York	Drew	5 - 5	3,000
Salford	Drew	9 - 9	6,100
Runcorn	Won	9 - 7	3,000
Cumberland League	Won	52 - 10	4,000
Leigh	Lost	11 - 14	6,000
Dewsbury	Lost	0 - 15	2,000
Yorkshire	Won	24 - 11	3,500
Hunslet	Won	12 - 11	6,000
Aberdare	Won	37 - 10	5,000
Warrington	Lost	3 - 10	5,000
Northern League	Won	10 - 9	6,000
Hull Kingston Rovers	Lost	16 - 21	7,000
Lancashire	Won	20 - 6	4,000
Barrow	Won	21 - 5	6,500
Halifax	Lost	8 - 12	6,000
Swinton	Won	10 - 9	1,500
GREAT BRITAIN	Drew	22 - 22	2,000
at Park Royal, London			
Treherbert	Won	6 - 3	4,000
Wakefield Trinity	Lost	13 - 20	3,000
Leeds	Won	14 - 10	12,000
Oldham	Lost	5 - 11	15,000
ENGLAND	Lost	9 - 14	7,000
at Huddersfield			
Widnes	Won	13 - 2	1,000
Wigan	Lost	7 - 10	4,000
Batley	Lost	5 - 12	2,000
Welsh League	Lost	13 - 14	6,000
Ebbw Vale	Won	9 - 8	5,000
Wigan	Lost	8 - 16	8,000
GREAT BRITAIN	Lost	5 - 15	22,000
at St. James Park, Newcastle			
Keighley	Drew	8 - 8	1,000
Hull	Lost	8 - 9	10,000
ENGLAND	Drew	17 - 17	3,000
at Glasgow, Scotland			
Cumberland	Lost	2 - 11	2,000
Broughton Rangers	Lost	12 - 14	12,000
St. Helens	Lost	0 - 9	1,500
Warrington	Drew	8 - 8	7,000
GREAT BRITAIN	Lost	5 - 6	9,000
at Villa Park, Birmingham			
Huddersfield	Lost	3 - 5	9,677
Barrow	Lost	3 - 11	6,000
Merthyr Tydfil	Lost	13 - 15	4,000
ENGLAND	Lost	7 - 14	4,500
at Everton			
Lancashire	Lost	14 - 19	4,000
Widnes	Won	55 - 3	1,200

The first Kangaroos undertook a truly massive tour. Under the captaincy of Denis Lutge, the Australians played 45 matches, of which 17 were won, 22 were lost with 6 drawn.

Top try scorer was Jimmy Devereux with 17. "Dally" Messenger kicked 65 goals and, with ten tries to his credit, he was easily the top points scorer. The Eastern Suburbs second-row forward Larry O'Malley, put in most appearances, toiling his way through 35 matches.

The Test matches ended with Great Britain successful by way of two wins and a draw. The drawn match played at London's Park Royal only realised a paltry 2,000, whereas the first Test at St James Park, Newcastle produced the best "gate" of 22,000.

Keepsake of voyage **R.M.S. MACÉDONIA**
Péninsular Oriental Co

Postcard of the "Macedonia", the ship that brought the first
Kangaroos to England in 1908.

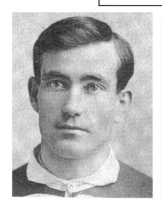

Two famous Australian threequarters
who found fame in England after the
tour:

Left: **Jimmy Devereux** top try scorer
on the tour who joined Hull F.C.
Right: **Albert Rosenfeld** who signed
for Huddersfield. His 80 tries, scored
in season 1913-14, will probably
remain a record for all time!

William "Birdie" Dixon, a try
scorer for Oldham against the first
Kangaroos. Also known as
"junior", he was so named
because he played at the same time
as another William Dixon who
joined the club first and was
slightly older. They came to be
known as Billy and Birdie.

A tour cap from the 1908 Kangaroos tour.

This cap was awarded to **Pat "Nimmo" Walsh** for his inclusion in the 1908 tour. A native of
Newcastle, N.S.W., Walsh was a tough and talented forward whose non-selection for the Australian
Rugby Union team some years earlier was one of the stepping stones of discontent that led to the
eventual formation of the professional game in New South Wales and Queensland.

1911 1911
1911 1911

OLDHAM R.L.F.C

NEW ZEALAND
RUGBY LEAGUE

November 11th 1911.
OLDHAM 14 AUSTRALIA 8

MONDAY. SEPTEMBER 18. 1911.

THE AUSTRALIAN TOURISTS.

The first official team of Australian Northern Union footballers who have just arrived in England.

The Great Britain team had played two Test matches in Australia the previous summer winning both to retain the Ashes. Oldham forward Bert Avery, who was selected to play loose-forward in this afternoon's game, played in the first Test in Sydney which generated a crowd of 42,000, a record for any Northern Union game played in either hemisphere.

The clash had caught the imagination of the Oldham supporters as the Aussies, although there were four New Zealanders included in the squad, had lost just one of their 14 matches played on tour so far, including victories over Lancashire, Yorkshire, Wales, England and against Great Britain in the first Test. It wasn't known then, but the tourists would go on to win two and draw one of the three match series to take the Ashes for the first time, although it would be a further 51 years before another Australian outfit would win this prize on British soil.

The Roughyeds were the new rugby league champions, having bolstered their side by paying a world record transfer fee to Salford for the Great Britain captain and three-quarter James 'Jumbo' Lomas. The Oldham backs for the big match included George Smith, the New Zealand vice-captain, Australian internationals Syd Deane, Tom McCabe and George Anlezark, British captain James Lomas and the former England rugby union full-back Alf Wood, who would be selected to play against the tourists in the second Test.

The kick-off was delayed for 15 minutes as the tourists had been delayed by fog on their journey from Manchester up to a mist shrouded Watersheddings.

[EWSPAPER.]   MONDAY, SEPTEMBER 18, 1911.   Sent prepaid to any address for 1½d. pa. 3s 3d half-yearly; 6s. 6d. yearly in advance.

THE AUSTRALIAN TOURISTS.

The first official team of Australian Northern Union footballers who have just arrived in England.

Back Row (left to right): C. Savoury, P. M'Cue, W. Noble, A. Broomham, J. Murray, C. M'Murtrie.   Second Row: V. Farnsworth, G. Gillett, R. Stuart, D. Frawley, C. Russell, H. Gilbert, R. Craig.   Third Row: E. Courtney, R. Williams, C. M'Kivat, C. H. Ford (manager), J. Quinlan (manager), F. Woodward, C. Sullivan, W. Farnsworth.   Fourth Row: W. Cann, P. Burge, A. Holloway, A. H. Francis, T. Berecry.   Front row: S. Darmody, C. Fraser, W. Neil, H. Hallett.

Photo by Kerry & Co., George-st., Sydney.

A remarkably well preserved newspaper photograph of the tourists from September 1911.

26

November 11th 1911.
OLDHAM 14   AUSTRALIA 8

The match against the 1911 Australian tourists was subject to great anticipation in Oldham due to the fact that they arrived in the town having suffered just one defeat (Wigan) and one draw (Hunslet) in their previous 14 games.

It was a misty Watersheddings that greeted the tourists as they took the field a quarter of an hour after the match was due to start owing to the touring party being delayed by a much denser fog as they travelled up from Manchester.

Tour captain Chris McKivat won the toss for Australia and chose to receive first possession. Joe Ferguson duly kicked-off. The ball was fielded by Albert Broomham who kicked the ball directly into touch which resulted in the first scrum of the match on the Australian twenty-five yard line. The visiting forwards came away from the scrum in a rush which was defused when Alf Wood scrambled the ball into touch. Next it was Oldham's turn to go on the offensive. Half-backs George Anlezark and Tommy Brice moved the ball out to Jim Lomas who broke clear only for his winger George Cook to miss the final pass.

The Australians responded and, after their compatriot Syd Deane had fumbled a pass, Broomham got clear only for Cook to redeem himself by checking his opposing winger's progress with a timely ankle-tap. Viv Farnsworth was proving a danger in open play and it took a good tackle from George Smith to prevent him from scoring. Arthur Francis was unsuccessful with a penalty attempt which occurred just prior to Oldham almost taking the lead. After a kick from McKivat was charged down by Anlezark, Lomas dribbled forward then dropped on the ball for what appeared to be a good try. However, the referee disallowed the effort ruling that the ball had already crossed the dead-ball line.

North Sydney wingman Albert Broomham, the first of the Kangaroos to see action at Watersheddings on the 1911 tour.

Two minutes later Oldham did register the first score when Billy JARDINE kicked a penalty goal. This seemed to act as a wake-up call for the tourists who set about their endeavours with renewed vigour. Broomham kicked cleverly over Cook's head and then re-gathered the ball only to be foiled by another fine piece of defence by Wood. The Australians were now in the ascendancy and the pressure finally told when another good break by the elusive Farnsworth created a try for Howard HALLETT. The conversion attempt by Francis was unsuccessful. It did not take Oldham long to hit back. In fact only two minutes later Courtney was pulled up for offside and this time WOOD put over the goal to restore a one point lead for Oldham.

Just before half time the Australians regained the advantage when, direct from a scrum, McCue fed the ball

*The ex-Australian international **E.A. "George" Anlezark** whose controversial try swung the game in Oldham's favour.*

to Farnsworth who sent out a peach of a pass to GILBERT. The centre hit the ball at top speed which carried him through the home defence for a great try which was warmly applauded by the Oldham crowd. FRANCIS tacked on the conversion to give the Kangaroos a half time lead of eight points to four. As the teams left the field referee Smith was implored by the spectators to *"play the game"*, as it seemed that a blind eye was being turned to a number of knock-ons and forward passes by the tourists.

The third quarter was dominated by the defences of both teams but just before the hour mark a kick ahead left the ball nestled over the Oldham line with Farnsworth, Gilbert and Broomham in hot pursuit only for an Oldham defender to make the ball dead in the nick of time. From the resumption McKivat went close and it seemed the Australians were taking control of the match.

The course of the game changed on a controversial decision that this time favoured the Roughyeds. After a scrum near half-way Anlezark burst forward and sent a clever punt behind Fraser. The two players then chased the ball to the Australian try line and although it appeared that Fraser was the first to ground the leather, to the amazement of the crowd ANLEZARK was awarded the try. WOOD converted to give Oldham the lead once more. The Oldham full-back was in great form and again saved his side with a crunching tackle on Russell who looked odds on to score.

*The South Sydney pair, **Howard Hallett** and **Herb Gilbert** who were the Australian try scorers. Here pictured side by side as they appeared in the official tour brochure.*

The next score came after Tommy Brice had dribbled the ball up to half-way. Fraser knocked on in trying to retrieve possession and from the resulting scrum Oldham were awarded a penalty. The position was fifty yards out from the posts and also half way to the touch line. A tremendous distance! Nevertheless, up stepped Joe FERGUSON who pointed to the posts to notify that he was going for goal. Always a man for the big occasion, the kick proved successful and according to reports *"still had good height when it crossed the bar"*. This mammoth effort by the Oldham captain deflated the visitors who succumbed once more with ten minutes to go when Lomas broke clear, drew in the remaining cover and sent COOK over for a "walk in" at the corner. The try went unimproved to leave Oldham the victors by fourteen points to eight.

OLDHAM:
A. Wood; G.W. Smith, S. Deane, J. Lomas, G. Cook; T. Brice, E.A. Anlezark.
W. Biggs, J. Ferguson, A. Smith, T. McCabe, W. Jardine, A. Avery.

AUSTRALIA:
C. Fraser; A. Broomham, H. Hallett, H. Gilbert, C. Russell; C.H. McKivat, V. Farnsworth;
W.A. Cann, E. Courtney, R. Craig, A.R.H. Francis, P.A. McCue, R. Williams.

Attendance: 10,500   Referee: Mr. A. Smith

Yours sincerely
Vivian Farnsworth

W. FARNSWORTH,
Newtown, N.S.W.

Outside half-back. Represented N.S.W. (Union Code) v. Queens-land, 1909. Came over at the time of "Wallaby" stampede.

Remarkably elusive in attack and unrivalled as a defender. Considered the finest player in his position who has ever played in Australia. Also a cricketer of note, having represented N.S.W. in the summer game; a brilliant batsman.

Represented N. S. W.		v. Queensland,	1910-11
,,	,,	v. New Zealand,	1911
,,	,,	v. England,	1910
,,	Australia	v. England,	1910
,,	Australasia	v. England,	1910

Age 23. Height 5ft. 7in. Weight 11st. 6lb.

Viv Farnsworth, another Australian who, along with his brother Billy, was enticed to stay and play for Oldham after the tour. Billy went on to become the professional for Oldham Cricket Club.

After the match the teams were treated to an *excellent tea* at the Friendship by Mr. & Mrs. Winterbottom, after which there was the usual round of speeches and toasts. However, it was reported that the tourists did not take the defeat in good order and left in something of an unsportsmanlike manner after the "King's toast".

This was actually billed as an "Australasian" tour but there were in effect only four New Zealanders in the party. It is thought that the reason behind this was that, whereas the first New Zealand "All Golds" tour produced a healthy profit, the subsequent "first Kangaroos" outing was something of a financial disaster. The four players from New Zealand were forwards Arthur Francis, George Gillett and Charlie Savory, along with half-back Frank Woodward.

The jersey was sky blue in colour with the badge incorporating both the Kangaroo and a fern leaf within a maroon letter "A", thus incorporating elements of recognition for the New South Wales, Queensland and New Zealand bodies.

It was a most satisfactory tour. The Kangaroos lost only five and drew two of the 35 matches played therefore making the Oldham victory all the more noteworthy. The Test series was secured for Australia by two wins and a draw. However, the choice of venues all outside of the north of England heartland produced disappointing attendances.

Chris McKivat led the tour by example appearing in most matches. He skippered the side for 31 out of the 35 games. Howard Hallett topped the try count with 20 followed by Viv Farnsworth with 18. New Zealander Arthur Francis kicked 49 goals which combined with his nine tries made him leading overall scorer with 125 points.

The 1911-12 Australasian Tour	Result	For	Ag	Att
Midlands/Southern England	Won	20	11	3,000
at Coventry				
Yorkshire	Won	33	13	4,000
Broughton Rangers	Won	8	18	12,000
Lancashire	Won	25	12	5,000
Wales	Won	28	20	7000
Widnes	Won	23	0	5,000
St. Helens	Won	16	5	12,000
England	Won	11	6	6,000
Hunslet	Drew	3	3	4,000
Northern League	Won	16	3	6,000
Wigan	Lost	2	7	25,000
Swinton	Won	28	9	4,000
Hull	Won	26	7	6,000
GREAT BRITAIN	Won	19	10	5,317
at St. James' Park, Newcastle				
Oldham	Lost	8	14	10,000
Leigh	Won	13	12	6,000
Wakefield Trinity	Won	24	10	5,000
Cumberland	Won	5	2	6,000
Barrow	Won	44	8	6,500
Runcorn	Won	23	7	2,000
Huddersfield	Lost	7	21	17,000
England	Lost	3	5	3,000
Salford	Won	6	3	4,000
York	Won	16	8	1,500
GREAT BRITAIN	Drew	11	11	8,000
at Tynecastle Park, Edinburgh				
Wales/West England	Won	23	3	1,000
Rochdale Hornets	Won	18	6	4,500
Halifax	Won	23	5	10,000
Warrington	Won	34	6	8,500
GREAT BRITAIN	Won	33	8	4,000
at Villa Park, Birmingham				
Leeds	Won	8	6	1,000
Hull Kingston Rovers	Won	5	2	7,000
Barrow	Won	22	5	1,500
Batley	Lost	5	13	2,000
Northern League	Won	20	12	2,000
Runcorn	Won	54	6	1,500

The 1911-12 tour badge.

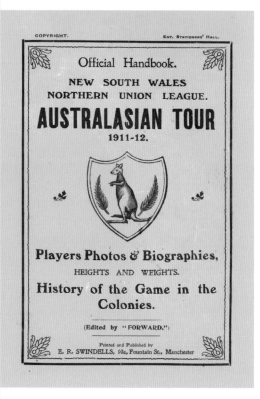

A copy of the official handbook of the tour issued by the Northern Union and printed in Manchester.

OLDHAM v. AUSTRALIANS

STEWARTS PATRIOTIC OVERCOAT OFFER

Here's a special offer for next Saturday's match—and there's two special reasons for it too. First, we want to extend the glad hand of friendship to our kith and kin from over-seas, and secondly, in view of the great interest evinced in the visit of The Colonials we feel that some special recognition from The King Tailors and Football Tailors is but right and proper. Our offer is:

2 Coats for every 2 tries-- both teams alike

or in more precise phraseology: We will present one of our Famous Overcoats to every Oldham or Australian Player who scores 2 tries, and in addition we will give an extra Coat to any Spectator each scorer brings along with him. Play up, Boys!— there's no limit, 2 Coats or 20 are all the same to Stewarts, The King Tailors. All we want is a keen, honest, sportsmanlike encounter—and may the best team win!

And Mr. Spectator, when you've welcomed your favourites into the arena, may we ask for just "three more" for The Kangaroos. Remember, as Kipling puts it, "They're sons of the great white mother"—striving for the honour of the same old flag tho' flown beneath the Southern Cross. Give them a hearty, rousing reception too—a bit of real old Lancashire.

Stewarts
THE KING TAILORS,
83, YORKSHIRE STREET,

Branches in most large towns between London and Aberdeen, including Bolton, Preston, Rochdale, Blackburn, Liverpool, Derby, Leicester, Swansea, &c., &c.

A tempting offer for the players of both the Australian and Oldham teams from the local outlet of Stewarts, the "King" tailors. This advertisement appeared in the local papers during the week leading up to the match on the rather intriguing date of November 11th, 1911.

Arthur "Bolla" Francis:
The New Zealand goal-kicking, second-row forward, who top scored for the 1911 Australasian tourists.

1911 tour captain
Chris McKivat

Alf Wood:
Produced a fine display on defence for the Roughyeds.
Full-back Alf would continue to be a thorn in the Australians' side especially for his heroics in the famous "Rorkes Drift" Test in Sydney in 1914

George Cook:
Scored a late try to seal the Oldham victory.

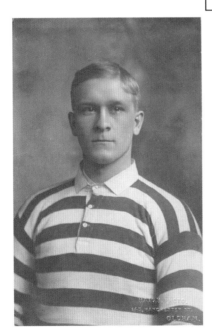

Left: **Sid Deane** *and right:*
Tom McCabe *who, along with George Anlezark, formed a trio of ex - Kangaroos in the* **Oldham** *team for the 1911 tour match.*

1921 1922
1921 1922

OLDHAM R.L.F.C

AUSTRALIA RUGBY LEAGUE TOUR

NEW ZEALAND RUGBY LEAGUE

November 26th 1921.
OLDHAM 5 AUSTRALIA 16

A BROKEN RECORD

Oldham Defeated by the Australians

GLIMPSES OF BRILLIANCE

C BLINKHORN THE SPEEDY THREE QUARTER

TUESDAY, JANUARY 17, 1922.

OLDHAM'S RECORD

ONLY TEAM TO BEAT ALL TOURISTS

January 16th 1922.
OLDHAM 15 AUSTRALIA 5

Oldham played the Australians twice during the 1921-22 tour making up for the fact that it had been ten years since the Kangaroos had last visited Watersheddings. The First World War had intervened of course but by the time the second of those two matches against Oldham had been played Great Britain had won back the Ashes, lost them again, and won them back for a second time!

The Ashes - lost here during the 1911-12 series - had been reclaimed in Australia back in 1914 when the Lions won a three match series by two Tests to one, not arriving home until seven weeks after the outbreak of the war. Oldham's three tourists, full-back Alf Wood, three-quarter Billy Hall and forward Dave Holland had each played in the third and deciding Test which is now enshrined in rugby league folk-lore as the "Rorke's Drift Test".

It seemed that the guns had hardly stopped smoking before the British again toured down-under. Oldham provided three players to the 1920 squad, full-back Alf Wood – who, at the age of 36, became the oldest player to tour – the very talented Welsh three-quarter Evan Davies and Oldham-born forward Herman Hilton. The Kangaroos, billed very much as the underdogs, snatched back the mythical trophy when they won the first two Tests of a three match series.

A year later the Australians were back here and by the time the second of the two matches against the Roughyeds was due to be played the Lions had won the first and third Tests to again reclaim the Ashes. The Australians, who had so far won 14 of their 17 matches against club sides, faced tough opposition from the Roughyeds for this, the first of the two games. The Watersheddings side had appeared in three consecutive Lancashire Cup finals and by the end of the 1921-22 season would sit at the top of the rugby league winning 29 and drawing one of their 36 matches. Of the 13 players who had faced the Australians ten years earlier only stalwart forward Joe Ferguson remained to play against them this time.

The tourists, who were billeted in Harrogate, arrived at Oldham's Clegg St. railway station and after being welcomed by the Oldham president Mr. Tom Taylor a light lunch was taken at the nearby Café Monico. Oldham were at full strength, the team including British tourists Herman Hilton, Billy Hall, Alf Wood and Evan Davies, international forwards Rod Marlor and, of course, Ferguson. Australia had suffered a blow when star winger Harold Horder was ruled out after picking up an injury in the previous game against St Helens.

The 1921-22 tourists on board ship, en route to England.

November 26th 1921.
OLDHAM 5   AUSTRALIA 16

The visit of the 1921 tourists was as eagerly anticipated as were the previous visits of the Kangaroos. Their compatriot, former tourist and Oldham favourite E.A. "George" Anlezark, was amongst the welcoming party to greet the tourists on their arrival. The touring party arrived from their headquarters just after mid-day. When their train arrived in Oldham the visitors were immediately conveyed to the Café Monico for lunch before travelling on to Watersheddings.

Both sides were well represented with the notable absence of Harold Horder from the Australian ranks, the famous international having been injured in the previous game at St Helens. Oldham were the first team to come on to the pitch which had been covered with straw to protect it from frost. They were followed by the Australians who turned out in light blue jerseys. Included in the team was hooker Sandy Pearce who had toured with the first Kangaroos back in 1908 and, now aged 38, was making his second appearance at Watersheddings. The local press stated that *the entrance of the teams was captured by Kinematographers"*. Before the start the Kangaroos treated the crowd to their usual war-cry.

Joe Ferguson kicked off for the home team and, after the Australians failed to deal with the kick effectively, an early bout of Oldham pressure culminated with a penalty attempt by the same player. However, the chance was missed and the next serious action featured Cec Blinkhorn, the Australian right wing, being brought down just short of the line.

The early exchanges showed the Aussie forwards to the fore in the scrummaging department while the Oldham six fared better in loose play. Oldham took the lead on thirteen minutes when the tourists were caught offside and Ernie KNAPMAN landed a goal from just inside the Australian half of the field. The Kangaroos then enjoyed a spell on attack with wingers Blinkhorn and George Carstairs both going close. Relief came for the Roughyeds when Herman Hilton and Willie Thomas dribbled the ball away up to half way. The Australian defence dithered in trying to control the situation which let in the home forwards to secure possession and Maurice TIGHE was on hand to back up his pack to good effect, grasping hold of the ball to score an unconverted try.

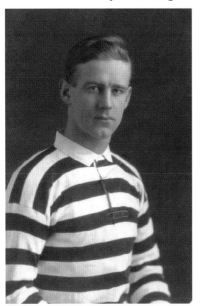

*Full-back **Ernie Knapman** who opened the scoring.*

Just when it seemed that Oldham were gaining the upper hand an attack by the home side broke down on the visitors twenty-five yard line. BLINKHORN scooped up the ball and with Knapman out of position, having linked with the attack, he raced away through three-quarters the length of the field for a try. It appeared that the Oldham defence was somewhat distracted as no one gave chase. Soon afterwards, the Australians increased their advantage when Frank BURGE scored from what the home side maintained was a forward pass from Charles Fraser. Worse was to follow when the referee signalled that the conversion by Duncan THOMPSON was successful. Apparently the kick was from an easy position and the official must have assumed that the kick would inevitably succeed. The touch judges (and the crowd) failed to agree but the score was allowed to stand.

Oldham put their misfortune behind them and finished the half on attack. Reg Farrar got away and kicked past Rex Norman. Tighe made up ground well to take the ball, only to be held up in a last gasp tackle. The home scrum-half had opportunity to unload the ball but a lack of support meant that the chance was lost. Then Jim Finnerty was held close to the line before a failed penalty attempt by Ferguson brought the first half to an end with the tourists ahead by eight points to five.

In the second period Oldham pulled Bob Sloman out of the pack to play as an extra three-quarter. This tactic brought more Oldham pressure but the Australian tackling was up to the task and when Dick Vest fielded a kick by Billy Hall, some snappy passing by the tourists led to Carstairs putting BURGE over for his second try. Jim Craig failed with the goal attempt, as did Ferguson when Oldham were awarded a penalty for a deliberate knock on by Fraser. Thompson, the Kangaroos scrum-half was now running the show as his team began to take control of the game. First the tricky half-back broke clear and only a forward pass prevented the visitors from extending their lead. Then a magnificent handling movement by no fewer than eight players ended up with Carstairs held on the line. After regaining possession, the home team had Evan Davies to thank for a relieving clearance kick which took play back to the half-way line.

Oldham looked like scoring when Ferguson dribbled the ball past Norman, but this time Burge displayed his defensive skills by being on hand to make the ball dead. Oldham continued to press the Australian line but poor finishing allied to the fact that the tourists

Cec Blinkhorn and Frank Burge who each scored two tries as the 1921 Kangaroos became the first touring team to defeat Oldham. (Caught here in caricature by Hull cartoonist Ern Shaw.)

now were also employing five three-quarters were enough to keep the Roughyeds at bay. The last score of the match came, not unexpectedly, after another break by Thompson. This time he was supported by BLINKHORN and the fleet-footed winger had the necessary pace to outstrip the Oldham cover for his second try. Fittingly it was THOMPSON who converted to give his side the spoils by sixteen points to five.

For Oldham, Maurice Tighe, Herman Hilton and Bob Sloman were the pick of the day. However, the man of the match was undoubtedly Thompson, ably supported by his two- try colleagues, Burge and Blinkhorn.

OLDHAM:
E. Knapman; J. Finnerty, W. Hall, E. Davies, R. Farrar; A. Bates, M. Tighe;
J. Collins, J. Ferguson, T. Rees, R. Sloman, H. Hilton, W. Thomas.

AUSTRALIA:
R. Norman; C. Blinkhorn, J. Craig, R. Vest, G. Carstairs; C. Fraser, D. Thompson;
W. Schultz, S. Pearce, F. Ryan, F. Burge, W. Richards, R. Latta.

Attendance: 15,344   Referee: Mr J. Speight - Wakefield

IS THIS YOUR PHOTO ?

IF SO, CALL ON US FOR YOUR PRIZE

This photograph of the crowd for the Australian game at Watersheddings on November 26th 1921 appeared in the "Oldham Standard" the week after the match. If you were the lucky circled figure you could claim a reward from the newspaper's office. The gift? A ten shilling voucher redeemable from any of the businesses which advertised in the "Standard". A considerable prize in 1921.

After the match the teams assembled at the Oldham Central Conservative Club for the post match festivities, where the tourists were in much demand for autographs. Oldham club president, Mr. G.W. Holden, conceded that, on the day, the best team had won. In the concluding speeches he stated that he hoped the visitors would return with a kindly thought for Oldham Football Club. In reply the tour manager Mr George (S.G.) Ball said he was proud to be associated with the first touring team to win at Watersheddings. He went on to add that, "*Who in Australia, particularly the Eastern states, had not heard of the famous Oldham Football Club?*" The official had certainly done his homework for he went on to recite the names of all the Oldham players who had ever toured down under and gave special mention to Tom McCabe who, having relocated to Australia as a young man, brought much needed expertise of the Northern Union game which led to him becoming a tourist with the first Kangaroos, before he returned to enjoy a successful spell with Oldham. Charles Fraser, who skippered the Kangaroos on the day, recalled having played in Oldham in 1911 and had assured his team-mates that a good time was guaranteed on their visit.

The final word was with E.A. Anlezark who said he regarded himself as an Australian first and an Oldhamer second and was glad to say that the Oldham club had given the Kangaroos *"a gradely do!"* The evening was brought to a close with a rendition of "Auld Lang Syne" followed by the Aussie war-cry.

Charles "Chook" Fraser who captained the Kangaroos at Oldham in the match at Watersheddings on November 26th, 1921.

Back Row.—W. Richards, H. Caples, A. Latta, N. Potter, C. Blinkhorn, R. Townsend, N. Broadfoot, E. S. Brown.

Third Row.—S. Pearce, F. Burge, Rex Norman, R. Vest, G. Carstairs, C. Prentice, W. Schultz, J. C. Ives, J. Craig.

Second Row.—E. McGrath, C. Fraser (Vice-Capt.), W. A. Cann, L.A. Cubitt, S. G. Ball, J. Watkins, H. Horder.

Front Row.—B. Gray, D. Thompson, F. Ryan, H. Peters, A. Johnson.

Again promoted as an Australasian tour, this time in reality there was just one New Zealander in the 28-man party, five-eighth (stand-off half), Bert Laing who must have joined up with the tour party after the official photo above.

January 16th 1922.
OLDHAM 15   AUSTRALIA 5

This second encounter at Watersheddings for the 1921-22 Kangaroos was organized mid-tour with the match against high-flying Oldham probably arranged to boost the tour receipts before the long journey home. The match was played on a Monday afternoon with a 2.45pm kick-off. The Kangaroos must have been feeling the strain coming to Watersheddings at the end of an arduous tour and just two days after an almighty, series-deciding clash with Great Britain in the third Test at Salford. As chance would have it, Oldham went into the match having had a blank weekend due to the postponement of their scheduled game at Bradford. Consequently, the Roughyeds must have been better prepared than their antipodean rivals, notwithstanding the loss of skipper Herman Hilton, who was rested after putting in a sterling performance in the Test match. He was replaced in the pack by Welshman Thomas Rees. The Australians put out a strong side including star wingmen Harold Horder and Cecil Blinkhorn, and centre Edwin Brown, who was making only his third appearance after being injured early in the tour. It was a wonder that the match took place at all after heavy snow over the weekend threatened to cancel the fixture. However, groundsman Sam Ogden and a team of volunteers worked through the Sunday night and Monday morning to clear the pitch with the aid of horse-drawn carts. The inclement weather kept the attendance down, nevertheless six thousand hearty souls made their way up the hill to take in the spectacle.

*Star winger **Harold Horder** was in the Australian team for this second meeting with Oldham on the tour...*

The conditions, later described as the worst of the tour, did not make for good open rugby. What there was of it came in the first half. Stand-in forward REES gave Oldham the lead when he stormed over for a try after a clever inside pass from scrum-half Maurice Tighe, who in turn failed with the conversion attempt. The advantage was increased when centre Evan Davies made good ground after receiving a wide pass. He handed the ball on to Reg FARRAR who rounded Horder, for a fine try improved by Ernie KNAPMAN. The Kangaroos responded with the best score of the match. As in the previous game, Duncan Thompson was causing Oldham no end of problems. A deft pass from the Aussie scrum-half got Horder away. Frank Burge was there in support and the move was finished off by BLINKHORN who had crossed from the opposite wing. Jim Craig missed the conversion but the Oldham spectators were generous in their applause for what was a splendid try. Half-time duly followed with the score Oldham eight, Australia three.

The second half was a defence-dominated, irritable affair. After a number of altercations between the teams, referee Mr Robinson of Bradford, finally lost patience and dismissed Bob Sloman and Clarrie Ives for fighting. Two KNAPMAN penalty goals, the latter after a "mark" (a free-kick awarded after a clean catch from a kick by an opponent) by stand-off Jerry Donovan, were countered by a solitary success by THOMPSON for Australia. Horder was injured and played out the last quarter at full-back. Just before the final whistle FARRAR scored his second try after following up a dribble by Jack Collins. The score went unconverted to leave Oldham winners by fifteen points to five.

*... but it was the Oldham favourite, **Reg Farrar,** who stole the show with two tries.*

OLDHAM:

E. Knapman; E. Thomas, W. Hall, E. Davies, R. Farrar; J. Donovan, M. Tighe;
F. Brown, A. Tomkins, R. Marlor, R. Sloman, T. Rees, J. Collins.

AUSTRALIA:

R. Norman; H. Horder, R. Vest, E. Brown, C. Blinkhorn; J. Craig, D. Thompson;
F. Ryan, C. Prentice, R. Latta, J. Ives, R. Townsend, F. Burge.

Attendance: 6,000   Referee: Mr. R. Robinson - Bradford.

Compared with previous games against the touring teams the after-match festivities were somewhat simpler. Nevertheless it was reported that a convivial atmosphere pervaded the pavilion where the teams and officials took tea. What is more, Sloman and Ives were seen to be sharing a drink together and apologising to each other for their earlier indiscretion.

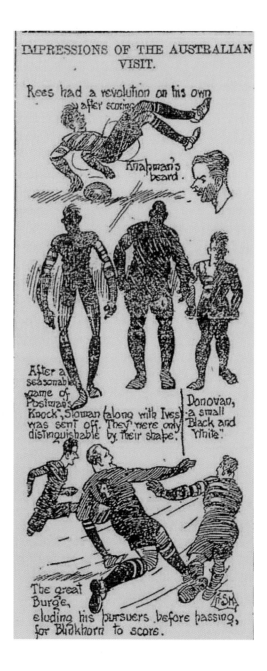

The Green Final's cartoonist "ASM" (left) gives his interpretation of some of the proceedings at Watersheddings on January 16th and (below) alludes to the great interest in the first match in November, as the father of the little girl is put in mind of Mr A.J. Swann, the Oldham secretary, who would have dealt with ticket applications.

Overheard in the Park last Sunday (?)
"Oh! Daddy, do come and look at the swans."
"Ah, that reminds me I've forgotten to write for a ticket for the Australian match."

A grand souvenir of the match in January 1922. - A collection of autographs from both teams.
Not only the Australian stars: Cec Blinkhorn, Duncan Thompson, Harold Horder, Les Cubitt etc but
also some of Oldham's greatest: Billy Hall, Evan Davies, Bob Sloman, along with Tom Sellers, then
on the Oldham F.C. committee and a veteran of many years service to the club going back to his
playing days when he turned out for the Roughyeds in the first season of the Northern Union in
1895. "One of the lads", indeed!

The 1921-22 Australian Tour	Result	Score		Att
Salford	Won	48	3	9,000
Keighley	Won	29	0	5,500
Hull Kingston Rovers	Won	26	6	13,000
Bradford Northern	Won	53	3	3,000
GREAT BRITAIN	Lost	5	6	31,700
at Headingley, Leeds				
Widnes	Won	28	4	11,000
Broughton Rangers	Won	18	6	17,000
England	Lost	4	5	12,000
Wigan	Won	14	6	24,308
Leeds	Won	11	5	14,000
Wakefield Trinity	Won	29	3	6,000
Batley	Won	33	7	6,000
Warrington	Lost	5	8	16,000
York	Lost	3	9	5,000
GREAT BRITAIN	Won	16	2	21,504
at The Boulevard, Hull				
Bramley	Won	92	7	1,500
Rochdale Hornets	Won	16	2	12,000
Swinton	Lost	0	9	6,000
Huddersfield	Won	36	2	12,000
St. Helens	Won	16	8	6,000
Oldham	Won	16	5	15,344
Lancashire League	Won	29	6	17,000
Barrow	Won	24	15	8,000
Yorkshire	Won	24	8	6,000
Wales	Won	21	6	13,000
Lancashire	Lost	6	8	6,000
Dewsbury	Lost	6	13	6,000
Leeds	Won	17	4	5,000
Hull	Won	21	10	12,000
Widnes	Won	17	8	12,000
Halifax	Won	35	6	12,000
Hunslet	Won	19	10	3,174
Cumberland	Won	25	12	5,000
GREAT BRITAIN	Lost	0	6	22,000
at Weaste Ground, Salford				
Oldham	Lost	5	15	6,000
St Helens Recreation	Won	16	5	5,000

*Oldham's **Herman Hilton**, hero of the Ashes deciding victory at Salford.*

*Star of the tour: **Duncan Thompson** of North Sydney.*

Of the 36 games played 27 were won and nine lost. Undoubted stars of the tour were the North Sydney trio, wingers Cec Blinkhorn and Harold Horder, along with the talented scrum-half Duncan Thompson. Blinkhorn scored a remarkable 39 tries, including nine in the record win against Bramley. Horder scored 35 and Frank Burge 30. Thompson topped the goal count with 49. The try-hungry Blinkhorn made most appearances with 29 and Sandy Pearce turned out 20 times at the age of 38.

The Test series was settled in the decider at Salford after Britain had won the first and Australia the second. Oldham's Herman Hilton put in a sterling performance and scored a try in the six nil victory.

1926 1926
1926 1926

OLDHAM R.L.F.C

October 23rd 1926.
OLDHAM 15   NEW ZEALAND 10

GREEN FINAL. SATURDAY, OCTOBER 23. 1926.

"ALL BLACKS" DEFEATED

Oldham's Superior Tactics in a Sternly-Contested

Game

It had been 19 years since the Kiwis had toured here although Great Britain had played matches against New Zealand during the 1910, 1920 and 1924 tours down-under. Oldham three-quarter Sid Rix, full-back Ernie Knapman and forward Albert Brough had all played against New Zealand during the 1924 series which the Lions lost by two Tests to one.

They, and fellow tourist, the giant forward Bob Sloman, would all play in today's match. By the time they came to Watersheddings the Kiwis had lost the first Test by 20 points to 28 but had won nine of their eleven matches against club sides. Oldham, who had gained a reputation as cup-kings, would this season appear in their fourth consecutive Challenge Cup final.

In 1926, the New Zealand Rugby Union took legal action, trying to stop their Rugby League counterparts from using the name, the "All Blacks". The NZRL however, felt that they had equal rights to the name and were keen to keep on using it. The jersey worn on the 1926 tour was still all black in colour but the fern was now replaced by the kiwi emblem and this eventually became the name adopted by the media to identify the New Zealand rugby league tourists. Despite the league initially discouraging its usage, the name stuck and is now the accepted norm.

The tour itself was controversial in so much as seven of the players objected to the strict disciplinary regime adopted by the manager, Mr. E.H. Mair, on the voyage to England and, although the differences were settled (after they were threatened to be sent straight back home), the ill feeling remained throughout the tour. So much so, that in December, five of the original seven refused to turn out against Yorkshire.

Although the attendance at Oldham was very good, this was not the case for other matches on the tour. The press were quick to pick up on the negative feeling in the New Zealand camp and it was thought that the subsequent bad publicity led to the small crowds.

The 1926 Kiwis pose for the camera before the match at Rochdale which ended in a narrow victory for the tourists by 11 points to nine.

October 23rd 1926.
OLDHAM 15   NEW ZEALAND 10

On the day of the match the 1926 Kiwis arrived at Clegg Street railway station at 12.25 p.m. They were then taken to the Duke of Edinburgh public house, in the town centre, for lunch. Amongst the ex-players in attendance were Tommy Cash, R.L. Thomas, Arthur Lees, Jim Parkinson, Bill McCutcheon and former Kiwi international G.W. Smith. The lunch was provided by Bulloughs Ltd of Yorkshire Street, and reports of the function told of an excellent repast!

The weather up at Watersheddings was fine as tour manager, Mr G. Ponder, led the tourists on to the field. The visitors then proceeded to perform the "Haka". The Oldham team stood in line and at the completion of the Maori "War Dance" the Roughyeds responded with three cheers for their opponents.

Oldham captain Bob Sloman won the toss and Kiwi half-back Wilson Hall took the kick-off to set the game in motion. The first action saw Oldham forward Jack Read on a rousing dash into the New Zealand half. This was followed by a series of kicking exchanges as both teams sought to gain territorial advantage. The play was very much end to end stuff and, after Ernie Knapman missed a penalty attempt for Oldham, opposing full-back Charlie Gregory started a fine move by the Kiwi back division which covered three-quarters of the length of the field. Back came Oldham after Hall had been penalised for a scrum infringement. Sloman broke through and put the supporting Ambrose Baker over for a try which was disallowed, the final pass having been ruled to be forward.

Oldham were now getting on top and it took some desperate defence by the visitors

to keep their line intact. First, Joe Corsi was forced into touch just short of the line. This was followed by Gregory just beating Sid Rix to touch down the ball after an astute kick ahead by Tom Holliday. The pressure was finally relieved when Oldham stand-off half

Above:
Joe Corsi *evades a New Zealand opponent after taking a pass from the grounded* ***George Hesketh***...

Left:
... and then races away from three of the Kiwis on the way to score the first Oldham try of the match.

Fred Ashworth, the Cumbrian born Oldham forward who scored the decisive try for the Roughyeds.

Ivor Jeramiah, was penalised for incorrectly playing the ball. About the same time Corsi retired injured and with the extra man it was New Zealand's turn to go on the attack. Fortunately for Oldham Corsi soon returned to the action, his reappearance greeted with cheers from the Watersheddings crowd. On 25 minutes Oldham took the lead, thanks to a penalty goal from Albert BROUGH. The visitors had a chance for an immediate reply but Craddock Dufty missed a penalty attempt.

Ten minutes later the home advantage was increased when Hesketh and Albert Brough worked a move from a scrum to put CORSI on a try scoring run to the corner. KNAPMAN converted from the touch line. Oldham finished the half well on top and after fielding a New Zealand clearance kick KNAPMAN was on the mark again, this time with a drop goal. Half-time fell with the Roughyeds leading by nine points to nil.

Brough started the second half, which continued where the first period had finished with a bout of Oldham pressure. However, it was the Kiwis who opened the scoring twelve minutes into the new half. Right winger, Lou Brown broke clear to pave the way for his centre Benny DAVIDSON, to score. DUFTY converted to reduce the arrears to four points.

Oldham hit back and, after Rix had a score disallowed for off-side, HOLLIDAY went over for an unconverted try. Still the tourists weren't about to give up and, after Knapman spilled the ball, the Kiwi captain Bert AVERY followed up to register a try which was converted by DUFTY. The score was now just 12 - 10 in Oldham's favour.

The game was finally settled when, after a good break by Brough, Fred ASHWORTH went over in a forward rush (when the massed ranks of the forwards would drive or dribble the ball towards the opponents' try-line) for an unconverted touchdown. There was a humorous incident when the conversion attempt struck the referee, Mr. H. Swift of Halifax, full in the face. Needless to say, no goal resulted and Oldham ended up winners by fifteen points to ten.

Overall the match was played at a furious pace with many "end to end" incidents and some vigorous tackling. Sloman, Corsi, Brough and the ever-inventive Hesketh were the pick for the Roughyeds, whereas for the tourists, full-back Gregory had a splendid game, ably supported by Avery and Gardiner in the forwards.

Green Final cartoonist "ASM" portrays **George Gardiner** *of the 1926 Kiwis.*
Notice with this and other images regarding this tour the term "All Blacks" was still very much in evidence in connection with the New Zealand thirteen-a-side code.

GARDINER, leader of the All Blacks' war song

OLDHAM:
E. Knapman; S. Rix, A. Higgs, T. Holliday, J. Corsi; I. Jeremiah, G. Hesketh;
J. Read, J. Scaife, F. Ashworth, R. Sloman, A. Baker, A. Brough.

NEW ZEALAND:
E.C. Gregory; L. Brown, B. Davidson, J. Sanders, W.L. Desmond; H. Brisbane, A.W. Hall;
L. Mason, E. Herring, G. Gardiner, H. Avery, C. Dufty, H. Thomas.

Attendance: 16,000   Referee Mr. H. Swift - Halifax

The after-match festivities took the form of a mayoral reception where the club president, Mr. W.H. Greaves and the mayor, Mr. F. Pollard, poured praise on the tourists and brought to mind the old days of Baskerville's pioneers in 1907. Mr. G.H. Ponder, the tour manager, replied for the New Zealand party. He congratulated Oldham on their victory and thanked the match officials. Co-manager of the tour Mr E.H. Mair thanked their hosts for recalling the Baskerville team and added that he was glad to see G.W. Smith again and how popular he was in Oldham. At the conclusion of the function Oldham secretary Mr G. Kilner presented Mr. Mair with a copy of the programme and reception menu for the first visit of the Kiwi tourists in 1907. Mr. Mair thanked the Oldham club for their thoughtfulness and said that these items would be much prized back in New Zealand. Thereafter the tourists departed for their tour HQ in Harrogate.

> *The cartoon below suggests that the New Zealanders were happy with the gate receipts, if not the result and vigorous nature of the match.*

Two superb action photographs from the match against New Zealand in 1926.
Above: Kiwi half-back **Hector Brisbane** gets a kick away as the Oldham pack closes in. The
Oldham players from left to right are: **Jack Read, Jack Scaife, Ambrose Baker and Albert
Brough**.
Below: **Fred Ashworth** moves in to tackle one of the New Zealanders. Other Oldham players
from left to right: **George Hesketh, Ambrose Baker, Tom Holliday and Ivor Jeremiah**.

Opposite: Both of these photographs combined into one collective image, captured in water
colour by Stephen Bennett.

B. DAVIDSON, an All Blacks' centre.

Another portrayal by "ASM".
This time of New Zealand centre,
Benny Davidson.
A try scorer for the 1926 Kiwis at
Watersheddings.

The 1926 New Zealand Tour	Result	Score		Att
Dewsbury	Won	13	9	13,000
Leigh	Won	23	16	12,000
Halifax	Lost	13	19	13,000
Rochdale Hornets	Won	11	9	7,590
Barrow	Won	19	16	5,500
Widnes	Won	15	5	6,000
GREAT BRITAIN	Lost	20	28	14,500
at Central Park, Wigan				
York	Won	19	11	3,099
Warrington	Lost	5	17	5,000
Bramley	Won	35	12	unknown
Hull	Won	15	13	12,999
Bradford Northern	Won	38	17	4,000
Oldham	Lost	10	15	16,000
Leeds	Won	13	11	4,000
St. Helens Recreation	Lost	14	28	6,000
Salford	Won	18	10	3,500
Huddersfield	Lost	10	12	5,000
GREAT BRITAIN	Lost	11	21	7,000
at The Boulevard, Hull				
Wigan Highfield	Won	14	2	2,000
Batley	Lost	17	19	3,000
Keighley	Won	21	3	3,861
Swinton	Lost	14	16	12,000
Wales	Lost	8	34	18,000
St. Helens	Lost	12	22	2,000
Wigan	Lost	15	36	9,000
Yorkshire	Lost	16	17	3,000
Hunslet	Lost	12	13	unknown
Pontypridd	Won	17	8	unknown
Broughton Rangers	Won	32	8	5,000
Wakefield Trinity	Won	29	24	6,000
Hull Kingston Rovers	Lost	15	20	7,500
Lancashire	Lost	3	28	7,000
Cumberland	Won	18	3	4,200
GREAT BRITAIN	Lost	17	32	6,000
at Headingley, Leeds				

Above;
Tom Holliday *(left) and* **Joe Corsi.**
Both try scorers for Oldham
against the 1926 Kiwis.

Although the Test series was lost three nil, it was a case of "fifty fifty" for the 1926 New Zealanders with 17 wins and 17 defeats from their 34 match tour.

Herbert Avery scored most tries with 23 while full-back, and sometimes second-row forward, Craddock Dufty topped the goal count with 42. Skipper Avery truly led from the front and his total of 29 appearances was only bettered by hooker Ernie Herring with 30.

Perhaps an indication of the "forward power" on this tour is the fact that, allied to the above statistics, forwards George Gardiner and Len Mason scored a further 18 tries between them.

1929 1929 1929 1929

OLDHAM FOOTBALL CLUB
SAPERE-AUDE

OLDHAM R.L.F.C

AUSTRALIA RUGBY LEAGUE TOUR

NEW ZEALAND RUGBY LEAGUE

November 2nd 1929
OLDHAM 10 AUSTRALIA 18

Australia
v.
Oldham
— SATURDAY, —
November 2nd, 1929.

The "Aussies" in Oldham

W. SHANKLAND

T. GORMAN (capt.)

The Australians had hosted two consecutive Lions tours since they were last here during the 1921-22 season. Great Britain had retained the Ashes in 1924 when they beat the Kangaroos by winning two out of the three match series in their own backyard and then, in 1928, repeated the feat. Oldham forwards Bob Sloman and Albert Brough, along with backs Ernie Knapman and Sid Rix, toured in 1924 but in 1928 Sloman was the only Oldham player selected.

Of the four only Sloman would play in today's game. Knapman had left the club and had been replaced at full-back by former Welsh rugby union international Tommy Rees who had played in the first Test at Craven Park, Hull where the Australians murdered the Lions 31-8. Of the 15 matches played so far they had lost only two.

H. STEINOHRT

G. TREWEEKE

F McMILLAN

Mr. A. HENNESSEY

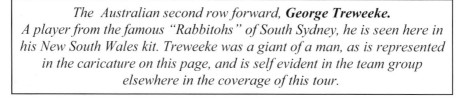

*The Australian second row forward, **George Treweeke**.*
A player from the famous "Rabbitohs" of South Sydney, he is seen here in his New South Wales kit. Treweeke was a giant of a man, as is represented in the caricature on this page, and is self evident in the team group elsewhere in the coverage of this tour.

November 2nd 1929.
OLDHAM 10   AUSTRALIA 18

A huge crowd of over 19,000 had gathered at Watersheddings for the event. The numbers were swelled by a considerable number of officials from other clubs who were taking the opportunity to view the tourists, who had acquired a reputation for open play and super fitness. Also in attendance were the selectors for the second Test which was to be played the following week at Headingley.

Hopes for ideal conditions were dashed when the rain started an hour before the start of the match. By kick-off time this was reduced to a drizzle. The teams entered the field to the strains of "Land of Hope and Glory", played by the Oldham Rifle Band. The Australians, who were playing in green and gold shirts and blue shorts, won the toss and elected to receive the ball.

Home hooker Jack Scaife took the kick to start the match and what a sensational start it was! The ball was fielded by one of the Australian forwards who immediately

Oldham stand-off **Jack Oster** *caught the Aussies napping with an interception try within the first minute.*

passed out to his captain, Tom Gorman. However, the ball never reached the tourists' skipper as, quick as a flash, Jack OSTER nipped in to intercept the pass and race round Frank McMillan to score near the posts. Barely twenty seconds had gone by when the tricky Oldham half-back touched down. Tommy REES made no mistake with the easy conversion and Oldham led by five points to nil. The Aussies soon hit back and a good run by stand-off Eric Weissel looked like producing a score but Gorman put down the final pass. Oldham took play back into the Australian half from where Rees was unsuccessful with a long range penalty attempt. The teams seemed evenly matched in the early exchanges and opposing full-backs Rees and McMillan engaged in a number of kicking duels.

The weather was hampering open play with the result that the tackling was becoming more and more vigorous, until Mr Peel lost patience and cautioned Harry Entwistle and George Bishop for "rough play". This prompted the tourists to get their act together somewhat and on a number of occasions they were unlucky not to score. First, loose-forward Wally Prigg snapped up a loose ball only for Herb Steinohrt to mishandle in a good position. Then Joe Busch put Bill Shankland away for the wingman to cover half the length of the field only to fall to a great tackle from Rees. Next, Gorman produced a gap from which Prigg actually got over the line only to lose the ball as he turned toward the posts. Prior to this REES had kicked a penalty goal after another indiscretion by Bishop and it was with a rather fortunate seven points to nil lead that Oldham left the field at half-time.

As in the first period Oldham were first on attack in the second half after Gorman fumbled possession, Abe Johnson dribbled the ball to the line only for McMillan to get across and make the ball safe. After this scare the tourists immediately rallied. George Treweeke made a break for Bill SPENCER to score a try which was converted by WEISSEL. The Australian three-quarters were now beginning to dominate proceedings and twice Shankland was brought down just short of the line. Oldham forward Harry Entwistle had to leave the field for a time due to a damaged finger and in his absence the visitors registered their next score. Weissel made a break and, after a bout of inter-passing with

SHANKLAND, the winger, this time, was not to be denied and his unconverted try gave the Kangaroos a one point lead.

Just as the match entered the final quarter Roughyeds' scrum-half Jack Reynolds was hurt which led to his swapping places with winger Johnson. At this stage Oldham were well and truly in the wars and things got worse when full-back Rees had to retire from the field. The Welshman soon returned but only in time to see Vic ARMBRUSTER increase the tourists' lead with a further try converted by WEISSEL. Oldham reduced the arrears to three points when RIX scored but the conversion attempt by Johnson, substituting for the injured Rees, failed. It was left to the tourists to complete the scoring when SPENCER went over for his second try after a scintillating break covering half the length of the field. The final goal by WEISSEL brought matters to a close with the Australians victorious by eighteen points to ten.

OLDHAM:
T. Rees; S. Rix, E. Thomas, J. Stephens, A. Johnson; J. Oster, J. Reynolds;
J. Read, J. Scaife, A. Clayton, F. Ashworth, H. Entwistle, E. Watkins.

AUSTRALIA:
F. McMillan; W. Shankland, T. Gorman, C. Fifield, W. Spencer; E. Weissel, J. Busch;
W. Steinohrt, G. Bishop, P. Madsen, G. Treweeke, V. Armbruster, W. Prigg.

Attendance: 19,284   Referee: Mr. F. Peel - Bradford.

Photograph taken on Oldham Town Hall steps last Saturday on the arrival of the Australian Rugby football team. Mr. Sunderland, the Australians' team manager, who later in the day had an accident in Union Street and is now in Oldham Royal Infirmary, is seen right in front with the small boy, who is known as Oldham's mascot.

Above: Newspaper photograph of the tourists on the Oldham town hall steps complete with the original caption.

After the game the tourists were transported to the Union Club on Union Street in the town centre in the same charabanc that had brought them from their headquarters in Ilkley. Upon arrival, no sooner had the tour manager Harry Sunderland stepped down from the vehicle than he was knocked down by a passing car. Several of the tour party and Oldham officials rushed to Mr Sunderland's aid where it was found that he was bleeding profusely from a head wound. He was taken to Oldham Royal Infirmary and remained there for a week.

This event cast something of a gloom over the post-match reception, which was attended by the Mayor Councillor H.W. Tupman and Mayor "elect" Alderman I. Crabtree. The mood was lightened later in the evening when reports were received that Mr. Sunderland was feeling better and sitting up talking to friends.

Left :
Winger **Bill Spencer** *scored two tries for the 1929 Kangaroos at Watersheddings.*
Right:
Great Britain international **Sid Rix** *replied with one for the Roughyeds.*

The Green Final edition the week after the match in 1929 and cartoonist "ASM" gives his impressions of the action at Watersheddings.

Official Souvenir Programme

Australia

v.

Oldham

— SATURDAY, —
November 2nd, 1929.

Price 2d.

J. ALLAN HANSON & SON. LTD., PRINTERS. OLDHAM.

Bill Shankland: A try scorer for the Kangaroos at Oldham in 1929. Bill would go on to play with distinction for Warrington, so much so that he is in their "Hall of Fame". He later became an accomplished professional golfer and twice finished third in the British Open.

Above: 1929 tour badge. This was given to Jean Ferguson (the young daughter of former Oldham legend, Joe) by the tour vice-captain Paddy Maher after the match.

P. MAHER
(Vice-Captain).

Thanks !

We desire to gratefully acknowledge with thanks, the kindness of "Monk," of the "Daily Express," Messrs. Hirst, Kidd and Rennie Ltd., "Green Final"; "The Daily Mail"; and the Warrington Football Club, for the loan of the various blocks and caricatures used in this programme.

Mr. J. L. DARGAN
(Joint Manager)
Australian Team.

The official programme was a special issue printed in light blue complete with illustrations of some of the notable characters from the tour.

Two random groups of the 1929 Kangaroos. (left to right) Above: **Bill Brogan, Jack Kingston, Bill Spencer, George Treweeke, Arthur Henderson, Eric Weissell, Cec Fifield.**
Below: **Tom Gorman, Bill Shankland, Herb Steinohrt, Frank McMillan, Joe Busch.**.

The 1929-30 Australian Tour	Result	Score		Att
Rochdale Hornets	Won	36	3	6,521
York	Won	32	11	4,729
Batley	Won	27	5	6,000
Widnes	Won	37	13	6,400
Broughton Rangers	Won	21	8	6,514
Lancashire	Won	29	14	24,000
Wakefield Trinity	Lost	3	14	9,786
Keighley	Won	15	9	3,000
GREAT BRITAIN	Won	31	8	20,000
at Craven Park, Hull				
Castleford	Won	53	2	4,000
Huddersfield	Won	18	8	18,560
Leigh	Won	19	16	8,000
Barrow	Won	13	10	10,000
Leeds	Lost	7	8	10,000
Hull	Won	35	2	10,000
Oldham	Won	18	10	19,284
GREAT BRITAIN	Lost	3	9	31,402
at Headingley, Leeds				
Bradford Northern	Won	26	17	7,000
St Helens	Drew	18	18	9,500
Yorkshire	Won	25	12	7,011
Halifax	Won	58	9	8,440
Swinton	Lost	5	9	9,000
Northern League	Lost	5	18	9,987
Cumberland	Lost	5	8	3,500
Glamorgan and Monmouthshire	Won	39	9	3,000
St Helens Recreation	Won	22	8	9,000
Northern League	Won	32	22	9,690
Warrington	Lost	8	17	12,826
Hunslet	Lost	3	18	12,000
Hull Kingston Rovers	Won	10	5	12,000
Wigan (aban 65 minutes)	Won	10	9	8,000
GREAT BRITAIN	Drew	0	0	33,809
at Station Road, Swinton				
Salford	Won	21	5	8,000
GREAT BRITAIN	Lost	0	3	16,743
at Athletic Grounds, Rochdale				
Wales	Won	26	10	16,000
at Wembley				

Probably the most talked-about tour ever, it will always be remembered for the extra Test match played to settle the series after the Test teams had played out one win each and a scoreless draw. The third Test at Swinton ended in drama when Joe Busch went over for a try in the corner, only for the effort to be disallowed on the intervention of the touch judge who ruled that local favourite Fred Butters had nudged the Australian wingman into touch. Oldham's Jack Oster played in this match, one of the most controversial in the history of international Rugby League.

The extra Test was played at the Athletic Grounds, Rochdale on January 15th 1930. Another close encounter, the match was again heading towards a scoreless conclusion until, with just six minutes to go, the Leeds winger Stan Smith, just recently signed from Wakefield, finally breached the Australian line for the decisive try. The match finished with Great Britain the victors by the narrow margin of three points to nil.

The tourists won 24, drew two and lost nine of the 35 match itinerary. Bill Shankland (23 tries) and Eric Weissel (56 goals) topped the scoring, while Jack Kingston and Frank McMillan shared the most appearances with 26 each.

Tom Gorman: Centre three-quarter from Toowoomba and the first Queenslander to captain the Australians.

This tour was also the first time the famous green shirts with a gold "V" were worn by the Kangaroos.

1933 1934
1933 1934

OLDHAM R.L.F.C

NEW ZEALAND
RUGBY LEAGUE

September 9th 1933.

OLDHAM 6 AUSTRALIA 38

SOUND DEFEAT FOR
OLDHAM

Official Souvenir Programme

Australia
v.
Oldham
—SATURDAY,—
September 9th, 1933.

The "Kangaroos" carried too heavy a punch for Oldham last Satur.

Gibb

Brown

January 10th 1934.

OLDHAM 5 AUSTRALIA 38

Great Britain had retained the Ashes when they won the 1932 series played in Australia by two Tests to one. For the first time the Oldham club failed to have any players selected but the club's President George 'Fred' Hutchins was again appointed joint tour manager, a similar position to the one that he had held for the 1928 tour.

The 1933-34 Kangaroos, under the captaincy of full-back Frank McMillan, played this, their first of two matches against the Roughyeds, early into the tour but they had already built a reputation for playing expansive and entertaining rugby league. Oldham, whilst they won the Lancashire Cup in 1933, were going through a transitional period and would end the season 18th in the league, the club's lowest position since a single division had been introduced back in 1905. No Oldham players would be selected for the Test series but former England rugby union international Ted Sadler, playing at loose-forward today, would represent England against the Aussies in a promotional match held in Paris.

THE "KANGAROOS" - AUSTRALIAN TEAM, 1933-4
R. STEHR. · S. PEARCE. A. RIDLEY. P. MADSEN. F. CURRAN. H. DENNY. C. PEARCE
M. GLASHEEN. R. MORRIS. W. PRIGG. F. O'CONNOR. L. HEIDKE. J. DOYLE. J. GIBB. J. LITTLE.
C. SMITH. J. WHY F. LAWS. H. SUNDERLAND F. McMILLAN. W. WEBB. F. NEUMANN. A. FOLWELL. D. BROWN.
(V CAPT.) (MNGR) (CAPT.)
(MNGR)
V. THICKNESSE. F. GARDNER. L. MEAD. F. GILBERT. V. HEY F. DOONAR.

The Oldham side that defeated Wigan in the Lancashire Cup semi-final in October 1933.
Back row:
J. Reynolds,
S. Bardsley,
L. Lewis,
J. Scaife,
J. Read,
J. Stephens,
A. Givvons.
Front row:
A. Clayton,
F. Ashworth,
T. Rees,
E. Sadler,
A. Taylor,
E. Hodgson.

September 9th 1933.
OLDHAM 6   AUSTRALIA 38

Frank McMillan leads out the 1933-34 Kangaroos from the Watersheddings tunnel. The teenage sensation Dave Brown is fourth in the line (in headgear).

There was just a slight breeze as Oldham took the field to the strains of "Land of Hope and Glory", to be followed by the Australians led out by captain Frank McMillan, being greeted with "Advance Australia Fair". Both teams received a rapturous welcome from the crowd of over 15,000.

Oldham captain Trevor Thomas won the toss and decided to take advantage of what little wind there was and subsequently the tourist scrum-half Les Mead was prevailed upon to set the game in motion. The same player was soon into the match and attempted to dart through to the line after the Australians took the first scrum. Back came Oldham and, following a few vigorous exchanges, Tommy Rees was off target with a penalty attempt awarded for rough play. The Roughyeds continued to press and after good work by Jack Reynolds, wingman Albert Taylor kicked ahead and took play to near the visitors' line. After further pressure a penalty was awarded and REES gave Oldham the lead on five minutes.

However, the tourists hit back almost immediately. The ball was swung out to the right wing where Alan RIDLEY outpaced the Oldham defence and eluded the covering Reynolds to score a fine try. Dave BROWN converted to push Australia into a three point lead. Oldham dominated the next phase of the match and were awarded another penalty after a foul on Alex Givvons. Rees missed the goal attempt but the home side continued to press and were unlucky when winger Llewellyn Williams was pulled down inches short after good work by Sam Bardsley and Taylor in the build-up. The tourists put in a solid defensive stint to keep Oldham at bay and were not afraid to throw the ball about even close to their own line. Ridley again got away on a winding run which took him from one side of the field to the other, leaving a trail of Oldham players in his wake only to be denied at the last by a solid tackle by Rees.

As half-time approached the visitors turned up the heat and it was somewhat against the run of play when REES reduced the arrears with his second successful penalty goal. Stirred into action, Australia again hit right back. All of the three-quarter line

Oldham's only points came from the boot of Wales and Great Britain international, Tommy Rees.

65

A superb panorama of Watersheddings taken during the match against the Australians in September 1933.

Over 15,000 had packed into the ground to watch Frank McMillan's Kangaroos.

Photo courtesy of Terry Williams.

*A tense moment from the match on September 9th 1933. A scrum breaks up and both teams scramble for the ball. Oldham players left to right: **Alex Givvons**, **Ted Hodgson**, **Fred Ashworth**, **Les Lewis** (No 5) and **Ted Sadler**. Tour vice-captain, **Wally Prigg, can be seen** in the scrum cap.*

combined in the best move of the match so far to send Wally PRIGG over for the score. Again BROWN converted. Then, in the very last minute of the half, second-row forward Jimmy GIBBS side-stepped his way through for another try. BROWN added the conversion to leave the visitors fifteen points to four to the good at the interval.

The Australians started the second half as they ended the first - in complete control. Neumann was tackled just short by Reynolds and, although Oldham took play into their opponents' half, the relief was short lived, for soon Brown was scooting through a gap from which he drew the tackle of Rees to give the supporting Cliff PEARCE a thirty yard dash to the posts. BROWN had no trouble adding the extra points.

To their credit Oldham continued to plug away and Givvons, aided by ex-rugby union international, Ted Sadler, was instrumental in setting up a position from where REES kicked another penalty goal. The same pair again combined to take the Roughyeds close once more. Once again the Oldham pressure seemed to wake up the tourists who finished the game much the stronger. Further tries were added by BROWN, Dan DEMPSEY and PRIGG, who was somewhat fortunate when he and Taylor chased down a kick only for a freak bounce to take the ball away from the Oldham man straight into the hands of the tourists' loose-forward. RIDLEY scored the final try following a dashing run to the Oldham posts after Mead had intercepted near the Australian line. BROWN converted three of these scores to produce a final result of Oldham 6 Australia 38.

The delight of the visitors was somewhat marred by an injury to prop-forward Herb Denny who dislocated a shoulder in the second half of the game. However, after treatment at Oldham Royal Infirmary, he was allowed to travel with his team-mates back to their HQ in Ilkley.

OLDHAM: T. Rees; L. Williams, S. Bardsley, A. Taylor, L. Lewis; J. Reynolds, A. Givvons; J. Read, J. Scaife, W.T. Thomas, E. Hodgson, F. Ashworth, E. Sadler.

AUSTRALIA: F. McMillan; A. Ridley, D. Brown, C. Pearce, F. Neumann; V. Hey, L. Mead; M. Masden, D. Dempsey, H. Denney, J. Gibbs, R. Stehr, W. Prigg

Attendance: 15,281   Referee: Mr. A. Brown - Wakefield

On the morning of the game the touring party had been received at the Town Hall by the Mayor, accompanied by several Oldham officials. After the match the reception was held at the Union Club and after the initial toast to His Majesty the King, Mr. G.F. Hutchins gave "To our Australian visitors" which prompted a spontaneous approval.

The tour manager Harry Sunderland stood up to reply but seemed rather emotional and re-seated himself and let co-manager Mr. W. Webb take over. The Australian official thanked Oldham for their hospitality and was glad to say that Watersheddings had provided the best crowd of the tour so far. Having regained his composure Mr. Sunderland again rose and apologised but went on to explain that as he got up to speak he realised that this may be the last time he would visit the fine rugby town of Oldham and was saddened at the prospect. He went on to say that he considered himself to be very fortunate to be involved with the tour and eloquently stated, "*I have more than a man's share of privilege and happiness.*" He thanked Mr. Hutchins for arranging the playing of "Advance Australia Fair" before the match saying that this was a wonderful gesture that would be read about and appreciated all over Australia. The mood in the room was quite jocular and at one point Mr. Sunderland held up a photograph of Watersheddings in the snow as a warning to what his players might expect later in the tour.

The captain, Frank McMillan, gave his thanks to the Oldham official Jim Parkinson and put it to his players that he should be made "one of the boys". A gesture to which his colleagues roared their approval.

*Les Lewis makes the tackle on **Frank McMillan,** as the Oldham hooker **Jack Scaife** comes across in support and **Alan Ridley** (25) moves inside.*

"Kangaroos" With a "Kick"

Another of the cartoons so popular in the pre-Second World War era. This time it is "Snooker" from the Oldham Standard who gives an interpretation of the first of two thrashings handed out to the Roughyeds by the Kangaroos on the 1933-34 tour.

A copy of the match statistics submitted to the Rugby Football League by the Oldham club after the match on September 9th 1933.

The match programme, a similar issue to the one for the 1929 tour.

THE RUGBY FOOTBALL LEAGUE.

TOUR of the AUSTRALIANS - 1933-34.

FOR RECORDS AND STATISTICAL PURPOSES ONLY, PLEASE FILL IN THE
DETAILS ASKED FOR BELOW AND RETURN TO THIS OFFICE NOT LATER THAN
FIVE DAYS FOLLOWING THE DATE OF THE MATCH.

84 Grange Avenue,   JOHN WILSON,
LEEDS.   Secretary.

MATCH AT   Oldham

versus   Australians   DATE   September 9th   1933.
GROSS GATE RECEIPTS £ 1217 : 19 : 6.   TAX £ 203 : 13 : 5.
TOURISTS SHARE   £ 710 : 0 : 3.   ATTENDANCE 15,281.

RESULT OF MATCH.

AUSTRALIA.   Goals 7 Tries 8   Points 38
             Goals 3 Tries 0   Points 6
SCORERS, (AUSTRALIA)   Brown 7 goals, 1 try.
                       Ridley 2 tries, Prigg 2 tries, Gibb 1 try,
                       Pearce 1 try, Stehr 1 try.
-do- (HOME TEAM)   Rees 3 goals.

AUSTRALIAN TEAM   McMillan
             Ridley, Brown, C.Pearce, Nenmann,
                     Hey, Mead,
             Madson, Dempsey, Denny, Gibb, Stehr, Prigg.
HOME TEAM   Rees.
             Williams, Bardsley, Taylor, Lewis,
                     Givvons, Reynolds,
             Hodgson, Scaife, Read, Ashworth, Thomas, Sadler.
OFFICIALS   Mr. A. Brown, Wakefield.
             Mr. J. Parr, Mr. Taylor.
COMMENTS

Price 2d.

OLDHAM FOOTBALL CLUB

Official Souvenir Programme

Australia
v.
Oldham
—SATURDAY,—
September 9th, 1933.

J. Allan Hanson & Son Ltd., Printers, Cross Street, Oldham.

January 10th 1934.
OLDHAM 5 AUSTRALIA 38

So impressed were the tourists by the reception they received in Oldham, that a second match was arranged and in spite of the fact it was a dull January afternoon with a 2.45pm kick-off, a respectable crowd of 5,000 gathered at Watersheddings to witness the event.

Prop-forward Mick Madsen captained the tourists, duly won the toss and elected to take first use of a strong wind. Jack Stephens set the game in motion and, although the visitors had the best of the early exchanges, the first really exciting movement of the match came Oldham's way when Ted Sadler picked up at a scrum and put Tom Egan away, he in turn handed on to Stephens. The Oldham centre veered out to the wing but his attempted inside pass was intercepted. Next it was the visitors' turn to go forward and only a last-ditch smothering tackle from Sadler denied centre Cliff Pearce.

It was not long, however, before the tourists opened their account. Les Mead and Joe Doyle combined well to put Fred GARDNER clear and the speedy wingman crossed for the opening try. Dave BROWN added the goal and from there on it was more or less one way traffic with further tries from PEARCE, MEAD, Vic HEY and BROWN, who converted two more of these scores. Oldham's only respite came when STEPHENS sold an outrageous dummy to Ridley to cross for an unconverted try, which produced a half-time score of

THE TOURISTS IN OLDHAM

A hazy photograph taken on a cold January day at Watersheddings.
This image of a scrum breaking up is the only known pictorial record of the Australia game against Oldham played on January 10th 1934.

twenty one points to three for Australia.

The second half continued in much the same vein and the tourists clocked up five more tries from Alan RIDLEY, Sid PEARCE, Ray STEHR, and BROWN, with the final score coming from acting skipper MADSEN. BROWN only managed to convert one of the tries with a REES penalty goal the only Oldham reply to make the final score: Oldham 5 Australia 38.

Notwithstanding the severity of the beating the Oldham players, to their credit, kept going until the end against obviously, vastly superior opposition, none more so than the debut-making young hooker Edgar Brooks, who here embarked on a lengthy and notable career with the Roughyeds.

OLDHAM: T. Rees; W. Whitworth, S. Bardsley, J. Stephens, F. Marsh; T. Egan, J. Heywood; J. Read, E. Brooks, A. Clayton, F. Ashworth, W.T. Thomas, E. Sadler.

AUSTRALIA: A. Smith; A. Ridley, D. Brown, C. Pearce, F. Gardner; V. Hey, L. Mead; M. Madsen, J. Little, R. Stehr, J. Doyle, S. Pearce, W. Prigg

Attendance: 5,000   Referee: Mr. A. S. Dobson - Featherstone

In keeping with tradition there was an post-match reception which was held at the Friendship Hotel, where entertainment was provided by "Tony and Marie", Jack Hibbert and an orchestra!

The Aussies presented the Oldham official, Jim Parkinson, with a tour jersey and his son Tom with a tour tie. Continuing the gesture, Harry Sunderland took off his own tie and handed it over to the Oldham official, G.F. Hutchins. In return Mr. Parkinson presented skipper Frank McMillan with a set of mini clogs and a photo taken on the occasion of the last Australian visit with a request that it should be handed on to the captain of the 1929 tour, Tom Gorman. The proceedings were concluded with a special performance of the Australian version of the haka for young Tom Parkinson.

Edgar Brooks, the local born Oldham hooker who made his debut in the second match against the Kangaroos. Edgar went on to play 293 games for the Roughyeds.

The 1933-34 tour shirt presented to Jim Parkinson is now in the Oldham Rugby League Heritage Trust collection and can be seen at the bottom centre of the photo.

71

The 1933-34 Tour	Result	Score		Att
St Helens Recreation	Won	13	9	8,880
Leigh	Won	16	7	4,600
Hull Kingston Rovers	Won	20	0	7,831
Bramley	Won	53	6	1,902
Oldham	Won	38	6	15,281
Yorkshire	Won	13	0	10,309
Barrow	Won	24	5	12,221
Lancashire	Won	33	7	16,576
Wigan	Won	10	4	15,712
Castleford	Won	39	6	4,250
Halifax	Won	16	5	10,358
GREAT BRITAIN at Belle Vue, Manchester	Lost	0	4	33,000
Bradford Northern	Lost	5	7	3,328
Warrington	Lost	12	15	16,431
Hunslet	Won	22	8	6,227
Salford	Lost	9	16	15,761
Widnes	Won	31	0	6,691
Wakefield Trinity	Won	17	6	5,596
Bradford Northern	Won	10	7	9,937
Northern League	Lost	5	7	3,158
Swinton	Lost	4	10	13,341
GREAT BRITAIN at Headingley, Leeds	Lost	5	7	29,688
Keighley	Won	14	7	3,800
Huddersfield	Won	13	5	7,522
London Highfield	Won	20	5	10,541
Broughton Rangers	Won	19	0	5,527
Leeds	Won	15	7	5,295
St Helens	Won	20	11	5,735
Rochdale Hornets	Won	26	4	3,603
Cumberland	Lost	16	17	5,800
GREAT BRITAIN at Station Road, Swinton	Lost	16	19	10,990
York	Won	15	7	6,500
Hull	Won	19	5	16,341
Wales	Won	51	19	10,000
England in Paris	Won	63	13	5,000
Oldham	Won	38	5	5,000
England at Gateshead	Lost	14	19	15,576

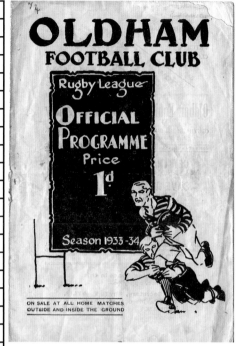

The regular club issue programme was utilised for the second tour game played on January 10th 1934.

The great **Dave Brown**

Alan Ridley *Top try scorer for the 1933-34 Kangaroos*

Although 27 of the 37 games on tour were won, the Test series went to Great Britain three - nil. However, the combined winning margins for all three Tests amounted to just nine points, demonstrating what closely fought encounters they were. The undoubted star of the tour was the young centre sensation Dave Brown. He amassed a total of 285 points from 114 goals and nineteen tries. Alan Ridley topped the try count with 25 and the honour for most tour appearances was shared by Brown and vice-captain Wally Prigg with 32 each.

73

A year earlier the Lions had retained the Ashes in Australia by winning the second and third Test matches. Oldham players failed to gain selection for the tour for only the second but consecutive time.

The 1937 Kangaroos, captained by loose-forward Wally Prigg - who was making his third and final tour – had, by the time they arrived at Watersheddings, played eleven matches against club sides losing to only Halifax and Salford. On the other hand, for the last three seasons, Oldham had languished in a mid-table league position. That being said, the Australians paraded a strong team packed with Test players for the match at Watersheddings.

*Right: **Harry Sunderland**, here in 1937 for his third tour as Australian manager. One of the game's great administrators.*

Below: The reception menu card for the after match dinner at the Union Club, complete with signatures of the tourists on the back cover.

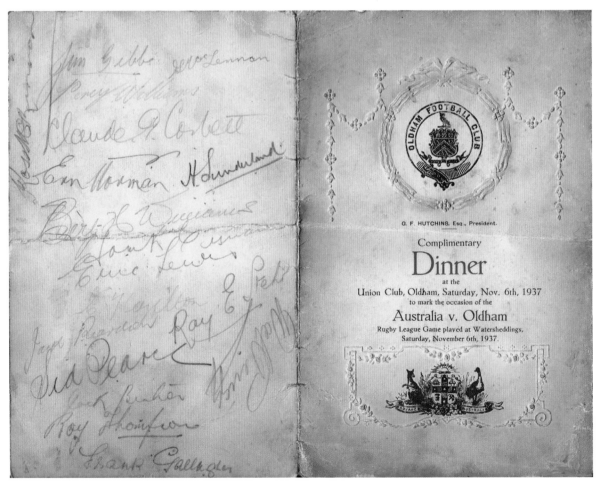

November 6th 1937.
OLDHAM 6   AUSTRALIA 10

The Australians paid Oldham the compliment of turning out a strong side with only three changes from that which contested the first Test. The Roughyeds were handicapped by the absence of full-back Tom Rees and three-quarters Fred Marsh and Graham Macrae. It was a grey November afternoon with a slight drizzle which greeted the tourists as they took the field. They entered the arena led out by tour vice-captain Jack Reardon, to the strains of "Advance Australia fair".

The visitors kicked-off and were soon showing their defensive prowess as they kept Oldham pinned down. The Roughyeds did make some progress through their kicking game but Australia looked the more dangerous side. A crunching tackle by Harry Barnes on Ernie Norman brought a roar from the crowd and after Laurie Ward cut through the middle from full-back it took a good effort from the home team defenders to crowd Jack Beaton out at the corner-flag.

The match had begun at a rousing pace which would continue for the entire eighty minutes. However, the intense fervour of both the Roughyeds and the Kangaroos endeavours did little to reflect on the finer points of the game. It was a case of the Australians' pace and guile versus the dominance and strength of the dogged Oldham forwards. For the most part the match featured

Jack Reardon leads out the 1937 Kangaroos at Watersheddings.

the tourists forever trying to coax a score only to be met by the most resolute defensive strategies from the men in red and white.

After Bob Cattlin had forced a handling error from Harry Pierce, the agile Givvons jinked through and handed on to the supporting Lew Rees but even the Welshman's fifteen stone frame couldn't dent the massed green wall that was the Australian defensive line. Oldham continued to press and Fred Hall got over only to be brought back for a forward pass. Eventually, the pressure brought results when the visitors were penalised for playing the ball incorrectly and ASHWORTH landed the goal to give Oldham the lead.

This seemed to wake up the tourists who followed up the restart kick at pace and forced a handling error which, after some swift passing, culminated in Ross McKINNON coming in on a diagonal run to score near the posts. BEATON added the conversion. Oldham got back to within a point when Percy Williams was penalised for "feeding" at a scrum and ASHWORTH was again on target with the kick. The same player narrowly missed with a third attempt a short time later. For the visitors Ward was in inspired form at full-back but the tourists were reduced to twelve men when Ray Stehr limped off with a leg

injury just before half-time which followed with the score finely balanced:
Oldham 4 Australia 5.

The second half commenced with Stehr back in the fray. Norman and McKinnon had changed positions at centre and stand-off. The pattern of the first half continued with the defensive efforts of both sides prevailing. The first scoring chance went to the visitors when Oldham were penalised but Beaton, who was vigorously barracked by the home support, was off target with his goal attempt. The Aussie winger tried to make amends soon after with a dashing run down the left and looked all over set to score until he was brought down by a flying tackle from Verdun Rhydderch. The diminutive Welshman repeated the feat some time later when, this time, he bundled the burly Pierce into touch some ten yards from the corner flag.

However, the Australians were now in control and in spite of some more heroic tackling, notably by Givvons on Stehr and Les Partridge on Les Heidke, their endeavours finally brought reward. It was second row forward Herb NARVO who capitalised on a momentary defensive lapse by the tiring Roughyeds to gallop thirty yards to score the decisive try which WILLIAMS converted. The highlight for Oldham was a superb solo effort from left wing Norman Holt. He set off on an exciting break by sidestepping away from two Australian defenders well inside his own half of the field. After further progress up the left flank he cut in diagonally for the posts only to fall victim to the weight of numbers of the Kangaroo cover. Alas, Oldham's only material response was a third penalty goal from ASHWORTH and the Australian line was never seriously threatened again. The match therefore concluded with the score Oldham 6 Australia 10.

OLDHAM: L. Partridge; F. Hall, V. Rhydderch, C. Davies, N. Holt; H. Barnes, R. Smith; F. Ashworth, E. Brooks, L. Rees, R. Cattlin, A. Givvons, N. Pugh.

AUSTRALIA: L. Ward; D. McLean, J. Reardon, R. McKinnon, J. Beaton; E. Norman, P. Williams; R. Stehr, H. Pierce, L. Heidke, H. Narvo, E. Lewis, A. Norval.

Attendance: 12,265   Referee: Mr. A. Hill – Leeds

To-Day's "Emu"sement!

Dear old pals! Jolly old pals! Sticking together through all sorts o' weather!

AUSSY

AUSTRALIA
xxxxx
OLDHAM

A.S.M.

"Aussy," th Emu (p) laid at Watersheddings this afternoon. The result of the "hatching" will be found elsewhere in this paper.

"ASM" still going strong in 1937.

This cartoon appeared on the front page of the Green Final on the day of the game and was no doubt set in place before the report was phoned through.

The two figures portrayed in the top left of the drawing are tour manager Harry Sunderland and Oldham official George Hutchins.

While admitting that it was a stirring game full of vigorous play and determined defending, the press was also critical of the lack of adventure from both teams. The Oldham Chronicle report sardonically stated, *"It would have made a good cup final, but as an Australian match it will pass unglamorously into history unwept, unhonoured and unsung."*

The touring party was officially welcomed at the Town Hall after the match and went on to dinner at the Union Club. Mr. G.F. Hutchins, president of the Oldham club, presided over the proceedings accompanied by the Mayor, Councillor F Tweedale. Mr. Hutchins gave the toast *"To our Australian visitors"* and went on to recall the hospitality he had received when he managed the British touring team in Australia. Messrs. Savage and Sunderland, the joint tour managers, both responded positively with Harry Sunderland remembering the incident on the last tour and how affected he was when he thought it would be his last time in Oldham. "I'm glad to be back," he went on to say. Other notables in attendance were Jim Parkinson, Bob Wylie and the deputy Chief Constable, Mr. G. Musgrave.

The Australians were presented with inscribed souvenirs including wallets and tankards. They reciprocated with Kangaroo badges for the Oldham players, the referee and Mr. Wylie the Oldham Secretary. The touring party wound up their day by attending a dance at the Greenacres Co-operative Hall (Hill Stores), a function organised jointly by Oldham F.C. and the supporters club. Such was the interest that 900 tickets were sold and many were turned away at the door. The special visitors arrived at 9pm as the orchestra played "Advance Australia Fair". The evening was a huge success with the Oldham skipper, Fred Ashworth and the tour captain, Wally Prigg jointly undertaking the duties as MC for part of the evening. The Oldham Chronicle reported that *"everything went with a swing until midnight came all too soon."*

Caricatures of **Ernie Norman, Percy Williams** *and* **Jack Reardon** *as they appeared in the Oldham match-day programme.*

The 1937 Australian Tour	Result	Score		Att
Leigh	Won	11	9	5,000
York	Won	15	6	5,000
Newcastle	Won	37	0	4,000
Lancashire	Lost	5	7	16,250
Halifax	Lost	2	12	14,500
Yorkshire	Won	8	4	7,570
Wakefield Trinity	Won	17	10	8,696
Rochdale Hornets	Won	6	0	2,400
GREAT BRITAIN at Headingley, Leeds	Lost	4	5	31,949
Widnes	Drew	13	13	4,201
Hull	Won	22	12	15,000
Bradford Northern	Won	19	6	5,748
Salford	Lost	8	11	12,000
Wigan	Won	25	23	9,800
Oldham	Won	10	6	12,265
GREAT BRITAIN at Station Road, Swinton	Lost	3	13	31,724
Liverpool Stanley	Won	28	9	1,500
Huddersfield	Lost	7	17	9,383
Swinton	Lost	3	5	4,113
Warrington	Lost	6	8	12,637
Leeds	Lost	8	21	5,000
St. Helens XIII	Won	15	7	2,000
Barrow	Lost	8	12	8,153
GREAT BRITAIN at Fartown, Huddersfield	Won	13	3	9,093
Broughton Rangers	Lost	0	13	3,000

*The Australians perform their "war cry" on a grey November day at Watersheddings. Stand-off half **Ernie Norman** (No 16) is prominent with his back to the camera.*

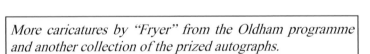

More caricatures by "Fryer" from the Oldham programme and another collection of the prized autographs.

BEATON
AUSTRALIA.

FRYER.

WAIRID
AUSTRALIA

HEIDKE
ONE OF
THE
AUSTRALIAN
HEAVY-
WEIGHT
FORWARDS

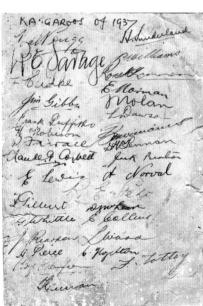

KA-GAROOS of 1937

Menu

Beneath our radiant Southern Cross,
We'll toil with heart and hands,
To make our youthful Commonwealth
Renowned of all the lands:
For loyal sons beyond the seas
We've boundless plains to share,
With courage let us all combine
To "Advance Australia Fair."

"You know your limitations—sit down."

Hors D'Œuvres :

"In league with France, Australia, New Zealand and England."

Soup :

ASPARAGUS.

"Refuse it not, it hath no tongue to vex you"—*Twelfth Night.*

Fish :

TURBOT AND "SAVAGE" SAUCE.

"Could not be 'harboured' in Sydney."

Poultry :

CAPON AND SAUSAGE.

"Let's go on with the game"—"*Sunderland*"in "*Alice in Wonderland.*"

PEAS, BAKED AND BOILED POTATOES.

"The Trainer's eye is watching how you run this course."

Sweets :

PINEAPPLE CREAM PUDDING.

"The Last TEST"

Cheese and Biscuits :

"Serenely full, the epicure would say, Fate cannot harm me,
I have dined to-day"—"*Macbeth.*"

"COO-E ON ILKLEY MOOR"

H.RET. KIDD & RENNIE LTD., PRINTERS, OLDHAM

Toast List

"The King"

Proposer - THE PRESIDENT.

"*When I forget my Sovereign, may my God forget me*"
———"Thurlow."

"Our Australian Visitors"

Proposer - Mr. G. F. HUTCHINS.

Responses - THE MANAGERS
(Messrs Hy. Sunderland
and R. Savage).

The inside pages of the menu card shown earlier.

Here we can see the "Toast List" and the menu itself. Headed by the words to "Advance Australia Fair", it is infused with humour, as well as Shakespearean quotes.

1947 1947
1947 1947

OLDHAM R.L.F.C.

NEW ZEALAND
RUGBY LEAGUE

October 25th 1947.

OLDHAM 8 NEW ZEALAND 18

OLDHAM'S BIG HAND FOR KIWIS

TOUR SOUVE

THE 1947-48 NEW ZEALAND LEAGUE

A VENTURERS PRESS PUBLICATION

WRITTEN & COMPILED BY STANLEY CHADWICK

This was the first New Zealand side to play at Watersheddings since they toured here in 1926 although Oldham had been allocated a match against the 1939 Kiwis who must rank as the unluckiest touring side ever. They arrived on the 29th of August 1939 and defeated St Helens on the 2nd of September, twenty-four hours after Germany invaded Poland! On the day following the match against Saints war was declared. All sport was stopped for a few days and following a match against Dewsbury on the 7th of September the New Zealanders sailed for home a week later.

Whilst there had been no Test matches played against the Kiwis in this country for over twenty years, the Lions had played regularly in New Zealand although the side that toured down-under in 1946 - and which included Oldham's Welsh forward Doug Phillips - played only one match against New Zealand who were surprise 13-8 winners.

The New Zealand side had already played the first Test at Headingley, losing by a single point in front of a 28,000 crowd but had progressed to beat Wales 28-20, despite the home side being roared on by 18,000 spectators. Oldham's ex-Llanelli forward Les Thomas played in both matches and would face the Kiwis for a third time today.

The teams, officials and the Mayor of Oldham get together for a pre-match photograph.

OLDHAM R.L.F.C

NEW ZEALAND

84

October 25th 1947.
OLDHAM 8   NEW ZEALAND 18

A splendid crowd of over 17,000 had come to watch the first post war touring team to visit Watersheddings. The 1947 Kiwis came to Oldham determined to be the first representatives of their country to lower the Roughyeds colours. That being said, there did seem to be a good rapport between the two camps which saw the two sides photographed together before the kick-off on the pavilion steps. In keeping with that gesture the teams took the field in pairs led by captains Norman Harris and Pat Smith.

However, once the game began the niceties were suspended for the duration of the action on the field of play and what a sensational start it was for the home side! New Zealand kicked-off into a strong wind and after Oldham had sent the ball back down-field, Ray Nuttall, the visiting full-back fumbled his catch. From the resulting scrum some slick handling saw skipper Norman HARRIS, cross the try line with several defenders hanging on. Home full-back Billy GRIFFITHS missed the conversion but soon afterward he made amends by slotting home a penalty goal after the tourists were pulled up for a scrummage offence. This stung the visitors into action to the effect that they were soon on level terms. The bulky forward C.C. Hancox split the home defence when he made a spectacular break up the field. The Oldham cover closed in but there was Ken MOUNTFORD up in support to take the slipped pass and score under the posts. NUTTALL put over the easy conversion.

Oldham made good use of the wind advantage with Ernie Large, Vince Kenny and Joe Mahoney all causing problems for the Kiwis. On the other side the left wing pairing of Maurice Robertson and Bill McKenzie looked dangerous and it was a break from the speedy winger that led to the next score. McKenzie had broken away from the Oldham cover and was left with just Griffiths barring his way to the line. The plucky Welshman launched himself at his rival with the result that the impact shook the ball from the New Zealander's grasp. Fortunately for the tourists the ball went backwards and Travers HARDWICK

A trio of tricky Kiwis: <u>*Left,*</u> ***Ken Mountford*** *usually a loose forward but filled in nicely at scrum-half at Watersheddings being on hand to score the first try.* <u>*Middle,*</u> ***C.C. (Claude Charles) Hancox*** *the "Man Mountain" whose bulky size masked his deceptive pace.* <u>*Right:*</u> ***Bill McKenzie****, speedy wingman from the Hornby club in Christchurch, he had a great match against Oldham.*

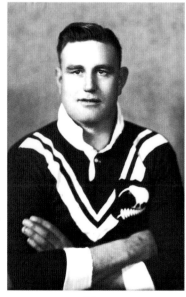
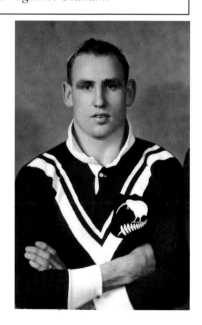

*It's mine! At the front from left to right: **Maurice Robertson, Norman Harris, Travers Hardwick** and **Tommy Ayres** scramble for the ball. At the rear Oldham's, **Wilf Frost** and **Les Thomas** along with Kiwis, **Charlie McBride** and **Bob Aynsley** look on with interest, as does referee Mr. Smith.*

reacted quickest to the situation scooping up possession to run fifty yards to the Oldham line. Again NUTTALL was on target for the extra two points. McKenzie needed treatment after his collision with Griffiths but he was soon recovered and causing more trouble for the Roughyeds. After the winger had once more taken play into the Oldham half, a kick for the line took a wicked bounce away from the luckless Griffiths and Dougie ANDERSON was on the spot to touch down. Once more NUTTALL was on the mark with the goal kick and half-time soon followed with the score: Oldham 5 New Zealand 15.

The Oldham supporters must have feared the worst for the second period with the Kiwis now having the wind at their backs and it did not take long for the lead to be extended. It was Mountford who broke from inside his own half before handing on to Des BARCHARD who finished off in style from 40 yards out. This time Nuttall was off target with the conversion attempt. To their credit Oldham did not let their heads go down. Prop-forward Jack Taylor put in a strong diagonal run out towards the right wing where he passed to Stan Inglesfield who in turn fired the ball back inside to MAHONEY, who managed to squeeze in at the corner. Griffiths made a good attempt for the extra points but the strong wind held the ball up short.

The Roughyeds took heart from this score and began to dominate the play. Ray Smith was dictating the tactics from scrum-half and Large looked likely to capitalise before he put down a potential try scoring pass. Another attack was foiled when Mountford nipped in to intercept an Inglesfield pass. As the match drew to a close Oldham continued to worry the Kiwi line with Kenny and Les Thomas prominent and there was a smart bout of inter-passing between Tommy Ayres and Harris but it was all to no avail. The New Zealanders' defence held firm and the victory was achieved by the score of eighteen points to eight.

OLDHAM:
W. Griffiths; S. Inglesfield, J. Mahoney, N. Harris, E. Large; V. Kenny, A.R. Smith; H. Ogden, W. Frost, J. Taylor, L. Thomas, N. Thompson, T. Ayres.

NEW ZEALAND:
R. Nuttall; R. McGregor, H.D. Anderson, M. Robertson, A.W. McKenzie; D. Barchard, K. Mountford; C. Hancox, R. Aynsley, C. McBride, P. Smith, J. Newton, T. Hardwick.

Attendance: 17,239   Referee: Mr F. Smith – Barrow

Left to right: **Dougie Anderson**, **Des Barchard** *and* **Ray Nuttall**, *all amongst the points scorers for New Zealand at Watersheddings in 1947.*

Norman Harris *prepares to tackle Kiwi wingman* Ron McGregor *as* Wilf Frost *and* Tommy Ayres *move across to provide cover for their captain.*

OLDHAM
v
NEW ZEALAND

Saturday, 25th October 1947
at
WATERSHEDDINGS,
OLDHAM.

Kick-Off 3 p.m.

Official Souvenir Programme 6d.

Above: Try scorer
Joe Mahoney;
Right: Goal kicker,
Billy Griffiths.
Along with Norman Harris they formed a Welsh trio that scored all the points for Oldham.

The tourists were entertained to dinner at the Town Hall where they were presented with silver serviette rings each inscribed with their initials and the Oldham coat of arms. The presentations were made by the Mayor, Councillor Joseph Berry. The Oldham vice-president Mr. F. Holt, alluding to the difficulties of the current time, stated, *"Goodwill and fellowship are not rationed and we give you an abundance..."* He went on to send his best wishes via the tourists to the ex-Oldham player Alan Laird, now back in his native New Zealand. Oldham stars of the past were in attendance with Bill McCutcheon, Joe Corsi and Sid Rix given a warm reception and a special cheer was reserved for when Oldham's own Kiwi hero G.W Smith was introduced to the gathering.

The tourists' co-manager, Mr Lance Hunter replied, again with reference to the hard times that prevailed, by saying, *"This team does not depend on finance for friendship, the game was played in a good spirit and the reception – wonderful!"* Mr Hunter then presented a Kiwi lapel badge to the Oldham committee members and a ball signed by both teams to the Mayor.

After the dinner the touring party were to be guests at a dance held in their honour, at the Greenacres Cooperative Hall (Hill Stores ballroom), by the supporters club.

EVENING CHRONICLE, Saturday, October 25. 1947

OLDHAM'S BIG HAND FOR KIWIS

Chronicle photograph.
NOT THE LATEST DANCE.—Just the Kiwis giving their famous warcry.

Always a good photo opportunity, the Chronicle lensman captures the scene as the Kiwis perform the "haka" on the Town Hall steps at the reception before the match.

Also shown a souvenir tour brochure for the tour published by the magazine "Rugby League Review".

1947 New Zealand Tour.	Result	Score		Att
St. Helens	Won	11	5	22,000
Swinton	Lost	6	8	12,148
York	Won	29	0	4,500
GREAT BRITAIN	Lost	10	11	28,445
at Leeds				
Castleford	Won	17	3	11,000
Hull Kingston Rovers	Lost	7	13	12,000
Bradford Northern	Won	17	7	17,519
Leigh	Won	10	5	15,000
Wales	Won	28	20	18,283
Wigan	Won	10	8	24,089
Oldham	Won	18	8	17,239
Hunslet	Lost	10	18	5,553
Hull	Lost	7	13	16,113
Batley	Lost	18	19	3,510
GREAT BRITAIN	Won	10	7	29,031
at Swinton				
Leeds	Won	23	16	8,864
Warrington	Lost	5	7	20,682
Halifax	Won	21	5	5,276
Huddersfield	Lost	7	12	8,872
Widnes	Lost	0	7	11,900
Dewsbury	Won	24	5	7,270
Workington Town	Won	12	7	10,722
Barrow	Drew	2	2	5,565
Wakefield Trinity	Won	30	3	11,595
Bramley	Won	31	3	3,100
Belle Vue Rangers	Won	19	3	10,000
GREAT BRITAIN	Lost	9	25	42,685
at Bradford				

The 1947 Kiwis gave a very good account of themselves. Although they lost the Test series by two games to one, the winning margin for Great Britain in the first match at Headingley was a single point.

Lennie Jordan recorded most tries with ten and Warwick Clarke topped the goal chart with 52. Of the 27 matches played 16 were won with one draw and ten defeats. Captain Pat Smith, along with Maurice Robertson made most appearances, each playing in 22 games.

Two of the original "All Golds", left **G.W. Smith** *and* **Arthur Kelly** *reunited to watch the 1947 Kiwis.*

THE NEW ZEALAND TOURISTS, 1947

Back Row:—R. Clark, K. Mountford, D. Anderson, A. W. McKenzie, G. Davidson, R. Nuttall, C. McBride, L. Jordan
Third Row:—R. Aynsley, L. Pye, J. Johnson, A. Gillman, C. Hancox, J. Newton, T. Hardwick, M. Robertson
Second Row:—L. Hunter, A. McInnarney, P. Smith, J. A. Redwood, A. Graham, J. Forrest, T. A. McClymont
         Manager.   *Captain.*   *Manager.*   *Vice-Captain.*   *Coach.*
Front Row:—W. S. Clarke, J. Haig, R. McGregor, R. Cunningham, D. Barchard.

90

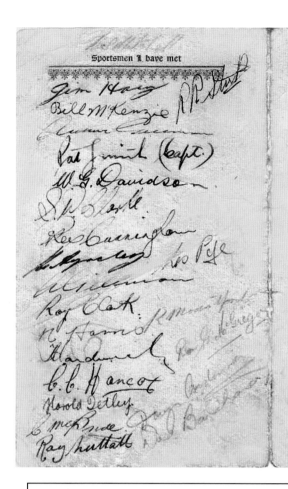

OLDHAM FOOTBALL CLUB

F. MILLS, Esq., PRESIDENT

Complimentary Dinner

at the

Town Hall, Oldham

on

Saturday, October 25th, 1947

To mark the occasion of the
OLDHAM v. NEW ZEALAND
Rugby League Game at Watersheddings, Oldham
SATURDAY, OCTOBER 25th, 1947

The menu card for the reception at Oldham Town Hall.

Toast List

THE KING
Proposer · · The President, F. Mills, Esq.

THE NEW ZEALAND TEAM
Proposer · The Vice-President, F. S. Holt, Esq.
Responses · · · · The Managers
A. Redwood, Esq. · L. Hunter, Esq.

Presentation of Souvenirs by
THE WORSHIPFUL THE MAYOR
(Councillor Joseph Berry, J.P.)

Menu

Hors d'oeuvres
or
Consomme Royal   Potage Vin Blanc

Filet de Plie Poche - Sauce Persil
or
Poulet Roti avec Farce

Pommes Duchess   Pommes Roti

Petit Pois

Fraise Melba

Charlotte Russe

Canape   Ecosaise

Cafe

OLDHAM FOOTBALL CLUB

OLDHAM R.L.F.C

AUSTRALIA RUGBY LEAGUE TOUR

NEW ZEALAND RUGBY LEAGUE

December 4th 1948.
OLDHAM 7 AUSTRALIA 27

The Australians' Tour 1948

RUGBY LEAGUE

1/- OFFICIAL SOUVENIR

Christmas and New Year

Happiness, Prosperity and Health in the New Year

GREEN FINAL

No. 20,319.   SATURDAY, DECEMBER 4, 1948.   Price 1½d.

CROWD GETS RUGBY THRILLS AT WATERSHEDDINGS

jury to Silva Spoils Great Gam

Aussies Sail Away Past Weaker Side

OLDHAM v AUSTRALIA

M.C.C. Win Easily.

Treble Centu for D. Comp

SPECTATORS at Watersheddings this afternoon were in

During the years following the Second World War the game boomed in Britain and 450,000 spectators flocked through the turnstiles to watch one or more of the 27 matches played by Colin Maxwell's Kangaroos. Oldham were going through a tough season and would end the campaign in the lower reaches of the league, but, regardless of that, almost 15,000 turned out to see the men in green and gold.

The Ashes had been retained two years earlier, when, down-under, the Lions won a three-match Test series by drawing the first and then winning the second and third matches. Oldham's second-row forward Doug Phillips, one of a record eleven Welshmen on the tour, played in all three games.

Oldham's match against the Australians had been scheduled to be played at the tail end of the tour and by that time the outcome of the Test series had been decided. The Lions had won the first Test played at Headingley, defeating the Kangaroos by 23-21 and had gone on to win the second, played at Swinton's Station Road, by 16 points to 7 to retain the Ashes, a trophy which they had now held for 28 years. As though reflecting the club's lowly league position no Oldham players were selected for the series.

Colourful brochure issued by the Rugby Football League to herald the visit of the 1948 Australians.

December 4th 1948.
OLDHAM 7   AUSTRALIA 27

A good crowd had gathered at Watersheddings on a mild December afternoon in anticipation of the first visit of the Kangaroos for over ten, war-interrupted years. Also this match was to be the debut for Oldham's new young Welsh scrum-half, Joe Silva.

The teams line up for the anthems before the start of the match.

After the traditional "war cry" the Australians kicked off. The early exchanges were full of vim and vigour and after only three minutes the Kangaroos' skipper, Colin Maxwell, was led from the field bleeding at the mouth after being met by a quartet of Oldham defenders. After being pinned down in their own quarter Norman Harris relieved the pressure with a clearing kick into the visitors' half. At the scrum which followed, Keith Froome was penalised only for Irving Barraclough's goal attempt to come back off the cross-bar. Back came the tourists and after just five minutes play stand-off Johnny HAWKE took advantage of some slack defending to scoot away from Barraclough and Bob Batten and score at the corner. Jack Horrigan missed the conversion attempt.

Silva was showing up well with his speedy service from the scrum and a spectacular flying tackle on Bobby Lulham. Maxwell returned to the fray but it was the Roughyeds who scored next. After good work by Tommy Leyland, Harris and Billy Mitchell had taken play deep into the Kangaroos half, but possession was subsequently lost. However, as the Australians moved the ball over to the right wing, Harry GLANVILLE nipped in between Vic Bulgin and Horrigan to intercept and race the twenty yards to score behind the posts. BARRACLOUGH added the goal to put Oldham in front. The lead did not last for long. Soon after the restart it became apparent that the visitors were playing at a pace that the home side were struggling to match and a rapid exchange of passes was finished off by LULHAM who scored at the corner. Horrigan was again off target.

Oldham were applying a more direct approach and after making steady progress up the field, Edgar Brooks was held just short after a lunge for the line. Likewise, Silva was only inches away as he attempted to wriggle over. The attack broke down when Leyland failed with a drop goal effort. Oldham were enjoying their best period of the game and BARRACLOUGH finally landed a penalty goal after previously just failing with two attempts in as many minutes. This sparked the Australians back into action, which resulted in HAWKE pushing off Harris to go over for his second try after Horrigan had made the initial break. FROOME took over the goal kicking duties and was successful with his first attempt. To add to the Roughyeds' woes Silva limped off after a heavy collision. Just before half-time there was a fracas that brought the flag-waving touch judge on to the field. The resultant penalty went Oldham's way but as Barraclough's effort sailed wide of the posts the

*There were just five minutes on the clock when **Johnny Hawke** evaded the attentions of **Bob Batten** and **Irving Barraclough** to dive over for the first Australian try. Number six **Bobby Lulham** was up in support if needed.*

half-time whistle blew with the score: Oldham 7 Australia 11.

Oldham brought Leyland out of the pack to replace the luckless Silva at scrum-half. The match resumed at a brisk pace with both teams showing up well, especially the visiting captain Maxwell who was causing much concern to the home defence. Inevitably, it was the visitors who turned the pressure into points. Some resolute defending, notably by Mitchell and Harris, kept the tourists at bay until Bill TYQUIN took a slick pass from Hawke direct from a scrum to go over. FROOME added the extra points. The Kangaroos were now on top gear and after Bulgin had failed with a drop goal attempt, the same player broke through the Oldham defence before handing on to Maxwell, who combined with Noel Mulligan to put Duncan HALL in for an unconverted try.

Oldham tried hard to come back, Batten was tried at scrum-half and Harris and Barraclough threatened the Aussie line, but it was the ever alert FROOME who broke away direct from a scrum to score a try which he converted himself. Mitchell was the next Oldham player to be given a go at the base of the scrum. However, none of the various home combinations could cope with the Australian half-backs. As the game drew to a close HALL crossed for his second try but Oldham battled away to the end and just before the finish Harris was held up just short of the Australian line to leave the final score: Oldham 7 Australia 27.

OLDHAM: I. Barraclough; R. Batten, W. Mitchell, N. Harris, H. Glanville;
J. Chalmers, J. Silva;
J. Pilkington, E. Brooks, H. Tomlinson, H. Ogden, J. Donegan, T. Leyland.

AUSTRALIA: V. Bulgin; J. Horrigan, C. Maxwell, L. Pegg, R. Lulham;
J. Hawke, K. Froome;
D. Hall, I. Benton, J. Holland, F. de Belin, N. Mulligan, W. Tyquin.

Attendance: 14,798   Referee: Mr. G. S. Phillips - Widnes

The after-match dinner was held at the Town Hall and as with the Kiwis the year before, the Australians were presented with an inscribed silver serviette ring by the Oldham President Mr. F.S. Holt who toasted the touring party and went on to introduce some of the celebrities present, including Alf Wood, Albert Brough, Bill McCutcheon and former Kiwi stars G.W. Smith and Arthur Kelly. In response Mr. E.J. Simmonds for the Australians spoke of the warmth and hospitality extended to them and expressed some sympathy for the plight of Oldham's scrum-half Joe Silva. He also presented pin badges to Mr Holt, the Secretary Bert Summerscales and the captain Norman Harris. The Oldham committee-man, Mr C.G. Hall also toasted the press for their expert reporting of the tour so far!

To the delight of the ensemble, the musical programme for the evening included Mr. F.S. Holt (baritone) with Mr. C.G. Hall at the piano.

It later emerged that it wasn't only Joe Silva who suffered in Oldham's cause that day. Left wing Harry Granville suffered a broken wrist in the very first tackle of the match! In total he appeared in twenty senior matches for the Roughyeds and in all the others he played at full-back.

Back Row: (left to right)   P. L. Tresidder (Press)   L. J. Furness (Trainer)   R. Dimond,   E. Brosnan,   A. Gibbs,   F. L. de Belin,
       J. F. Holland,   R. J. Rayner,   N. R. Hand,   D. Hall,   K. B. Schubert,   C. B. Hopkins
Middle Row: R. J. Maguire (Press)   T. L. Goodman (Press)   W. H. Thompson,   G. K. Froome,   J. N. Graves,   L. G. Cowie,
J. Horrigan,   H. A. Benton,   N. G. Mulligan,   D. A. McRitchie,   P. McMahon,   H. R. Matthews (Visitor)   W. F. Corbett (Press)
Seated: C. B. Churchill,   N. J. Hawke,   W. P. O'Connell,   I. W. Tyquin (Vice-capt.)   E. J. Simmonds (Business Manager)
       C. M. Maxwell (Capt.)   W. G. Buckley (Team Manager)   L. R. Pegg,   R. J. Lulham,   F. E. Johnson,   V. J. Bulgin

It's the Town Hall again and it seems everyone wants to be photographed with the 1948 Kangaroos.

An echo from a more thoughtful period of time.
A Christmas and New Year Greeting card specially printed for the 1948 Australian touring team.
This was sent to the Oldham hooker, Edgar Brooks and his family from the tour vice-captain Bill
Tyquin. The team group on the previous page was featured on the inside cover of the card.

1948 TOUR	AUSTRALIA		
MATCH	RESULT	SCORE	ATTENDANCE
Huddersfield	Lost	3 - 22	26,017
Belle Vue Rangers	Won	14 - 9	7,535
Hull	Won	13 - 3	16.616
Wakefield Trinity	Won	26 - 19	20,040
Leigh	Won	24 - 12	12,968
Salford	Won	13 - 2	16,627
Castleford	Won	10 - 8	14,004
GREAT BRITAIN at Headingley, Leeds	Lost	21 - 23	36,394
Cumberland	Lost	4 - 5	8,818
St Helens	Lost	8 - 10	20,175
Dewsbury	Won	14 - 4	13,614
Hull Kingston Rovers	Lost	12 - 17	7,614
Wigan	Lost	11 - 16	28,554
Barrow	Won	11 - 5	13,143
Leeds	Won	15 - 2	13,542
Warrington	Lost	7 - 16	26,879
GREAT BRITAIN at Station Road, Swinton	Lost	7 - 16	43,500
Bradford Northern	Won	21 - 7	13,287
Workington Town	Lost	7 - 10	13,253
Swinton	Won	21 - 0	5,849
Wales	Won	12 - 5	9,161
Yorkshire	Lost	2 - 5	5,310
Halifax	Won	10 - 8	6,520
Oldham	Won	27 - 7	14,798
Lancashire	Lost	8 - 13	11,788
Widnes	Won	18 - 8	10,761
GREAT BRITAIN at Odsal , Bradford	Lost	9 - 23	36,294

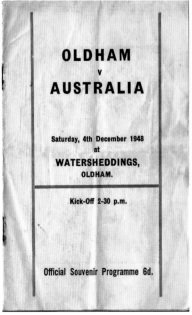

OLDHAM
v
AUSTRALIA

Saturday, 4th December 1948
at
WATERSHEDDINGS,
OLDHAM.

Kick-Off 2-30 p.m.

Official Souvenir Programme 6d.

An indifferent tour for the 1948 Kangaroos with 15 victories, and 12 defeats from the 27 match itinerary. Those losses included all three Tests and the three county games. The third Test was postponed in December because of fog and the tourists completed a ten match tour of France before returning for the Test match at Bradford in January.

Leading scorers were Jack Horrigan 13 tries, Johnny Graves 24 goals and most appearances went to fellow South Sydney player Jack Rayner with 19.

The 1948 Kangaroos
Fourth row: Hopkins, Johnson, Mulligan, Cowie, Furness (trainer), McRitchie, McMahon, Thompson, O'Connell.
Third row: Hawke, de Belin, Pegg, Dimond, Horrigan, Rayner, Holland, Hand, Schubert, Gibbs.
Second row: Brosnan, Hall, Tyquin, Simmonds (manager), Maxwell (captain), Buckley (manager), Bulgin, Benton, Graves.
Front row: Lulham, Churchill, Froome.

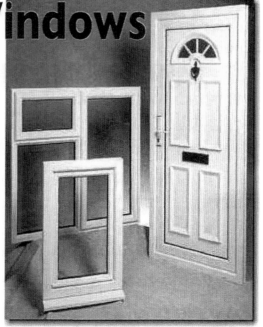

1951 1951
1951 1951

AUSTRALIA RUGBY LEAGUE TOUR

OLDHAM R.L.F.C

NEW ZEALAND RUGBY LEAGUE

September 29th 1951
OLDHAM 21 NEW ZEALAND 18

RUGBY LEAGUE

OLDHAM

FOOTBALL CLUB

. . . .

OLDHAM

v.

NEW ZEALAND

B. Mitchell
Sportsmen I have met

Complimentary Dinner

at the

Assembly Room

Central Fire Station, Oldham

on

Saturday, 29th September,

To mark the occasion of the

OLDHAM v. NEW ZEALAND

Rugby League Game at Watersheddings

SATURDAY, 29th SEPTEMBER

EVENING CHRONICLE, Monday, October 1, 1951

THIS WAS RUGBY TO DELIGHT ANY SPECTATOR

Stirrup played hero's role
in Oldham's great victory

YOU'VE got to applaud these Oldham players—they can play the best
ball with the best of teams, and if a number of lukewarm supporters are
won over to giving more support to Rugby League football after Saturday

At last Oldham were on the up. Back in 1948 when the Australians had hammered the Roughyeds by a 20 points margin the Oldham side were in the lower reaches of the league. This season Oldham would finish the season in fifth place, just one point outside a top four play-off slot.

 Oldham had recruited wisely since the match against the Kangaroos. A trio of Welsh forwards had arrived at Watersheddings - Charlie Winslade from the Maesteg Rugby Union Club, loose-forward Bryn Goldswain from Hull K.R. and the rugged Bryn Day from Belle Vue Rangers.

Ace marksman Bernard Ganley and the classy three-quarter Alan Davies had been signed from the Leigh amateur game, whilst mercurial half-back Frank Stirrup had arrived from Salford, utility man Frank Daley from the Leigh club and three-quarter Joe Warham from Swinton. Front-row forward Ken Jackson and winger Terry O'Grady were local born youngsters, whilst hooker Jack "Rubber Legs" Keith was signed from the Bush Electric amateur club in Leeds. Apart from Keith all had been selected to play in today's match against the Kiwis.

*Above: Tour captain **Maurice Robertson** introduces the Mayor of Oldham, Alderman Frank Lord, to his 1951 Kiwis.*

As you will see, this is just one of several fabulous photographs that exist from this exciting match.

September 29th 1951.
OLDHAM 21   NEW ZEALAND 18

In the time honoured tradition the Kiwis lined up in front of the main stand before the game to perform the "haka".

*Following the officials and dignitaries, **Bryn Goldswain** and **Maurice Robertson** lead out the teams. Oldham are in numerical order with **Bernard, Ganley, Joe Warham, Billy Mitchell** etc seen following their captain on to the field.*

The first serious action of the match saw Charlie Winslade break away and hand on to Alan Davies but the New Zealanders' line was saved by a timely interception from Jim Edwards. The visitors hit back and a cross kick from Andy Berryman looked certain to set up the first score only for Bevan Hough to fumble the ball as he tried to gather near the Oldham line. There continued to be an element of to and fro between the two halves before the Kiwis broke the deadlock when prop forward Cliff JOHNSON burst through several tackles to score under the posts. Jim HAIG added the conversion with just less than ten minutes played. The Roughyeds were thus stung into scoring action themselves. After being put in the clear by Davies, Terry O'GRADY rounded Berryman to score right in the corner. Ganley failed with the goal attempt.

It was a good open game with play fluctuating from end to end. It was a piece of trickery from Oldham's "Mr Football", Frank Stirrup, that put the Roughyeds in front. After the Kiwis were penalised it looked for all the world as if Bernard Ganley was going to go for a goal attempt but up stepped Stirrup who tapped the ball forward, inter-passed with Bryn Day and finally handed on to Joe WARHAM who sidestepped through for a try. Ganley again missed the conversion. Oldham were now playing some great football with Winslade leading the way. Even when Davies had to retire injured it did not stop the Oldham momentum and after some sustained pressure it was that man Stirrup again who masterminded the Kiwis' downfall. He broke away wide from a scrum whilst half-back partner Frank Daley came steaming up on the inside shouting for the ball. Seconds later Daley was occupying the attentions of several New Zealand defenders. However, STIRRUP never released the ball and crossed the line to score near the posts. This time GANLEY was on target to give the half-time score:
Oldham 11 New Zealand 5.

The packed Watersheddings' terraces look on as Oldham winger **Joe Warham** receives a pass from **Billy Mitchell** as **Bevan Hough** and **George Menzies** set off in pursuit.

Within a minute of the restart the crowd were cheering again when GANLEY landed a 45 yard drop goal. Next it was the now restored Davies who combined with Winslade for a fifty yard advance into New Zealand territory. This time the Kiwi defence held firm and a swift breakaway concluded with EDWARDS going over. HAIG missed the conversion but was on target with a penalty soon after to leave the visitors only three points in arrears. Oldham responded when O'Grady was unlucky as he fumbled the ball when trying to re-gather his own kick ahead. Les Anthony managed to heel the resulting scrum and when the ball was moved quickly to the right Billy Mitchell drew in the cover to send WARHAM over for his second try in spite of Johnson's despairing tackle. Ganley was just wide with the conversion attempt. The match continued in open style with Oldham always looking the more dangerous. The game was sealed when "*man of the match*" STIRRUP dummied his way through the defensive line then followed his kick through to score. GANLEY added the extra points and Oldham were home and dry.

*Despite the tackle from **Doug Richards-Jolley**, **Joe Warham** touches down for Oldham to the delight of **Charlie Winslade** (left) and **Bryn Day** and to the dismay of a posse of Kiwis.*

104

The New Zealanders, to their credit, plugged away to give the scoreline some respectability and even after Doug Richards-Jolley was carried off injured the tourists found enough reserves to go in for two late tries from Charlie McBRIDE and HOUGH, both were spectacular solo efforts from long range. HAIG converted one of the scores to leave the final result: Oldham 21 New Zealand 18.

OLDHAM: W. B. Ganley; J. Warham, W. Mitchell, A. Davies, T. O'Grady; F. Daley, F. Stirrup; K. Jackson, L. Anthony, B. Day, C. Winslade, T. Leyland, B. Goldswain.

NEW ZEALAND:
A. Berryman; J. Edwards, M. Robertson, T.O. Baxter, B. Hough; G. Menzies J. Haig; C. Johnson, D. Blanchard, W. McLennan, D. Richards-Jolley, C. McBride, A. Atkinson.

Attendance: 15,174   Referee: Mr. C. F. Appleton - Warrington

After the match the New Zealand party were guests of the Oldham club at a *"well arranged"* dinner held at the Oldham Fire Station Assembly Rooms. During the proceedings the Oldham President, Mr Arthur Caldwell, said the Kiwis were always a great attraction as the attendance and gate receipts had proved. He went on to say they were great ambassadors for the sport, which he thought was not sufficiently well known around the world.

Not this time, Joe!
*Two-try **Joe Warham** is well and truly collared by **Bevan Hough** and **Tom Baxter** with full-back **Andy Berryman** on hand if required.*

Above: **Alan Davies** *prepares to pass inside to* **Terry O'Grady** *as* **Charlie Winslade** *looks on.*
Below: **Charlie McBride** *dives over for a Kiwi try while* **Alan Davies** *and* **Frank Stirrup** *arrive too late to prevent the score.*

Both the joint tour managers reciprocated with niceties. Mr. D. A. Wilkie praised Oldham for the sportsmanlike manner in which they played the game and congratulated them upon their victory. Mr. T. F. McKenzie said that each place they visited tried to outdo the other with the kindness offered to the team. However, the welcome they had received from the Oldhamers when the coach pulled up at the Town Hall had really warmed the hearts of the lads. At one point during the dinner the fire alarm sounded giving the tourists a first-hand opportunity to see the Oldham brigade dash to their stations and turn out the fire engines. A task they apparently achieved in a matter of seconds.

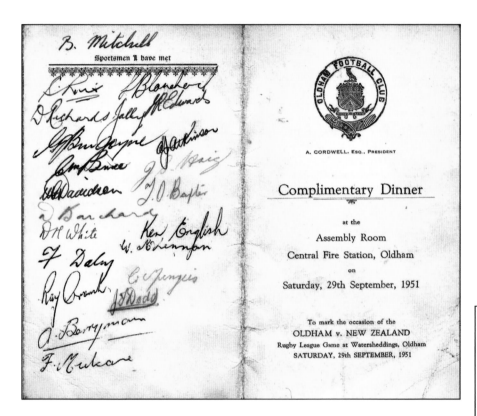

OLDHAM FOOTBALL CLUB

A. CORDWELL. ESQ., PRESIDENT

Complimentary Dinner

at the

Assembly Room

Central Fire Station, Oldham

on

Saturday, 29th September, 1951

To mark the occasion of the

OLDHAM v. NEW ZEALAND

Rugby League Game at Watersheddings, Oldham
SATURDAY, 29th SEPTEMBER, 1951

The menu card for the after-match reception at the Fire Brigade Assembly Room.

There is also the usual collection of Kiwi signatures, along with a few "guests".

Toast List

THE KING

Proposer   -   The President, A. Cordwell, Esq.

———

THE NEW ZEALAND TEAM

Proposer - The Vice-President, P. G. Carter, Esq.
Responses   -   -   -   The Managers
W. McKensie, Esq.   D. Wilkie, Esq.

Menu

Grapefruit with Marsala

Cream of Tomato Soup

Fillet of Sole Mayonnaise

Roast Turkey and Chipolata Sausage

Roast Potatoes   Creamed Potatoes

Carrots   Peas

Peach Shortcake

Cheese and Biscuits

Coffee

*"We hope with the clock's last chime
You'll all exclaim 'a lovely time'"*

Bernard Ganley manages to scramble the ball away from Maurice Robertson, George Menzies and Bevan Hough.

1951-52 New Zealand Tour			
Opponents	**Result**	**Score**	**Att**
Rochdale Hornets	Won	13 - 9	4,000
Halifax	Lost	12 - 18	15,000
Workington Town	Won	17 - 15	8,935
Oldham	Lost	18 - 21	15,174
Castleford	Won	10 - 9	6,600
GREAT BRITAIN	Lost	15 - 21	37,475
at Bradford			
Huddersfield	Won	34 - 12	9,859
Warrington	Won	19 - 13	18,889
Batley	Won	20 - 13	5,087
Bramley	Won	24 - 20	2,100
St Helens	Won	33 - 10	17,000
Leigh	Won	31 - 5	9,000
Barrow	Lost	5 - 9	13,319
Bradford Northern	Lost	8 - 13	29,072
Wigan	Won	15 - 8	13,500
York	Won	15 - 12	4,183
GREAT BRITAIN	Lost	19 - 20	28,246
at Swinton			
Wakefield Trinity	Won	26 - 18	8,850
Leeds	Won	19 - 4	16,000
Lancashire	Lost	12 - 13	7,313
Belle Vue Rangers	Lost	5 - 7	5,000
Hull	Won	28 - 8	9,000
Salford	Won	27 - 12	10,000
Yorkshire	Won	10 - 3	2,910
Wales	Won	15 - 3	8,568
Cardiff	Won	18 - 10	2,000
GREAT BRITAIN	Lost	12 - 16	18,649
at Leeds			
British Empire XIII	Lost	2 - 26	6,800
at Chelsea			

For the 1951 Kiwis, ably led by centre Maurice Robertson, it was a case of what might have been. The 28 match tour itinerary brought 18 victories and 10 defeats. Unfortunately, three of those setbacks were in the Test matches but the losing margins were just six points, one point and four points.

The series could hardly have been much closer. Indeed the six point defeat in the first Test was their biggest losing score until what one would imagine was a deflated set of players succumbed to a 26 – 2 reverse by a British Empire XIII in the last match of the tour.

Des White top scored with 63 goals and two tries, while Bruce Robertson, brother of the skipper, topped the try list with 13. White and Robertson (M), along with Charlie McBride, appeared in most games, each playing in 22 of the matches.

Bruce Robertson: *Top try scorer for the 1951 Kiwis.*

RUGBY LEAGUE

OLDHAM

FOOTBALL CLUB

• • • •

OLDHAM

v.

NEW ZEALAND

Saturday, 29th September, 1951

3-0 o'clock Kick off

• • • •

Price 6d

SOUVENIR PROGRAMME

1952 1952 1952 1952

OLDHAM R.L.F.C

AUSTRALIA RUGBY LEAGUE TOUR

NEW ZEALAND RUGBY LEAGUE

September 15th 1952.
OLDHAM 7 AUSTRALIA 7

TRAGIC SLIP ROBBED OLDHAM OF VICTORY

THE KANGAROOS WAR CRY

Aussie steamroller held up in Watersheddings thriller

Prior to the game commencing the Australians gave their famous war Cry. Here it is:—

Walla mullah, Woommera, Woommera, Illah,
Ganai, Berring, Warrang, Woorang,
Yallah, Yallah, Yarrah, Yarrah.
Ah. Jeleeba booga boorooloon,
Yarrahmeei meei meei.
Neeyarra, Neeyarra, Jeleeba, Carryoon,
Cooeewah, Cooeewah, Warr, Wooh!

The translation of which reads:—

We are fierce fighters descended...
beware, beware, bewar...
...they will be great...
go...
...b...
d!

OLDHAM FOOTBALL CLUB

PROGRAMME

The eighth Kangaroos visited Watersheddings as Ashes holders. Two years earlier the touring Lions had lost a series for the first time in thirty years when the Australians won two out of the three Test matches.

Prior to their match against Oldham the green and golds had won their first four matches - all against club sides - and by the completion of the tour had lost only three of their twenty-seven fixtures scoring a record 816 points. The only two club sides they failed to defeat were St Helens and Oldham.

Telephone Nos.: Office, MAIn 4865   Sec. MAIn 4998 (10 Grendon Avenue, Oldham)

Oldham Football Club

(MEMBERS OF THE RUGBY FOOTBALL LEAGUE)

SECRETARY:
H. SUMMERSCALES

PLEASE ADDRESS ALL COMMUNICATIONS TO
THE SECRETARY. PAVILION.
WATERSHEDDINGS, OLDHAM.

PAVILION, WATERSHEDDINGS,

OLDHAM

23rd Sept 1952. 19

Mr W Fallowfield.,
180 Chapeltown Road,
Leeds. 7.

Dear Sir.,

Oldham v Australian Tourists.,
at Watersheddings, Oldham,
Monday, 15th Sept 1952.

Gate receipts.,   £2856- 2- 3.
Entertainment Tax.   673-14- 6.

                          £2182- 7- 9.

65% to Tourists.,   £1418- 6- 0.
Oldham F.C.   764 1- 9

Attendance., 19.620.

        Cheque value £1418- 6- 0 was forwarded to the
Tourists, Friday, 19th Sept 1952.

        Yours faithfully.,

                Summerscales
                    Secretary.

Oldham's formal submission to Rugby League headquarters of the accounts for the 1952 tour match.

September 15th 1952.
OLDHAM 7   AUSTRALIA 7

Controversy shrouded the 1952 tour match at Watersheddings before a ball had been kicked or a tackle made. Very much at the last minute Oldham were told that they could not play three players who were due to take part in an England v Wales international later in the week. So late was the decision made known that many of those attending the match were unaware until the teams took the field.

Two of the players concerned were forwards, club captain Bryn Goldswain and fellow Welshman Bryn Day, along with speedy local wingman Terry O'Grady, selected for England. Ironically one of the players drafted in as a replacement was another Welshman, Les Anthony who, to be fair, was a regular member of the team throughout the season. However, the other two stand-ins were very new to senior rugby. Loose forward Alf Murray was making only his fifth start in the first team, whereas the "A" team forward John Watson being used as an emergency wing after the withdrawal of O'Grady and an injury to regular wingman, Lawrie Platt. Both local men, Watson, who was making only his second first team appearance, and Murray, did not let the side down.

The tourists, after an indifferent performance in defeating Whitehaven on the previous Saturday, put out a strong team, their only concern being that injuries to both regular hookers caused them to field a stand-in striker. A wonderful crowd of over 19,000 turned up for the Monday evening encounter. Frank Stirrup assumed the captaincy and led the teams out side by side with the Australian skipper, the legendary Clive Churchill.

Clive Churchill and *Frank Stirrup* lead out the teams followed by *Duncan Hall* and *Frank Daley*.

Notwithstanding their disappointment at the team changes, the home crowd were soon cheering as a penalty goal from Bernard GANLEY put the Roughyeds in front. The advantage lasted only a matter of minutes before a long distance effort from Noel PIDDING brought the scores back level. Oldham soon returned to the attack and a kick ahead, direct from a play the ball, caught the Aussies napping. They eventually made the ball safe but from the resulting scrum Frank Stirrup darted away diagonally, drawing three defenders with him. Just as they were about to pounce he slipped the ball out to the wing where WATSON finished strongly to cross the line for a try. GANLEY converted to put Oldham five points clear after nine minutes.

*Stand-in wingman, **John Watson** takes on Kanagroos, **Ken McCaffery** and **Dennis Flannery** (3).*

The rest of the half was dominated by tenacious defending from both teams. Penalties resulted but both Ganley (twice) and Pidding (three times) were out of luck with goal attempts. Churchill looked dangerous when coming into the line, as did winger Dennis Flannery. Still the Oldham line survived to leave the interval score: Oldham 7 Australia 2.

The visitors dominated in the early part of the second period. More penalties went their way but Pidding and Churchill were both off target. Oldham responded and a lightning breakaway finished with Sid Little diving on a loose ball over the Australian line. The score was ruled out when referee Brown decided an Aussie had got there first to make the ball dead. Back up to the other end they went and after Oldham were caught off-side PIDDING, at last, was successful with a penalty attempt. The visitors were now playing with confidence and Churchill looked certain to score when he sped away up the touch line. However, when all seemed lost, Murray flung himself full length and managed to tap the full-back's ankle, which caused him to topple over; whereupon several Oldham defenders came in to finish the job.

More pressure from the tourists saw centre Harry Wells cross the Oldham line only to be brought back for an obvious forward pass.

Australia continued to lay siege to the home line and with a quarter of an hour remaining they finally broke through. As luck would have it the score came from a mistake by hooker Jack Keith, who had provided his team with a good amount of possession against his inexperienced opponent, Charlie Gill. After being pinned down for some time in their own quarter, Keith tried a clearing kick which was charged down by a rush of green and gold shirts. Ken McCAFFERY gathered up the ball to go over for the equalising try. Luckily for Oldham the conversion from the hapless Pidding hit the post and bounced out. In the remaining minutes the ever tricky Stirrup went close for Oldham and in reply the impressive Flannery almost got over for the visitors. Tense right up to the last, the match finished level: Oldham 7 Australia 7.

OLDHAM:
W. B. Ganley; J. Warham, W. Mitchell, A. Davies, J. Watson; F. Daley, F. Stirrup; L. Anthony, J. Keith, H. Ogden, S. Little, A. Tomlinson, A. Murray.

AUSTRALIA:
C. Churchill; D. Flannery, H. Wells, N. Hazzard, N. Pidding; C. Geelan, K. McCaffery; D. Hall, C. Gill, B. Davies, H. Crocker, F. Ashton, A. Paul.

Attendance: 19,620   Referee: Mr. F. Smith - Barrow

*Kangaroo tied down! The Oldham pack combine to bring down **Charlie Gill**.*
***Harry Ogden** and **Les Anthony** make the tackle as **Sid Little**, **Arthur Tomlinson** (mostly hidden) and **Jack Keith** move in. **Dennis Flannery** watches in the background.*

Above: This time it's a Roughyed in trouble as **Ferris Ashton** and **Albert Paul** combine to put a stop to the progress of **Alan Davies**. Ouch!
Other players are **Frank Stirrup**, **Duncan Hall** and **Alf Murray**.

THE KANGAROOS' WAR CRY

Prior to the game commencing, the Australians will give their famous War Cry. Here it is :—

> Wallee, Mullarra, Choomooroo, Tingal,
> Nah, Nah, Nah, Nah;
> Canai, Barrang, Warrang, Warrang,
> Yallah, Yallah, Yallah, Yallah.
> Ah; Jaleeba booga boorooloong,
> Yarnah meei meei meei,
> Neeyarra, Weeyarra, Jeleeba, Cahwoon,
> Cooeewah, Cooeewah, Warr, Wooh.

The translation of which reads :—

> We are a race of fighters descended from the war,
> Beware, beware, beware, beware,
> Where we fight there will be great bloodshed,
> Go, go, go, go,
> We are powerful but merciful; are you friends?
> Good, good!
> The Kangaroo is dangerous when at bay,
> Come on, come on to death.

The regular match day issue programme for the 1952-3 season was used for the tour match. and contained within its pages the "war cry".

The press was lavish in its praise of the Oldham performance, not least for the three stand-in players. Watson the try-scorer, Murray, the-try saver and Anthony, who had a storming game in the thick of the fray. However, the major plaudits were reserved for Stirrup whose non-inclusion in the Great Britain squad had the critics baffled.

Prior to the match the touring party was afforded the usual hospitality at the Town Hall with a civic reception before being conveyed to Watersheddings.

1952 Australia Tour			
Opponents	Result	Score	Attendance
Keighley	Won	54 - 4	7,431
Hull	Won	28 - 0	15,364
Barrow	Won	26 - 2	16,045
Whitehaven	Won	15 - 5	9,253
Oldham	Drew	7 - 7	19,370
Halifax	Won	39 - 7	18,773
Wigan	Won	23 - 13	16,223
St Helens	Lost	8 - 26	17,205
Featherstone Rovers	Won	50 - 15	3,700
GREAT BRITAIN	Lost	6 - 19	34,305
at Headingley, Leeds			
Bradford Northern	Won	20 - 6	29,287
Warrington	Won	34 - 10	21,478
Leigh	Won	34 - 5	8,409
Swinton	Won	31 - 8	10,269
Hunslet	Won	49 - 2	3,273
Workington Town	Won	27 - 15	11,341
Doncaster	Won	41 - 13	2,452
Huddersfield	Won	27 - 9	25,494
GREAT BRITAIN	Lost	5 - 21	30,509
at Station Road, Swinton			
Wakefield Trinity	Won	58 - 8	7,239
Hull Kingston Rovers	Won	31 - 6	5,817
Lancashire	Won	36 - 11	5,863
Leeds	Won	45 - 4	29,335
Yorkshire	Won	55 - 11	3,737
Dewsbury	Won	22 - 7	2,485
Widnes	Won	18 - 7	7,411
GREAT BRITAIN	Won	27 - 7	30,509
at Odsal Stadium, Bradford			

This must have been a most frustrating tour for the 1952 Kangaroos and Australian rugby league as a whole, for of the 27 games played, 23 were won, three were lost, with one draw. Unfortunately for the tourists two of those three defeats were in the first and second Tests. Several of the club sides were absolutely thrashed by the free-scoring Kangaroos. It is to the great credit of St Helens that they not only beat the tourists but did so convincingly. Oldham, of course, claimed the draw in that tense battle at Watersheddings.

Teenager Brian Carlson scored 19 tries, while Noel Pidding landed 79 goals. Skipper Clive Churchill, vice-captain Duncan Hall and Arthur Collinson played in most matches with 17 appearances each.

1955 1955
1955 1955

OLDHAM R.L.F.C.

NEW ZEALAND
RUGBY LEAGUE

October 29th 1955.
OLDHAM 13   NEW ZEALAND 15

OLDHAM EVENING CHRONICLE   SPORTS EDITION

GREEN FINAL

No. 22,460   SATURDAY, OCTOBER 29, 1955   Price 2d.

BRIGHTER
for your
LIGHTER
PETROL-PAK   1/-
LIGHTER FUEL
CAPSULES LTD · STRETFORD · LANCS.

What! NO INCREASE in pric
Yates's Blue Label
Scotch Whisky   Yates's
Bottle .... 35/-   Irish Whisky
½ Bottle .... 18/8   Bottle 3
Noggin .... 8/10   ½ Bottle ....
½ Noggin ...... 4/7   Noggin ....
                       ½ Noggin ....
YATES'S WINE LODG
HIGH STREET, OLDHAM
ONLY BRANCH IN OLDHAM

VICTORY CHANT FOLLOWED BY SERIES OF TERRIFIC ATTACKS

Kiwis prove much too warlike fo
Oldham's tean

FOR the visit of the New Zealand touring team, Oldha
made one last-minute surprise change, Etty, who
recalled to the right wing, being replaced by John No
who moved out of the right centre position to accommod
Frank Daley. New Zealand exchanged the wing positi
bringing McNichol on to the right, with Bakalich on the l

NEW ZEALAND: McNichol,   guilty of standing off-side at
McKay, Baxter,   Sorenson,   the ball and one of these infri
Robertson, McLeu   Yates.   ments gave Oldham a chance
McDonald, Perry,   their score.   From an
OLDHAM: Si   in front of the
Davies, O'Grad   ed a penalty goa
Ogden, Reith   nich
Goldsw

Refere   M:
field!

As the   t
tions on th
another
O'Grady
while Da   t
the left

The
a cro
start
the
hug

r

THE RUGBY LEAGUE

*New Zealanders'
Tour 1955*

GREAT BRITAIN

OLDHAM FOOT

OLDHAM
versus
NEW ZEALAND
at
WATERSHEDDINGS, OLDHAM
on
SATURDAY, 29th OCTOBER
1955
KICK-OFF 3-0 p.m.

OFFICIAL   2/   SOUVENIR

Just over twelve months earlier the Lions had toured Australia and New Zealand where the Kangaroos regained the Ashes. Some pride was restored when the Kiwis were beaten in two out of a three Test series. Oldham winger Terry O'Grady played in the second and third Tests against the Kangaroos and in all three against New Zealand.

At the end of 1954 Great Britain had beaten the Kiwis 26-6 on the way to lifting the inaugural World Cup played in France. By the time the New Zealanders arrived at Watersheddings they'd lost seven of their fourteen matches including the first Test. Half-backs Frank Pitchford and Alan Kellett, three-quarter Johnny Noon and forward Jack Rogers were making their first appearance against a touring side whilst wearing Oldham's colours.

THE NEW ZEALAND RUGBY LEAGUE KIWIS OF 1955

Back Row—Menzies, Kilkelly, Maxwell, Yates, Moore, McNicol, Percy, Riddell, Hawes, Roberts

Middle Row—Belshaw, Bakalich, Sorensen, Bond, McDonald, Butterfield, Blanchard, Grey, Atkinson, Haggie

Front Row—Robertson, Denton, Siddle, Baxter, McLennan, Tetley, McKay, Creedy

The official 1955 New Zealand tour photograph as it appeared in the Oldham match day programme.

*The 1955 Tour captain **Tom Baxter** played in 23 out of the 27 games in England.*

October 29th 1955.
OLDHAM 13 NEW ZEALAND 15

Oldham were forced to make a late change when John Etty dropped out of the side. Johnny Noon moved over to the wing with Frank Daley coming into the team at centre.

It hardly seemed that the Kiwis had finished their famous war cry than they were opening the scoring. Shortly after the kick off Alister Atkinson intercepted a pass and raced 80 yards before being grounded just short of the line. However, just seconds later the ball went across the field to Vern BAKALICH who avoided Terry O'Grady's desperate attempt to tackle to dive in at the corner. Dick Haggie missed the conversion attempt.

*Maori forward **Johnny Yates** leads his team mates in the "haka", performed by the 1955 New Zealanders to over 14,000 people at Watersheddings.*

Oldham tried hard to respond and Frank Stirrup was prominent in most of the worthwhile attacking moves bringing his ball-handling and side-stepping skills into play.

The home side was unlucky when Jack Rogers was brought back for a forward pass after racing 25 yards to touch down and the misfortune was compounded when a short time later Ron McKAY took a pass from Bill Sorenson to score near the posts. This time HAGGIE had no trouble adding the extra two points.

Bad handling was costing Oldham dear but at least their defensive qualities improved enough to keep the lively Kiwis at bay. The Roughyeds missed a chance to get back in the game when Frank Pitchford broke through and put Noon away. However, the wingman's kick ahead went astray and the New Zealand defence recovered. The tourists were very quick in moving up at the play-the-ball and were often caught offside. From one such offence ROGERS opened the scoring for Oldham with a simple penalty goal. This gave confidence to the home team and within a matter of minutes they narrowed the lead further. Jack Keith, who was having a storming game in the loose, completely fooled the New Zealand defence with an outrageous dummy. This produced a gap which the Yorkshireman galloped through *en route* to the try line. The Kiwi defenders managed to stop him just short but Sid LITTLE was on hand to take the scoring pass and go over. Rogers missed the kick but Oldham were right back in it now and were unlucky when Noon "scored" only to have the try disallowed. Also, Pitchford twice went close but to no avail.

Then the Kiwis, whose ability to move the ball at speed was causing all sorts of trouble for Oldham, broke away at breathtaking pace which culminated in Robertson veering out to the wing before releasing a classic reverse pass to send BAKALICH on a run to the posts. HAGGIE converted without any trouble. Just before the interval the tourists were dealt a blow when Robertson had to retire with a shoulder injury. However, a further HAGGIE penalty goal left them with a useful advantage.

Half-time: Oldham 5 New Zealand 15.

*The first try of the match. In the background **Bryn Goldswain** can only look on as **Vern Bakalich** dives over in **Terry O'Grady's** tackle.*

When the match resumed the Kiwis had to adjust as Bruce Robertson was unable to continue. Nevertheless, they continued in attacking fashion and Johnny Yates went close only to lose possession after some desperate tackling. At last the home forwards seemed to get to grips with the task and both Little and Rogers were prominent with captain Bryn Goldswain also to the fore. Keith again fooled the visitors with his handling skills but like Noon in the first half his kick ahead failed to trouble the New Zealand line.

Next, Haggie failed with a long range goal attempt before play switched to the other end and after O'Grady narrowly failed to score, PITCHFORD darted through direct from a scrum without a hand being laid upon him. Rogers missed what was an easy conversion to leave Oldham seven points in arrears. Just before full time O'GRADY squeezed in at the corner after some snappy passing and this time ROGERS made amends for his earlier effort with a glorious conversion from the touch line. Oldham rallied for one last assault on the New Zealand line but time ran out on them and the Kiwis held on for victory with the final scoreline: Oldham 13 New Zealand 15.

OLDHAM:
F. Stirrup; J. Noon, F. Daley, A. Davies, T. O'Grady; A. Kellett, F. Pitchford;
H. Ogden, J. Keith, S. Little, J. Rogers, C. Winslade, B. Goldswain.

NEW ZEALAND:
R. Haggie; L. J. McNichol, R. J. McKay, T. O. Baxter, V. Bakalich;
W. Sorenson; B. E. Robertson;
B. McLennan, T. Kilkelly, J. E. Yates, G. S. McDonald, R. W. Percy, A. Atkinson.

Attendance: 14,700   Referee: Mr. T. Armitage – Huddersfield.

" How've they gone on?"

*"How've they gone on?",
says the little lad in the
cartoon printed in the
Monday edition of the
Oldham Chronicle on
October 31st..
Well, the two glum faced
Oldhamers convey the
message that the Kiwis
had won the match but
the financial returns
shown above would
suggest that secretary
Bert Summerscales
would have been pleased
with the takings from the
attendance of 14,700.*

OLDHAM EVENING CHRONICLE   SPORTS EDITION

GREEN FINAL

No. 22,460   SATURDAY, OCTOBER 29, 1955   Price 2d.

VICTORY CHANT FOLLOWED BY SERIES OF TERRIFIC

Kiwis prove much too warl

Oldham

FOR the visit of the New
made one last-minute su
recalled to the right wing
who moved out of the right c
Frank Daley. New Zealand
bringing McNichol on to the ri

NEW ZEALAND: Haggie; McNichol,
McKay, Baxter, Bakalich; Sorenson,
Robertson; McLennan, Kilkelly, Yates,
McDonald, Percy, Atkinson.

OLDHAM: Stirrup, Noon, Daley,
Davies, O'Grady; Kellett, Pitchford;
Ogden, Keith, Little, Rogers, Winslade,
Goldswain.

Referee: Mr. T. Armitage (Huddersfield).

As the teams took up their positions on the field Oldham made yet
another late change. Davies and
O'Grady made up the right flank
while Daley and Noon moved out to
the left.

The famous Kiwi war cry thrilled
a crowd of about 13,000 before the
start and right from the kick-off
the tourists went into the attack
suggested by their battle cry.

Atkinson intercepted a pass to
race eighty yards before he was
tackled short of the line. Seconds
later the ball crossed the field t

*A great action shot from the 1955 game shows **Frank Daley** and **Jack Keith** bringing down **Trevor KilKelly**. Others from the left **Bill McLennan**, **Charlie Winslade** and **Harry Ogden**.. The photo is shown above as it appeared in the "Green Final" and opposite is Stephen Bennett's interpretation in watercolour.*

125

The 1955 New Zealand Tour			
Opponents	Result	Score	Attendance
Blackpool Borough	Drew	24 - 24	12,015
York	Lost	16 - 20	8,174
Halifax	Lost	17 - 18	12,492
Yorkshire	Won	23 - 17	7,907
Wigan	Lost	15 - 17	19,386
Hull	Won	17 - 12	10,167
Barrow	Lost	13 - 17	7,098
Workington Town	Won	26 - 16	11,043
GREAT BRITAIN	Lost	6 - 25	21,937
at Station Road, Swinton			
Lancashire	Won	17 - 15	6,887
Leeds	Won	18 - 16	15,738
Featherstone Rovers	Won	7 - 6	5,100
Huddersfield	Lost	16 - 25	11,271
St. Helens	Lost	8 - 16	14,000
Oldham	Won	15 - 13	14,700
Leigh	Lost	13 - 14	3,400
Warrington	Lost	15 - 22	14,462
GREAT BRITAIN	Lost	12 - 27	24,443
at Odsal, Bradford			
Castleford	Won	31 - 7	2,440
Rochdale Hornets	Won	17 - 16	9,300
Bradford Northern	Won	11 - 6	5,271
Salford	Won	21 - 5	4,000
Wakefield Trinity	Won	27 - 16	4,838
Rugby League XIII	Lost	11 - 24	3,643
Keighley	Drew	11 - 11	4,200
Rugby League XIII	Won	28 - 15	3,643
GREAT BRITAIN	Won	28 - 13	10,438
at Headingley, Leeds			

In line with the usual custom the Mayor (Councillor H. Holt) laid on a reception at the Town Hall for the Kiwis before the game.

Another "so nearly" tour for the New Zealanders. The 27 matches produced 14 victories, two draws and 11 defeats. Most of the games the Kiwis lost were by very small margins. However, the first two Tests showed that Great Britain had the measure of the tourists with comfortable winning scorelines on each occasion.

Vern Bakalich had a great tour with 20 tries and Dick Haggie topped the goal charts with 48. Tour captain Tom Baxter led from the front playing in 23 of the games and the tourists had the satisfaction of a last Test victory at Leeds.

Below: A special, if somewhat cumbersome, (it was actually 7½ x 10 inch) programme was issued for the match, seen here with the official tour brochure.

1956 1956 1956 1956

OLDHAM R.L.F.C.

NEW ZEALAND
RUGBY LEAGUE

November 7th 1956.
OLDHAM 21 AUSTRALIA 2

KANGAROOS' WORST DISPLAY

Oldham pack crushed Aussies

OLDHAM FOOTBALL CLUB

PROGRAMME ··· THREEPENCE

OURISTS SAID TURNER WAS MAN WHO MOST WORRIED THEM

dham showed up Australia's
ailing

Australians have a lot to
n. In losing 21—2 to
dham yesterday, they
up weaknesses that if not
d will cost them more
ng defeats. And the
were the first to admit
ilings.

forward Tom Tyquin
ards: "The game has
us that we need to learn
more tricks. It is better
e find out now instead of
the first Test."

pectacle the game flopped
Despite a monopoly of the
g like their expected them
Aussies failed to produce
ttack was disjointed and

When the Australians last toured in 1952 they played a total of 27 matches but this time around the number of fixtures was reduced by almost a third. Out of the window went the clashes against the county sides and a number of clubs expressed their anger at not getting a tilt at the boys in green and gold, especially as Liverpool City, who had finished last season's campaign in the rugby league basement, had been awarded the opening game. As would have been expected the fixture against Oldham was retained, albeit that it was scheduled for a mid-week date as opposed to a more prestigious Saturday game.

By the time the Kangaroos arrived at Watersheddings they had won six of their nine matches played so far, losing to Leeds, Whitehaven and Warrington. None of the three Test matches had yet been staged but Oldham stars, scrum-half Frank Pitchford, prop-forward Ken Jackson and loose-forward Derek Turner had played for a Northern RL X111 at Hilton Park, Leigh; being beaten 19-15 by the Aussies.

Oldham would kick-off the game as Lancashire Cup winners, having defeated St Helens 10-3 at Central Park just a couple of weeks previously. Winger Terry O'Grady, centre three-quarter Alan Davies and Pitchford had represented Lancashire in the county championship, forward Sid Little had played for Cumberland and winger Dick Cracknell for Yorkshire.

FOUR ROUGHYED HEROES!

Back Row: (left) **Derek Turner**, *(right)* **Sid Little**
Front Row: (left) **Frank Stirrup**, *(right)* **Alan Davies**

Turner made his international debut in the second Test at Bradford, as did Little in the third at Swinton, when they both scored a try.
Davies played in all three Tests scoring a try in the first at Wigan, and was, in the absence of a regular goal kicker, the unlikely choice to put over two conversions in the third Test.
Stirrup again captained Oldham against the tourists. The creditable draw in 1952 was overshadowed by the awesome display of the champions elect this season.

Sid Little *goes over for the opening score of the match in the third, and Ashes-deciding, Test at Swinton. The try was converted by his Oldham team-mate, Alan Davies.*

Strangely the Great Britain selectors chose to play the Roughyeds' star second-row forward at prop. However, their overall decision was vindicated by a 19 points to nil scoreline.

November 7th 1956.
OLDHAM 21   AUSTRALIA 2

The 1956 Aussies just happened to come to Watersheddings at a particularly bad time. The match was played on a Wednesday and on the previous Saturday, while the tourists were making hard work of a two point victory at York, Oldham had gone down by a similar margin at Workington. Now the Oldham team of 1956-57 did not take defeat lightly and there is no doubt that coach Griff Jenkins had his boys fired up for the next game. So it was that Ken Kearney led his team on to the pitch to face the Roughyeds, who had not tasted victory against the Kangaroos for thirty-four years.

The match opened up with the usual vigorous exchanges with the two loose-forwards Derek Turner and Kel O'Shea making the biggest impression. At half-back Frank Pitchford was on top form and proving a handful for opposite number Cyril Connell. Indeed, it was an error from Connell that eventually produced the first score of the match. After the visitors' scrum-half had spilled the ball, winger Terry O'Grady was up to it in a flash, kicking ahead and giving chase along with Derek Turner. Clive Churchill appeared to have the situation covered but as the two Oldham men advanced, he misjudged the bounce of the ball and with all three of them scrambling on the ground up popped PITCHFORD to

*Confusion - While the ball bounces over the Australian try line the prone **Derek Turner** watches as **Clive Chuchill** brings down **Terry O'Grady**. However, out of the photo Frank Pitchford is quickest to react and races in to touch down for the first try of the match.*

ground the ball for a try. Bernard GANLEY added the goal to give Oldham a five point advantage after just six minutes.

The game was being played in an open manner with Alex Watson and Connell showing up well for the visitors. Likewise, O'Grady looked sharp for Oldham but it was Turner who was giving the Kangaroos the most trouble. Both Ganley and Churchill (twice) were off target with penalty attempts until, just after the half hour mark, the visitors were penalised at the scrum and this time GANLEY was on target. The tackling was as fierce as

Alex Watson *falls to a copybook tackle from* *John Etty*, *as* *Frank Stirrup* *left regains his balance and* *Bobby Banks* *comes up in support.*

ever and four minutes before half-time GANLEY kicked another goal, following a high tackle from the visitors, to give an interval score: Oldham 9 Australia 0.

Within a minute of the restart the Australians were again pulled up for rough play and up stepped GANLEY to again put the ball over the bar. There was no let-up from Oldham who took the game away from the tourists with a sparkling try two minutes later. O'Grady started the move with a cross-field run from his own quarter. Turner was on hand to take the ball and put in a precision kick ahead which Frank Stirrup took on the first bounce to speed away towards the visitors' line. The cover managed to get to him but a slick pass just before he was grounded gave John ETTY a chance and the powerful Yorkshire-man beat off the last shreds of defence to run in at the corner. Ganley failed with the conversion attempt. It was perhaps as well for the tourists that at least their hooker, and skipper, Kearney was dominating the scrum possession. The Kangaroos eventually got on the scoreboard when Oldham were caught offside and CONNELL put over the penalty kick. However, the effort was nullified almost immediately when, after another Australian indiscretion in the tackle on the half-way line, GANLEY thumped the ball home from fully fifty yards.

John Etty touches down in the corner to give Oldham a fourteen point lead early in the second half of the match.

Thanks to their scrum monopoly, the Aussies kept battering at the Oldham line only to be met with tremendous defence. Packmen Ken Jackson, Don Vines, Sid Little and Charlie Winslade proved to be an insurmountable barrier. As the match drifted towards full-time the Aussies looked well and truly beaten. Only Connell, who ran himself to a standstill, Watson and the ever impressive O'Shea looked up for the task. It was fitting that the last say went to the man of the match! TURNER had caused the tourists much concern right from the start and after he had weaved his way through the tiring defence and kicked ahead he was tackled from behind, whereupon referee Watkinson promptly pointed for an obstruction try. GANLEY converted to leave the final score: Oldham 21 Australia 2.

OLDHAM:
W. B. Ganley; T. O'Grady, D. Ayres, A. Davies, J. Etty; F. Stirrup, F. Pitchford;
K. Jackson, J. Keith, D. Vines, S. Little, C. Winslade, D. Turner.

AUSTRALIA:
C. Churchill; K. O'Brien, T. Payne, A. Watson, D. McGovern; R. Banks, C. Connell;
R. Bull, K. Kearney, W. Marsh, T. Tyquin, D. Furner, K. O'Shea.

Attendance: 8,956   Referee: Mr. T. W. Watkinson - Pendlebury

*One of the Aussies to emerge from the match with credit was loose-forward **Kel O'Shea** here seen in two newspaper cuttings. Left, taking the tackle from **John Etty** and **Ken Jackson** and (above) again in the thick of the action.*

1956 Australian Tour			
Opponents	Result	Score	Attendance
Liverpool City	Won	40 - 12	4,712
Leeds	Lost	13 - 18	24,459
Hull XIII	Won	27 - 14	17,172
Barrow	Won	25 - 11	9,888
Whitehaven	Lost	11 - 14	10,840
Bradford Northern	Won	23 - 11	2,743
Warrington	Lost	17 - 21	15,613
English League XIII	Won	19 - 15	7,811
York	Won	20 - 18	6,842
Oldham	Lost	2 - 21	8,458
Huddersfield	Won	20 - 10	12,127
GREAT BRITAIN	Lost	10 -21	22,473
at Central Park, Wigan			
Hunslet	Won	27 - 11	4,451
St Helens	Lost	2 - 44	15,579
GREAT BRITAIN	Won	22 - 9	23,334
at Odsal Stadium, Bradford			
Halifax	Lost	3 - 6	2,254
Wigan	Won	32 - 4	15,854
Wakefield Trinity	Lost	12 - 17	3,381
GREAT BRITAIN	Lost	0 - 19	13,515
at Station Road, Swinton			

OLDHAM FOOTBALL CLUB

PROGRAMME ··· THREEPENCE

There was no special issue programme for the 1956 match against Australia and the same design as for the 1952 game was still in use. Both of the examples shown are for the 1956 match. A few misprints, devoid of the green colouring, obviously slipped through the net.

OLDHAM FOOTBALL CLUB

PROGRAMME ··· THREEPENCE

The Mayor, Alderman T. Lyson, greeted the tourists at the civic reception at the Town Hall and after the game a buffet tea was laid on for the Kangaroos at the Café Monico on Union Street. The main talking point of the Australians after the match was the omission of Derek Turner from the recently announced squad for the first Test. The rugged Oldham loose-forward had given a typical, no-holds-barred, all-action performance that left him with concussion at the end of the match. Although the first Test was won by Great Britain, Turner did go on to play in the second and third games of the series which the Lions won two to one.

In a much shorter tour than any that went before, the 1956 Kangaroos won ten and lost nine of their games. The low point was the 44 - 2 thrashing at St Helens. They bounced back to hand out a 32 - 4 walloping to Wigan. However, the Test series went to Britain.

Most tries went to Ian Moir with seven, while Gordon Clifford kicked 34 goals. Manly's prop-forward Roy Bull made most appearances with 14.

Roy Bull

Clive Churchill "The Little Master" The legendary, South Sydney full back made his third appearance for the Kangaroos at Watersheddings in 1956.

132

ROGER HALSTEAD

My earliest recollections of touring teams coming to this area stretch back to 1959 - two years before I joined the Oldham Evening Chronicle and five years before I started to cover Oldham Rugby League Club. I worked for a Rochdale freelance firm and as an impressionable 18 year old, I was totally wrapped up in the magical world of newspapers and their coverage of my favourite sport, rugby league. It was a world in which I rubbed shoulders, for the first time, with boyhood heroes or top-brass of the game at local level.

One of those was Arthur Walker, showman chairman of Rochdale Hornets, who was later to defect to the "enemy" and become chairman of Oldham after the ginger-group coup of 1970. The '59 Kangaroos came to Rochdale to play the Hornets at the Athletic Grounds. Always keen to put on a show, Arthur hired a donkey, and a local band and led a parade of kids and young supporters from Rochdale town centre to the Athletic Grounds for the big match. He got the publicity he sought - and the procession of fans up Drake Street, behind Arthur, the band and the donkey, showed conclusively that when the Australians came to town it was indeed an occasion to savour.

Four years on - and now an Oldhamer by adoption - I was similarly fascinated by the work of my predecessor, Ken Ashton, in his Chronicle build-up to an October day at Watersheddings when the Aussies were coming to do battle with an Oldham team that was to finish the season as second division champions. An imaginative and highly-skilled pro, Ken could do the lot - write, sub-edit and come up with page designs that at times bordered on the gimmicky, but were never dull. He was also steeped in rugby league. He knew the sport inside out. His claim to fame as a player was that he had a season playing on the wing for Liverpool City 'A'. He was a flier.

As a St Helens lad, he was born and brought up in a town where only two things mattered - glass-making and rugby league. His top toy as a kid was a rugby ball, and there was nowhere in the world like Knowsley Road. It was his playground. His excitement in the first week of October,1963 at the pending arrival in Oldham of Reg Gasnier, Graeme Langlands, Johnny Raper and co knew no bounds. It swamped the entire Chronicle sports desk.

He turned the spotlight in one of his preview pieces on the brilliant Gasnier. Likening him to a submarine, with its speed, power and ability to lurk menacingly before striking stealthily to devastating effect, he told readers to look out for Gasnier's own version of "Up periscope". He wrote that the Aussie centre star could elongate his neck to take in an over-view of defenders ahead of him and when he did that it was time for opposing sides to worry. For all that, he wasn't going to write off Oldham's chances and his optimism was reflected in his preview headline (unusual newspaper practice, but Ken wrote AND subbed his own stuff): "Oldham can tie these Kangaroos down, sport." They didn't. The tourists won 12-4 and Oldham's only points came from a couple of goals by full-back Johnny Noon.

By the time the next touring team arrived at Watersheddings, in August, 1965, Ken had departed for the then Daily Sketch and yours truly was at the start of his second season covering Oldham affairs for the Chronicle. This time it was the Kiwis, and they scraped home 5-2, aided by a useful contribution from R. F. Christian, a direct descendant of Fletcher Christian of 'Mutiny on the Bounty' fame. A John Winton penalty goal provided the solitary score for Oldham.

The Kiwis were to come again six years later, winning 24-13, but the Oldham side had changed beyond recognition with only Mike Elliott, Ken Wilson and Kevin Taylor surviving from the '65 side.

Bob Irving starred in the '71 tour game, but he was already an established Great

Britain second-rower, having played in all three Tests when the Kangaroos were here in 1967. The second of those Tests was played at London's White City. Bert Jones, a leading Oldham official, and I travelled to White City by train and tube to give "our Bob" a cheer and he didn't let us down as he turned in a fantastic performance for an 18-year-old to keep his place in the third Test at Swinton. On the domestic front, Oldham worked hard to restrict the tourists to an 18-8 win at Watersheddings against an Australian side that included two forwards whose sons were to carve their own niche in Oldham sport many years later, Rasmussen (his boy became pro at Oldham Cricket Club) and Goldspink, whose son Brett played for the Bears in their Super League days. The game was a special occasion for several Oldham-born players in the side --- wingers Trevor Buckley and Joe Collins, hooker Kevin Taylor, prop Ian Howarth and front-rower Colin Smith, a substitute.

John Winton and *Des Foy* - *The first and the last points scorers for Oldham in the tour matches during the "Halstead Years".*

Another local boy, John Blair, hit the headlines when the Kangaroos won 44-10 at Watersheddings in 1973. Terry Clawson, a proven GB front-rower and a man the Aussies respected highly, had a magnificent battle with Arthur Beetson, but the lad who really got the better of the legendary Australian was the local lad, John Blair. Bob Gaitley and Peter Astbury were the Oldham halves, but John came off the bench to score a memorable try at the pavilion corner. "I'll never forget it for as long as I live," said John later. "I made a break just inside the Australian half and suddenly realised I was on my own, out in the open with a long way to run against some of the best players in the world. Beetson was chasing me, Bob O'Reilly, another fearsome forward, was threatening to get to me and Graham Eadie, the full-back, was covering across. I've never run as fast in my life."

He never ran as fast again, either, but the lessons he learned in Greenacres as a boy - it's better to puff and pant a bit than to get caught - stood him in good stead in a memorable moment for John as well as for nearly 3,000 Oldhamers.

The Aussies were back again two years later in a World Championship warm-up game, winning 20-10, but the best had yet to come - that fantastic effort by an Oldham side which came close to beating the Kangaroos in 1986.

I close my eyes and I can still see Colin Hawkyard going over for a try at the Hutchins end and Des Foy scoring in the pavilion corner. What a game! What an achievement by 15 Oldham heroes on one of those magical Watersheddings nights which will live on in the memory of thousands of Oldhamers. It was the night 'Bruiser' Clark had his best game in Oldham colours - one of three Australians who played their hearts out against their fellow countrymen. Gary Warnecke at centre and Stuart Raper at loose-forward also excelled against a star-spangled touring team that, for long periods, was knocked off its game by the sheer intensity and exuberance of the Oldham side.

At the first scrum all hell was let loose. It was later to emerge that it was an Oldham plan to unsettle the Kangaroos and to let them know they were in for a game. 'Bruiser', not known for his consistency, chose this game to reach his Everest.

The rest of the forwards responded -Terry Flanagan (at hooker), Neil Clawson, Mick

Worrall, David Hobbs, Raper and the two subs, Hawkyard and Tom Nadiole. Let Hawkyard take up the story of the first Oldham try against the meanest defence in world rugby league. "Mick Worrall made the break," he recalled, "and Gary Warnecke went with him. I came on the inside, Gary gave me the ball and I saw the line looming before me. It was magic."

Worrall (3) and Hobbs kicked goals; Foy's speed took him over when chasing a Raper kick in the closing seconds; just prior to this, it needed a solo try from the scrum to clinch victory for one of the finest touring sides ever to leave Australian shores.

At the end of the game the Oldham players were treated like heroes by a crowd of approaching 6,000. Little did we know then that an international team from down under on tour would never again grace Watersheddings.

Thanks for the memory.

Roger Halstead.

A selection of Roger's headlines.

1959 1959 1959 1959

OLDHAM R.L.F.C

NEW ZEALAND RUGBY LEAGUE

October 3rd 1959.
OLDHAM 14 AUSTRALIA 25

OLDHAM FOOTBALL CLUB

THE PAVILION :: WATERSHEDDINGS

Entertaining, yes. But

this game was a . . .

DISGRACE
TO RUGBY
LEAGUE

Great Britain had lost the World Cup and retained the Ashes since the Australians had last toured here in 1956. After a gruelling domestic season in which they had each played in over 45 matches Derek Turner, Alan Davies and Sid Little were selected for the 1957 British World Cup squad to be played in Australia. Competed for in a min-league format, Australia beat each of the other three competing nations to lift the trophy. Little and Turner played in all three of the Lions' matches whilst Davies was injured in the second match - against the Kangaroos - thus missing the final game against the Kiwis.

Davies, Little, Turner and prop-forward Ken Jackson were the four Oldham players selected for the 1958 tour, albeit Little and Turner both withdrew. Oldham's speedy scrum-half Frank Pitchford was added when Leeds scrum-half Jeff Stevenson also pulled out. Alan Davies played in the first Test, won 25-8 by the Kangaroos and in the Ashes decider, which the Lions won 40-17. Two Tests were also played in New Zealand. Davies and Pitchford played in the first, won 15-10 by the Kiwis, and then Davies - in the unusual role of stand-off - played in the second, won 32-15 by the British.

The 1959 Australians arrived at Watersheddings at a time of trauma for the club. The RFL had just levied accusations in respect of illegal payments (loans to players), which would culminate in ten Oldham committeemen being suspended. Later the management team were reinstated when it was decided by the courts that they didn't have a case to answer. Ace marksman and full-back Bernard Ganley had earlier kicked nine goals when Lancashire defeated the tourists 30-22, a match in which three-quarter Alan Davies also played. Oldham's stand-off Alan Kellett had scored a hat-trick of tries in Yorkshire's 47-15 defeat of the Australians at York. Recent signing Geoff Robinson, who had cost Oldham a world record transfer fee for a forward, was in the Roughyeds' second-row but the club's other costly Cumbrian star, Ike Southward, was out injured.

Left:
Ike Southward.
Oldham's Cumbrian winger was unfit for the game at Watersheddings but appeared in the second and third Test victories, scoring a try in the latter.

Right:
Alan Kellett.
On the losing side at Watersheddings but a hat-trick hero for Yorkshire county as the "White Rose" demolished the Aussies 47 - 15 at York.

October 3rd 1959.
OLDHAM 14   AUSTRALIA 25

Ever since the "All Golds" first entered the Watersheddings arena one hundred years ago, most people who attended the tour matches could still remember them for one reason or another. A spirited performance, a famous victory, or perhaps a crushing defeat. Those who were at the 1959 match, despite seven wonderful tries, would remember, more than anything else, the fights! Not just one mass brawl for there were several.

By the end of the decade Oldham had lost a number of star players but there was enough talent left (Bernard Ganley, Alan Davies, Frank Pitchford, Charlie Winslade) to trouble any team, international or otherwise. On the opposite side much was being made of a precocious young talent by the name of Reg Gasnier. However, what the teams contrived to serve up that day is still remembered with a wince and a shake of the head by those who where there.

History would have it that the trouble set in when Alan Kellett was chopped down by Brian Hambly. Ken Jackson was up for the next drive and within seconds there was a free-for-all involving as many as eight players from each team! From then on tension was high with niggling tactics the order of the day. Still, in the midst of the darkness there shone a jewel. After seven minutes GASNIER snapped up a fumbled Oldham possession to go in

for try number one. Brian CARLSON added the conversion. There wasn't much to choose between the teams and for the next quarter of an hour it was end-to-end stuff with neither side able to break the deadlock. Then, on twenty five minutes the ball was moved out swiftly by the Kangaroos from a scrum on their own twenty-five yard line until it reached GASNIER. The centre then turned on the pace to scorch through the Oldham defence for his second score. CARLSON was again on target for the extra two points and later added a penalty goal to put the visitors twelve points ahead.

*The magical **Reg Gasnier** scored a hat trick of tries at Watersheddings. This was a precursor for his Test debut at Swinton a few weeks later when the fleet-footed centre again touched down three times.*

The Roughyeds were brought back on track by two of their most experienced players. Frank Pitchford unlocked the tourists' defence with a sixty yard break that brought the crowd to its feet; and Alan DAVIES got with him to finish off in style. GANLEY added the conversion and just before the interval he kicked a penalty goal to leave the half-time score: Oldham 7 Australia 12.

The ill-tempered mood continued into the second period and within a few minutes of the restart CARLSON punished the Roughyeds for their continued indiscretions with another goal. However, the penalties were not all going one way and six minutes later GANLEY responded for Oldham. Australia increased their lead on the hour mark. GASNIER was again on hand to finish off, this time from close range after taking a pass near the try line. Oldham protested long and loud that there had been an obstruction but the whistle stayed silent and the score was allowed to stand.

Still, Oldham would not bow down. When rugby football and not fisticuffs were on view the home side proved they also had some skill. A lively bout of passing culminated in DAVIES going over for his second try. The ever-reliable GANLEY put over the conversion to leave the Roughyeds just three points in arrears. Ironically, after Gasnier's sparkling performance it was the right wing pair who settled the match for the Kangaroos. First centre Ron BODEN went over and then five minutes from time CARLSON put the result beyond doubt with a try which he converted himself.

Two minutes from time the game erupted! Barry Muir had put in a late tackle on the Oldham hooker Jack Keith which went unpunished and when a minute later he did the same again on Pitchford the brawl started. Referee Charlie Appleton had already awarded Oldham a penalty, but the previously-lit fuse finally sparked the explosion with, once again, several players involved in fights.

When order was finally restored Mr Appleton pointed to the dressing rooms and rival scrum-halves, Pitchford and Muir, departed for the tunnel. A minute later the match was over, the Kangaroos triumphant. Oldham 14 Australia 25.

OLDHAM:
W. B. Ganley; V. Nestor, A. Davies, J. Noon, B. Pendlebury; A. Kellett, F. Pitchford; K. Jackson, J. Keith, R. Dufty, C. Winslade, G. Robinson, L. McIntyre.

AUSTRALIA:
D. Chapman; B. Carlson, R. Boden, R. Gasnier, K. Irvine; B. Clay, B. Muir; G. Parcell, I. Walsh, D. Beattie, R. Mossop, W. Delamere, B. Hambly.

Attendance: 17,621   Referee: Mr. C. Appleton – Warrington

Barry Muir (left) and Frank Pitchford.

Two fiery scrum-halves who finally wore out the patience of referee Charlie Appleton and were both dismissed just before the end of the match at Watersheddings in 1959.

"The Battle of Watersheddings"

The final incident that resulted in the sending off of Frank Pitchford and Barry Muir who can be seen tangling on the ground whilst fights erupt all around them.

Stephen Bennett

Above: **Roger Dufty, Alan Davies** and **Len McIntyre** *can only look on as* **Reg Gasnier** *dives over in* **Frank Pitchford**'s *tackle for one of his three tries at Watersheddings.*

Below: The extended photograph as it appeared in the Oldham Evening Chronicle on Monday October 5th 1959.
Opposite: Stephen Bennett's interpretation of the two images in water-colour.

Entertaining, yes. But this game was a . . . .
RACE TO RUGBY LEAGUE

1959 Australian Tour			
Opponents	Result	Score	Attendance
Leeds	Won	44 - 20	14,629
Rochdale Hornets	Won	27 - 14	10,155
Warrington	Won	30 - 24	17,112
Lancashire	Lost	22 - 30	15,743
Salford	Won	22 - 20	11,008
Yorkshire	Lost	15 - 47	7,338
Widnes	Won	45 - 15	9,381
Oldham	Won	25 - 14	17,630
Leigh	Lost	17 - 18	11,932
St Helens	Won	15 - 2	19,156
GREAT BRITAIN	Won	22 - 14	34,964
at Station Road, Swinton			
Cumberland XIII	Won	13 - 8	7,463
Barrow	Lost	9 - 12	8,488
Hull XIII	Won	29 - 9	15,944
Bradford Northern	Won	29 - 8	4,126
Halifax	Won	17 - 5	8,274
Featherstone Rovers	Lost	15 - 23	7,671
Wigan	Lost	9 - 16	24,466
GREAT BRITAIN	Lost	10 - 11	30,301
at Headingley, Leeds			
Swinton	Won	25 - 24	5,021
Wakefield Trinity	Lost	10 - 20	17,615
Huddersfield	Won	21 - 7	2,349
Hunslet	Won	12 - 11	8,061
GREAT BRITAIN	Lost	12 - 18	26,089
at Central Park, Wigan			

The 24-match itinerary saw the 1959 Kangaroos win 15 and lose nine of the games played. The first Test was won but the other two went to Great Britain, although it took a late try in the second match at Leeds to deny Australia the Ashes.

The phenomenal Reg Gasnier scored most tries with 15. Keith Barnes topped the goal chart with 52 but most points went to Brian Carlson with nine tries and 39 goals. There was no points for Rex "Moose" Mossop. However, the Manly "hardman" played in most matches with 19 appearances.

Right: **Keith Barnes:** *Captain and main goal kicker of the 1959 Kangaroos.*

In spite of all the bad blood exhibited during the game it seems that all went well at the civic reception and after match dinner , both held at the Town Hall.

Reports stated… *"when the game was over the players were not slow to meet each other with a healthy handshake."*

Referee, Charlie Appleton was less impressed… *"after that lot they all shake hands and leave me holding the baby!"*

OLDHAM FOOTBALL CLUB
THE PAVILION :: WATERSHEDDINGS

SEASON · 1959-60
OFFICIAL PROGRAMME · · 3d.

Match programme:
Again just the regular issue for the 1959-60 season.

1961 1961
1961 1961

OLDHAM R.L.F.C

NEW ZEALAND
RUGBY LEAGUE

September 4th 1961.
OLDHAM & ROCHDALE 10
NEW ZEALAND 8

'Boo' crowd took
biscuit for bad
sportsmanship

THE NEW ZEALAND TOUR — 1961

OLDHAM & ROCHDALE HORNETS
versus
NEW ZEALAND
WATERSHEDDINGS, OLDHAM
on
MONDAY, 4th SEPTEMBER
1961
KICK-OFF 6.30 p.m.

SOUVENIR PROGRAMME SIXPENCE

OLDHAM & ROCHDALE HORNETS FOOTBALL CLUBS

The Committee and Directors of the above Clubs

invite you to the match against

The New Zealand R.L. Tourists

at Watersheddings, Oldham   Kick-off 6.30
on Monday, 4th September, 1961   Kick-off 7.0 p.m.

Afterwards: Reception at Oldham Town Hall, at 9.0 p.m.

RUNNING
BUFFET

H. SUMMERSCALES,
Secretary, Oldham F.C.

The sixth New Zealand side to visit Watersheddings did so early in the tour. Only a handful of matches had been played and so the tourists had not yet slipped into top gear.

Because the tour had been limited to 20 matches (including Test, county and other representative fixtures) a number of the games were scheduled to be played against combined club sides; hence the integration of Rochdale Hornets and Oldham players. Already the alarm bells had begun to ring when only 7,000 turned up at Headingley to support a combined Leeds, Hunslet and Bramley side when a fixture against the Leeds club itself would have been expected to attract a crowd in excess of 12,000.

The gate for the combined Hornets/Oldham match was 8,795 when six years earlier 14,700 had turned out to support Oldham against the Kiwis. Seven Oldham players and six from Rochdale wore the Roughyeds' change strip of white shirts and navy blue shorts.

Left: Tour captain for the 1961 Kiwis, **Don Hammond**

Right, the skipper of the combined Oldham / Rochdale Xlll, **Frank Pitchford.**

1961 NEW ZEALAND TOURING TEAM

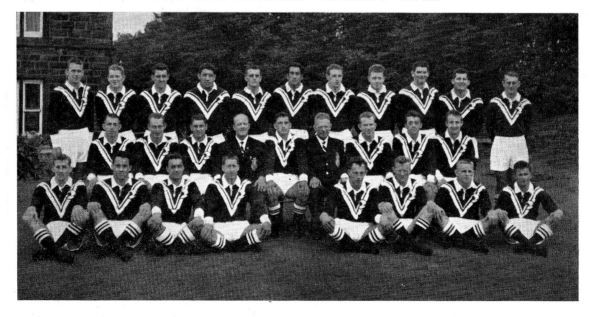

Left to right. Back Row: R. Cooke, A. N. Amer, G. R. Bailey, H. K. Emery, M. L. Cooke, S. K. Edwards, R. G. Hart, G. M. Kennedy, N. T. Tiller, J. R. Butterfield, B. T. Hadfield. Middle Row: G. S. Farrar, J. G. Patterson, J. E. Fagan, C. Siddle (Manager), R .D. Hammond (Captain), W. Telford (Coach), R. H. G. Duffy, J. P. Ford, K. R. McCracken. Front Row: B. E. Castle, R. W. Harrison, R. W. Bailey, W. L. Snowden, W. R. Harrison, J. A. Bond, B. S. Lee, B. T. Reidy.

September 4th 1961.
OLDHAM & 10 NEW ZEALAND 8 ROCHDALE HORNETS.

On the 1961 tour a number of teams were joined up to play the New Zealanders. Castleford and Featherstone, Whitehaven and Workington and a Manchester Xlll of Swinton and Salford, being examples. So it was that the Roughyeds and the Hornets joined forces to take on the Kiwis. The match took place at Watersheddings with Oldham providing seven players to Hornets' six. The combined team wore white shirts and navy shorts.

Reg Cooke - on target with four goals for the Kiwis.

The only try-less game in the history of Oldham versus tourist encounters, the sparse reporting of the action leaves one to believe that this was not one of the highlights of the genre. Actually from a personal point of view it was the first tour match I ever attended, aged seven. I stood upstairs in the Hutchins stand and can still remember being excited at the prospect and don't recall being too disappointed. Nevertheless, much was made in the press of prolonged slow handclapping and booing from the spectators. Indeed Test hooker Jock Butterfield, who watched this match from the stands, went on record as saying he had never heard such a degree of bad sportsmanship from the spectators at any match he had witnessed before.

The match was totally dominated by the forwards with Mel Cooke, the Kiwi skipper on the night, leading by example with a determined and robust display. Although the New Zealand half-backs, Graham Farrar and Graham Kennedy, looked to be "*on the top of their game*" they were starved of enough possession to make much impact. The Oldham supporters were eager to see the potential of Hornets' winger Trevor Simms but likewise, the ex-St Helens flyer also had little opportunity to show his class. The Oldham half-back pair of Alan Kellett and Frank Pitchford had been selected for the combined team and much was expected of them. However, on the night it was truly a case of sixes and sevens for the home half-backs with Kellett thought to be perhaps wary of his impending appearance for the Yorkshire county side against the tourists just two days later. Geoff Robinson played a solid game for the combined pack but Winslade looked somewhat tied down in his new position at prop-forward. Ironically as a ball-playing second-row the "Big Charlie" that the Oldham public knew and loved could have been the key to unlock the New Zealand defence.

So it was that penalty goals became the order of the day for the evening's scoring. The first two shots for the combined Xlll were entrusted to the Rochdale full-back Bill Atherton but both missed the target. In contrast Reg COOKE was finding no difficulty with four successful attempts. During that sequence the Oldham / Rochdale captain Frank Pitchford switched over to team-mate Johnny NOON for the goal kicking duties and the Oldham centre did not disappoint. Come the day, cometh the man! Five wonderful strikes gave the combined team victory. The fourth of them was an absolute beauty. It seemed that when the ball left the boot it was destined for nearer the corner flag than the posts. Not so! It seemed that "Noonie" had judged the wind to perfection and the ball curled in to sail neatly between the uprights.

For all the penalties it was not an over-aggressive match, although the game did appear to heat up somewhat following a foul by Brian Lee on Jim Parr in the 52nd minute, though nothing to compare with the events of Australia match two years earlier.

OLDHAM / ROCHDALE:
W. Atherton*; T. Simms*, J. Noon, A. Walsh*, T. Unsworth*; A. Kellett, F. Pitchford; W. Payne, L. McIntyre, C. Winslade, G. Robinson, J. Parr*, B. McGurrin*.
* Rochdale players

NEW ZEALAND:
R.W. Harrison; A.N. Amer, R.S. Cooke, G.R. Bailey, J.P. Ford; G.M. Kennedy, G.S. Farrar; S.K. Edwards, J.G. Patterson, W.R. Harrison, B.S. Lee, R.G. Hart, M.L. Cooke.

Attendance: 8,795   Referee: Mr T. Watkinson –Pendlebury

THE NEW ZEALAND TOUR — 1961

OLDHAM & ROCHDALE HORNETS
versus
NEW ZEALAND
at
WATERSHEDDINGS, OLDHAM
on
MONDAY, 4th SEPTEMBER
1961
KICK-OFF 6-30 p.m.

SOUVENIR PROGRAMME SIXPENCE

Match winner!
John Noon *won the match for the combined Oldham and Rochdale team with five beautifully taken penalty goals.*

A disappointing tour saw the Kiwis win only eight games from the 20 match itinerary. However, this did include the first Test which kept interest in the series right up until the last match. Roger Bailey scored 12 tries with Jack Fagan topping both the goals (43) and points (89) chart. Jock Butterfield and Maunga Emery both played in 17 of the 20 matches.

148

The 1961 Kiwis

at Watersheddings

R.W. Harrison

A.N. Amer

R.S. Cooke

G.R. Bailey

J.P. Ford

G.M. Kennedy

G.S. Farrar

S.K. Edwards

J.G. Patterson

W. R. Harrison

B.S. Lee

M.L. Cooke

R.G. Hart

1961 New Zealand Tour			
Opponents	Result	Score	Attendance
Widnes / Liverpool	Lost	6 - 9	9,050
Manchester XIII	Lost	7 - 19	6,926
Castleford / Featherstone	Won	31 - 20	5,744
Leeds XIII	Won	24 - 9	7,085
Oldham / Rochdale H.	Lost	8 - 10	8,795
Yorkshire	Lost	11 - 21	6,750
Barrow	Won	36 - 11	6,647
Lancashire	Lost	13 - 15	9,332
Huddersfield / Halifax	Won	31 - 11	7,251
Rugby League XIII	Lost	20 - 22	5,271
Warrington	Won	21 - 9	8,959
Great Britain	Won	29 - 11	16,540
at Leeds			
Hull / Hull K.R.	Lost	6 - 17	8,125
Wigan	Lost	6 - 28	25,483
Whitehaven / Workington	Won	10 - 9	4,970
St Helens	Lost	10 - 25	21,680
Great Britain	Lost	10 - 23	19,980
at Bradford			
Leigh	Won	15 - 4	6,984
Wakefield Trinity	Lost	7 - 20	16,558
Great Britain	Lost	19 - 35	22,558
at Swinton			

Trevor Simms, a Hornets player at the time and a future Oldham favourite.

One of the most mystifying elements in the research on all of the tour games is the complete lack of interest from the media in this match.

This newspaper cutting of a group of Hornets players and wives / girlfriends meeting the Kiwis at the after-match reception is one of the few images to survive.
New Zealanders Graham Farrar and Reg Cooke in the centre are surrounded by Gerry Unsworth, Alan Walsh, Trevor Simms and John Dickinson.

HORNETS MIX WITH KIWIS AFTER GAME

Ticket to the game at Watersheddings and after-match reception at the Oldham Town Hall, issued by the Oldham and Rochdale clubs.

OLDHAM & ROCHDALE HORNETS FOOTBALL CLUBS

The Committee and Directors of the above Clubs

invite you to the match against

The New Zealand R.L. Tourists

at Watersheddings, Oldham

on Monday, 4th September, 1961   Kick- off 7-0 p.m.   6-30

Afterwards: Reception at Oldham Town Hall, at 9-0 p.m.

H. SUMMERSCALES
Secretary, Oldham F.C.

RUNNING BUFFET

1963 1963 1963 1963

OLDHAM R.L.F.C.

NEW ZEALAND RUGBY LEAGUE

October 5th 1963.
OLDHAM 4 AUSTRALIA 12

URELY, AUSSIES ARE KIDDING ON THIS FORM

OLDHAM EVENING CHRONICLE · SPORTS EDITION
GREEN FINAL
No. 24,914 · SATURDAY, OCTOBER 5, 1963 · Price 3d.

GASNIER TRY ENDS ALI
OLDHAM HOPE

OLDHAM almost pulled the game out of the fire against the Australians with a storming finish after a sloppy first half in which they had frittered away chances. But just as Oldham looked set to score Gasnier stitched it up for the Tourists with a classy try.

ham were without player Frank Dyson who was rest knee injury Johnny Noon to full back with Brian Lord ing inside and Geoff Sims back on right-winger

promising until the final passes were dropped

Noon shot wide with another penalty and then failed to find

OLDHAM FOOTBALL CLUB
WATERSHEDDINGS · OLDHAM

OFFICIALS
President: H. GOODWIN, Esq.
Vice-President: S. STRETCH, Esq.
Hon. Treasurer: P. G. CARTER, Esq.
Committee:
Messrs. C. Bradley, A. F. Campbell, J. Errock, H. Hobson, G. F. Holden, H. Jones, T. E. Rees, R. L. Thomas, E. Watkins.
Club Doctors:
Dr. A. Campbell, Dr. A. R. Nettleton
Secretary: H. SUMMERSCALES
Pavilion Telephone No.: MAin (Oldham) 4865

OLDHAM v. AUSTRALIA
4   12
On SATURDAY, 5th OCTOBER, 1963
at Watersheddings, Oldham
Kick-off 3 p.m.

SEASON — 1963-64

Oldham's last encounter against the Australians had been four years earlier when the Reg Gasnier-inspired green and golds won a bruising encounter 25-14. The 1959 Aussies had failed to win back the Ashes when they lost the series by two Tests to one. Oldham's Alan Davies had played in the first match of the series at Swinton, won 22-14 by the Australians, and the Roughyeds' world record transfer fee winger Ike Southward had played in the second and third Tests, won 11-10 at Headingley and 18-12 at Wigan, a game in which he scored a try in the dying moments to secure the Ashes. The Lions later played hosts for the 1960 World Cup, beating France, New Zealand and Australia, thus wresting the trophy from the Kangaroos. Oldham centre Alan Davies was the only Oldham selection playing in all three matches, scoring a try against the Kiwis and two against the French. There was no Oldham contingent on the 1962 tour down under, during which Great Britain retained the Ashes by two Tests to one but lost both Test matches against the Kiwis.

When the fixtures against the latest batch of Kangaroos were awarded Oldham's performance during the 1962-63 season was disregarded. It was just as well. They'd won only nine of their thirty match First Division programme – their worst performance for over 80 years! The planners were well rewarded when over 11,000 spectators paid to watch.

The Australians hadn't yet come up against the Great Britain side but had lost both their matches against Lancashire and Yorkshire. Oldham winger Trevor Simms had scored one of Lancashire's three tries in their 13-11 victory at Central Park, Wigan. The selectors turned up at Watersheddings in numbers, reported to be watching prop-forward Charlie Bott, loose-forward Dave Parker, and hooker Len McIntyre who would eventually be selected for the second Test.

Left to right: **Charlie Bott**, **Dave Parker** and **Len McIntyre** *all watched by the selectors at Watersheddings in October 1963. As you can see, it was "Mac", pictured in his Great Britain kit, who got the nod to represent his country in the ill-fated second Test at Swinton where Great Britain were overwhelmed 12 - 50.*

October 5th 1963.
OLDHAM 4   AUSTRALIA 12

The 1963-64 season saw Oldham in the second division. However, in a bid to return to the top flight at the first attempt, a strong squad had been assembled. A team that would easily win the second division title, play in that epic Challenge Cup semi-final against Hull K.R. and give the classy '63 Kangaroos a good run for their money. Player-coach Frank Dyson had to pull out with a knee injury which meant John Noon switching to full-back with Brian Lord moving to centre and Geoff Sims coming in on the right wing. The tourists fielded a strong side with Ken Day coming in as a late call-up for the injured Kevin Ryan in the second row.

It was Oldham who opened the better with Noon linking up well with the attack. There was some considerable pressure on the Australian line which they met with robust defence. It was the maestro Reg Gasnier who got the Kangaroos back on track. Twice early in the game, he slipped the cover to lay on chances for Graeme Langlands and Peter

Dave Parker feels the strength of the Australian defence as he is tackled by two of the Kangaroos. Barry Muir watches from the left as Dick Thornett makes the tackle.

Dimond. The Roughyeds survived on both occasions and hit back in style when Brian Lord broke through and handed on to Peter Smethurst who gave Trevor Simms a chance only for Gasnier to prove he also had a solid defensive game with a try-saving tackle. After ten minutes Noon was wide with a penalty attempt after which the visitors began to take control. Loose-forward Johnny Raper made a break through the Oldham cover from inside his own half, Earl Harrison was in support to carry on the move and in turn handed on to LANGLANDS. The centre sped across the field and, with Oldham expecting a pass to Dimond, he straightened up to go through the gap and score under the posts. He also added the conversion.

The game was open and exciting with chances at both ends. Ken Irvine was unlucky to just put a foot in touch when put clear by Harrison and for Oldham, Smethurst missed a good opportunity when he put down a pass after good work by Jackie Pycroft. Indeed it was poor control of possession that was Oldham's biggest failing. Still, they persevered with the open play and after Geoff Robinson had dummied his way through the initial Aussie defence, Brian Lord took the ball, kicked ahead and seemed to win the race to touch down. However, referee Appleton disallowed the score. Barry Muir was being constantly lectured for his "feeding" technique at the scrums and after one indiscretion after twenty seven minutes, NOON put over a penalty goal to open Oldham's account. Stand-off Harrison was causing much trouble for the Oldham defence but a little indecisiveness with the final pass let him down on more than one occasion. Noon was unsuccessful with another penalty attempt and it took some stout defence, notably by Lord on Gasnier and Harry Major on Irvine, to keep the Oldham line intact. A minute before the interval LANGLANDS kicked another penalty to leave the half-time score: Oldham 2 Australia 7.

*Above: **Trevor Simms** steps inside **Ken Irvine** as **John Noon** backs up on the left.*

The Kangaroos set off well in the second period. Gasnier was again instrumental in getting Dimond clear and then it took a thunderous shoulder charge by Noon to deny Irvine at the corner. Next, Raper did well to put Dick Thornett over but the second-rower lost the ball as he tried to touch down. Harrison spoiled a glorious chance when he elected to send out a speculative long pass to the wing when he looked to have a clear run to the line. The match was evenly poised and there were some heated exchanges. Paul Quinn was cautioned after a foul on Charlie Bott and Smethurst and Langlands were constantly niggling each other. Hooker Len McIntyre, was having a fine game for Oldham, not only winning the possession battle in the scrums but also putting in a fine defensive display. Rival loose-forwards Raper and Dave Parker were both outstanding - the Aussie for his attacking skills and the Oldham man for some text book, hard and low tackles.

It was tense stuff as the match moved into the final quarter. Again Irvine was stopped just short after being overhauled by Oldham flyer Trevor Simms. Just ten minutes remained when NOON kicked his second penalty goal and a minute later Langlands was dismissed after another of many clashes with Smethurst. Now, with numerical advantage and only three points between the teams, Oldham pressed for the win. They pounded away at the Australian line only to find a solid wall of green and gold. The try that broke Oldham's hearts and sealed the match was a good one. As the game moved into the final

Geoff Sims (no 2), **Harry Major** and **Brian Lord** combine to bring down Aussie prop **Paul Quinn.**.

minute Ian Walsh and Day handled before the ball reached Raper. He in turn released GASNIER with a lovely reverse pass. The brilliant centre scythed through the middle to go sixty yards and score under the posts. IRVINE converted and it was with much relief for the tourists that the final whistle sounded soon after, with the final score:
Oldham 4 Australia 12.

OLDHAM: J. Noon; G. Sims, B. Lord, P. Smethurst, T. Simms; V. Nestor, J. Pycroft; C. Bott, L. McIntyre, K. Wilson, G. Robinson, H. Major, D. Parker.

AUSTRALIA: K. Thornett; K. Irvine, G. Langlands, R. Gasnier, P. Dimond; E. Harrison, B. Muir; P. Gallagher, I. Walsh, P. Quinn, R. Thornett, K. Day, J. Raper.

Attendance: 11,773   Referee: Mr. C. F. Appleton – Warrington.

SURELY, AUSSIES ARE KIDDING ON THIS FORM

Just in time ! Oldham full back Johnny Noon shoulder charges Aussie winger Ken Irvine into touch just when he threatens danger. Looking up from touch with a worm's-eye view is Trevor Simms. The Aussies won the match 12—4.

Were they kidding? - The newspaper headline suggests the 1963 Kangaroos might have been holding something back, having been held to such a low score by second division Oldham. Or was it that the Roughyeds just put up a good show ?

Trevor Simms tackles Ken Irvine as Peter Smethurst and Geoff Robinson stand by to assist.

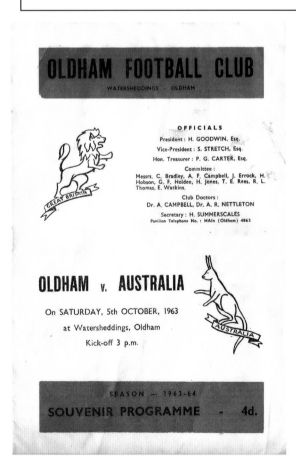

OLDHAM FOOTBALL CLUB
WATERSHEDDINGS · OLDHAM

OFFICIALS

President : H. GOODWIN, Esq.
Vice-President : S. STRETCH, Esq.
Hon. Treasurer : P. G. CARTER, Esq.

Committee :
Messrs. C. Bradley, A. F. Campbell, J. Errock, H.
Hobson, G. F. Holden, H. Jones, T. E. Rees, R. L.
Thomas, E. Watkins.

Club Doctors :
Dr. A. CAMPBELL, Dr. A. R. NETTLETON
Secretary : H. SUMMERSCALES
Pavilion Telephone No. : MAin (Oldham) 4865

OLDHAM v. AUSTRALIA

On SATURDAY, 5th OCTOBER, 1963
at Watersheddings, Oldham
Kick-off 3 p.m.

SEASON — 1963-64

SOUVENIR PROGRAMME - 4d.

This was the first time I saw an Australian touring team and with Oldham riding high at the top of the second division, immense interest was generated in the match. I was at the Town Hall to watch the tourists arrive and remember there was quite a crowd to see them greeted by the Mayor, Alderman J.H. Broadbent, everyone no doubt was looking forward to the afternoon's action with great anticipation.

Could the resurgent Roughyeds match the mighty "green and golds"? Well no, not quite, but they did give them an almighty fright. After the game it was on to the Hills Stores function room for a running buffet.

Left: the match programme with the special Great Britain / Australia cover.
This design was retained for the rest of the 1963-64 season.

156

1963 Australian Tour			
Opponents	Result	Score	Attendance
Warrington	Won	28 - 20	20,090
Huddersfield	Won	6 - 5	13,398
Yorkshire	Lost	5 - 11	10,324
Leeds	Won	13 - 10	16,641
Lancashire	Lost	11 - 13	15,068
St Helens	Won	8 - 2	21,284
Featherstone Rovers	Lost	17 - 23	7,898
Oldham	Won	12 - 4	11,338
Leigh	Won	33 - 7	9,625
Hull XIII	Won	23 - 10	10,481
GREAT BRITAIN	Won	28 - 2	13,946
at Wembley Stadium, London			
Rochdale Hornets	Won	3 - 0	8,637
Hunslet	Won	17 - 13	4,400
Wakefield Trinity	Won	29 - 14	15,821
Cumberland	Won	21 - 0	8,229
Barrow	Won	18 - 5	10,130
GREAT BRITAIN	Won	50 - 12	30,843
at Station Road, Swinton			
Castleford	Lost	12 - 13	7,887
Wigan	Won	18 - 10	11,746
Widnes	Won	20 - 9	6,509
Swinton	Drew	2 - 2	11,947
GREAT BRITAIN	Lost	5 - 16	20,497
at Headingley, Leeds			

A wonderful tour for the Kangaroos. They absolutely battered Great Britain in the first Test and humiliated them in the second to win back the Ashes.

From the 22 matches played Ken Irvine topped the try count with 17 and made most appearances, again 17. Most goals went to Graeme Langlands with 51 scored in 16 matches. This was the same number of appearances as Ian Walsh and, although Arthur Summons was the tour captain, it was the Sydney St. George hooker, Walsh, who led the team in all three Test matches.

*Above, **John Noon**: Once again the sole scorer of the Oldham points against the 1963 Kangaroos. This was John's fourth game against a touring side for Oldham.*

Left: Autographs of the Australians-property of a very proud M Turner in 1963 (and still in 2007).

1965 1965
1965 1965

NEW ZEALAND
RUGBY LEAGUE

August 31st 1965.

OLDHAM 2 NEW ZEALAND 5

Souvenir Programme 1/-

OLDHAM

v.

NEW ZEALAND

TUESDAY, 31st AUGUST, 1965

Kick-off 6.30 p.m.

OLDHAM FOOTBALL CL

ENCLOSURE SEAT (Pavilion Side)

BLOCK **B** ROW **F**

SEAT No 8

OLDHAM v NEW ZEALAND

At Watersheddings, Oldham

Tuesday, 31st August 1965

Kick-off 5.30 p.m.

THIS STUFF WON'T WIN KIWIS
ANY FRIENDS

The Kiwis were still cock-a-hoop after defeating the Lions in both Tests played in New Zealand during the 1962 tour and further bolstered by the fact that the Australians had won back the Ashes during their tour here in 1963.

Bill Snowden's men had only played four matches before their fixture at Watersheddings but had already gained a reputation for producing unattractive football, a stigma that they would suffer throughout the tour. However, back on that balmy, late summer, evening at Watersheddings here was an insight into the clinical mental toughness that would become so much a part of the game down under a dozen or so years in the future.

Pin badge souvenir of the 1965 New Zealand tour.

Wellington Press (Oldham) Ltd.

OLDHAM FOOTBALL CLUB

ENCLOSURE SEAT (Pavilion Side)

BLOCK **B**   ROW **F**   SEAT No **8**

OLDHAM v NEW ZEALAND

At Watersheddings, Oldham

Tuesday, 31st August, 1965

Kick-off 7-0 p.m.

6/6

John Stringer
Secretary

Grandstand seat ticket for the 1965 Kiwi tour match at Watersheddings.

Two veterans from the 1961 New Zealand touring side and still mainstays of the Kiwi pack in 1965. Left **S.K. (Sam) Edwards** and right **H.K. (Maunga) Emery**. These two Maori prop-forwards formed the backbone of the tourists' front row.

160

August 31st 1965.
OLDHAM 2   NEW ZEALAND 5

This was the earliest date that Oldham ever entertained a touring team and the balmy August Tuesday evening produced a decent crowd of over 10,000. On the previous Saturday the Roughyeds had produced an impressive performance to defeat Wigan 23 – 8 at Central Park. On the same day the Kiwis won at Halifax 24 – 12. Oldham suffered a set-back when talented youngsters Tom Warburton and Bob Irving were both declared unfit. This brought in Tom Canning for his first start in the senior team, although he was selected at stand-off rather than his usual scrum-half position.

Right from the start it became obvious that the visitors had come to win at all costs and the pattern was set for eighty minutes of no risk, forward-dominated rugby from the New Zealanders. Open play was at a premium and what there was of it tended to come from Oldham. Unfortunately, the Kiwi hooker Colin O'Neil gave his team the lion's share of possession and a lack of ball control added to the home side's problems. Oddly enough the tourists' half-back combination of Paul Schultz and Bob Irvine looked a lively pair but were content to turn the ball back inside to the forwards rather than utilise the three-quarters.

Peter Smethurst "up-ends" Kiwi loose forward **Jim White** *closely watched by* **Colin O'Neil**, **Charlie Bott** *and* **Kevin Taylor** *with* **Ken Wilson** *in the foreground.*

The only action of particular note in a truly dull first half was a bout of inter-passing by the Oldham forwards in which they turned the ball one way then the other with a raid down the left flank. The New Zealand line held firm throughout aided by some dubious 'spotting' tactics. Indeed, the speed with which the tourists were moving up at the play-the-ball gave Oldham little scope to move the ball in a positive fashion. The only points in the half came three minutes before the break when Jack FAGAN landed a penalty goal to leave the interval score: Oldham 0 New Zealand 2.

The second period was better. Not much, but at least there was some sprinkling of possession reaching the three-quarters of both teams. Four minutes into the new half home full-back John WINTON levelled the scores with a penalty goal. However, it didn't take the Kiwis long to regain the lead when, for once, the visitors showed a bit of ambition. Prop-forward Sam Edwards drove into the Oldham line and after drawing in several defenders, a neat pass put second-row man Kevin DIXON away. The West Coast forward showed a good turn of pace to outstrip the left side of the Oldham defence and veer away from Winton to score. The conversion attempt was missed and with over thirty minutes still to go New Zealand had delivered the *coup de grace*!

Oldham did try to hit back and produced two good chances. Stan McLeod and John Donovan combined well to produce an opening on the right wing but as Donovan shaped to pass to the supporting Canning, the Oldham man was pulled back before he received the ball. The resulting penalty was scant reward for the best bit of rugby in the whole game, especially when Winton put the kick wide. Another opportunity presented itself after Kevin Taylor quickly heeled from a scrum in the Oldham half. The half-backs Bill Broomhead and Canning, moved the ball swiftly to Stan McLeod who broke through the initial cover and sent what seemed to be a try-scoring pass to Donovan. Alas, Winton came into the attacking

*The ball eludes **John Donovan** and **Brian Langton**.*

line and took the ball which gave Brian Langton that extra yard he needed to make the tackle. He duly nailed the Oldham man and when Winton sliced an easy penalty attempt soon after it summed up an indifferent day for the Rhodesian-born full-back.

*The try that sealed the match. **Kevin Dixon** dives clear of the despairing tackle of **John Winton** to score the only try of the game. In the background **Jim McCormack** and **Trevor Simms** can only watch.*

Although Donovan saw some of the action, the other wingers, Trevor Simms for Oldham and Langton and Roy Christian for the Kiwis might have been better off watching from the stands. "Big" Jim McCormack in the backs and Peter Smethurst in the forwards strove might and main for the Oldham cause, whereas, for the tourists, Schultz and Edwards were the stars in what was in truth a game to forget. Final score: Oldham 2 New Zealand 5.

OLDHAM:
J. Winton; J. Donovan, S. McLeod, J. McCormack, T. Simms; T. Canning, W. Broomhead;
C. Bott, K. Taylor, K. Wilson, P. Smethurst, S. Whitehead, D. Parker.
SUBS: M. Elliott, J. Hill.

NEW ZEALAND:
J. Fagan; R. Christian, G. Kennedy, R. Strong, B. Langton; P. Schultz, R. Irvine;
S.K. Edwards, C. O'Neil, E. Moore, R. D. Hammond, K. Dixon, J. White.
SUBS: R. Bailey, R. Orchard.

Attendance: 10,333   Referee: Mr. L. Gant - Wakefield

*John Donovan breaks away from the Kiwi defence as **Stan McLeod** comes up in support and **Charlie Bott** watches from afar.*

The attendance of over 10,000 was excellent for a mid-week fixture only Wigan and St. Helens had better crowds for the club matches on this tour.

1965 New Zealand Tour			
Opponents	Result	Score	Attendance
Other Nationalities	Won	15 - 7	1,200
Bradford Northern	Lost	15 - 28	8,373
Warrington	Won	14 - 7	8,162
Halifax	Won	24 - 12	6,730
Oldham	**Won**	**5 - 2**	**10,333**
Wigan	Won	17 - 12	12,583
Widnes	Lost	3 - 8	9,450
Hull Kingston Rovers	Won	21 - 11	7,540
St. Helens	Lost	7 - 28	11,270
Leeds	Won	28 - 13	5,782
Yorkshire	Lost	8 - 15	14,814
GREAT BRITAIN	Lost	2 - 7	8,497
at Swinton			
Leigh	Won	10 - 5	4,840
Barrow	Won	20 - 10	5,081
Whitehaven	Lost	7 - 12	3,208
Castleford	Won	7 - 6	5,702
Hull	Won	11 - 8	6,591
Lancashire	Won	21 - 10	8,781
Rochdale Hornets	Won	10 - 4	7,075
GREAT BRITAIN	Lost	9 - 15	15,849
at Bradford			
Swinton	Lost	7 - 14	8,345
Wakefield Trinity	Lost	4 - 16	7,484
GREAT BRITAIN	Drew	9 - 9	7,919
at Wigan			

After the match the tourists received a reception at the Town Hall where the players and officials were presented with a diary for 1966 each inscribed with their name.

The Kiwis won thirteen games, lost nine and made one draw which came in the final Test.

Roger Tait kicked most goals with 30 and his three tries also made him top points scorer. Perhaps a reflection of the tour is seen in the fact that the most tries were the seven scored by prop-forward, H.K. "Maunga" Emery. Centre three-quarter, Graham Kennedy made most appearances with 19.

Roger Tait: top scorer for the 1965 New Zealand tourists.

Below, the match programme and a set of New Zealand autographs secured for the author by the former Oldham favourite Alex Givvons.

KIWIS v OLDHAM 1965-6

Souvenir Programme   1/-

OLDHAM

v.

NEW ZEALAND

TUESDAY, 31st AUGUST, 1965
Kick-off 6.30 p.m.

1967 1967
1967 1967

OLDHAM R.L.F.C.

NEW ZEALAND
RUGBY LEAGUE

November 11th 1967.

OLDHAM 8 AUSTRALIA 18

AUSSIES' DEFENCE TOO
GOOD FOR OLDHAM

OLDHAM
v.
AUSTRALIA

SATURDAY, 11th NOVEMBER,
1967

Souvenir
Programme 1/-

The Australians had held on to the Ashes when they beat the 1966 Lions in two out of the three match Test series although all three had been tight affairs. Some consolation was gained when Great Britain won both Tests against the Kiwis.

Before the 1967 Kangaroos breezed into Watersheddings two Test matches had already been played. Again they were both closely contested and Oldham's young second-row forward Bobby Irving had played in each. The Lions won the first Test played at Headingley, 16-11, but then allowed the Kangaroos to hit back when they won the second Test played at London's White City Stadium, 17-11.

Oldham were having a torrid time during the 1967-68 campaign, destined to finish 22nd in a division of thirty. The only respite would come in the Challenge Cup when a second round replay against Bradford Northern generated a crowd of 18,500. In contrast only 3,329 bothered to turn up on a wet November Saturday afternoon to watch the Australians. 11,600 at Warrington, 11,000 at Hull KR, 22,700 at Wigan, 17,200 at St Helens, 10,000 at Widnes, 14,000 at Bradford, 8,500 at Barrow but a paltry 3,329 at Watersheddings! There was only one crowd lower – 2,600 at Rochdale Hornets.

Australian Rugby Football League Board of Control

165 PHILLIP STREET, SYDNEY

'PHONES: 28-8565

Private: 81-2083

All communications
should be addressed to
The Hon. Secretary
H. R. MATTHEWS
Box 4415, G.P.O.
Sydney, Australia

KGS/DH

10th February, 1967.

Mr. W. Fallowfield,
Secretary,
The Rugby Football League,
180, Chapeltown Road,
LEEDS, 7. ENGLAND.

Dear Sir,

1967 Tour of England - Itinerary

We acknowledge receipt of your letter of the 27th January, submitting a provisional itinerary for the Tour of England, which was discussed at a Meeting of the League held on even date.

In response, we desire to advise you that as the Sydney First Grade Competition has been increased to twelve Teams, it is impossible for our Season to conclude any earlier than the 16th September.

It was therefore felt that we would not be in the position to commence the Tour of your Country any earlier that the 30th September. You will be fully aware that in doing this, it will be impossible for the Team to embrace the Tour of your Country and France and be home in time for Christmas.

It has been customary in the past to conclude the English section of the Tour after the Third Test and we feel that this should apply in the case of the coming Tour and also that the fixtures against Leeds and Wigan should be included in the early part of the itinerary.

With kind regards,

Yours faithfully,

A/HON. SECRETARY.

An interesting letter from the Australian R.F.L. regarding the 1967 tour.

Notice the request for the games against Leeds and Wigan to be included towards the beginning of the tour.

One would imagine that this would be in the hope that an early fixture would ensure these matches be played in better weather thus further boosting the attendance of what was likely to be the two best supported club games.

November 11th 1967.
OLDHAM 8   AUSTRALIA 18

A grey, dull afternoon awaited the teams as they took to the field and continuous rain for some hours before the kick-off left the conditions very heavy indeed. The tourists had been beaten at Castleford earlier in the week and, eager to get back on track, fielded a strong team for the visit to Watersheddings.

Tommy Warburton found touch right from the kick-off to give Oldham a good field position. Martin Murphy linked up well with the three-quarters to take play up to near the Australian line, whereupon the visitors were caught offside for WARBURTON to give Oldham the lead with an easy penalty goal. The greasy ball was causing handling difficulties for both teams but the Kangaroos looked lively whenever they chose to move the ball. The Referee, Mr. Lawrinson, was not happy, on several occasions, with the Oldham scrummaging and John McDONALD levelled the scores after Tommy Davies had been penalised right in front of the Oldham posts. Murphy did well to cope with a kick through by full-back Les Johns, and as the tourists enjoyed a good spell of pressure, skipper Noel Kelly was hauled out for a lecture after he and McDonald up-ended Kevin Taylor.

The crowd already annoyed by several of the refereeing decision became incensed at the first Australian try. Johns put in a well judged kick ahead which Murphy appeared to

"Up and Over! **Kevin Taylor** *is up-ended by* **Noel Kelly** *and* **John McDonald**. *Other players from left:* **Ian Howarth, Bob Irving, Arthur Hughes** *and* **Tommy Davies**.

touch down safely over his own line. However, when Ken IRVINE followed up and did the same the score was awarded. McDonald missed the conversion. The anger of the crowd was fuelled further a few minutes later when Oldham captain Arthur Hughes broke from a scrum and sent Davies side-stepping past Les Johns to go under the posts, only for the try to be ruled out for a forward pass. Nevertheless, the home team stuck to their task and WARBURTON, who was having a fine game, landed his second penalty, a beauty from near the touchline, when the Kangaroos were again caught offside. Considering the conditions the play was quite open with excitement at both ends of the field. Warburton

Kevin Junee dives over the line beneath the posts in the Watersheddings gloom.

brought the supporters to their feet with a thrilling break, as did Murphy when he turned round and caught the highly rated McDonald, forcing him to fluff a pass to the supporting Johnny King.

Hughes was leading by example and after he put in a long range touch-finder, the field position was capitalised upon when WARBURTON put over a grand drop goal to put Oldham ahead. The Kangaroos were not daunted and after good yards had been made by Elton Rasmussen and Ron Coote, the Roughyeds' defence was caught napping when Kevin JUNEE shot through a gap from acting half-back to dive over beneath the posts. McDONALD added the goal. Then, just before half-time, the tourists demonstrated their pace; when an Oldham attack broke down and the ball was moved swiftly to KING who out-stripped Murphy to go in for an unconverted try, to leave the interval score: Oldham 6 Australia 13.

The hooking battle was going Oldham's way with Taylor providing a steady stream of possession for his team and, with Hughes and Warburton looking as good as anyone on the field, the home supporters were in good heart. Mick Mooney produced a good break which took him to within ten yards of the visitors' line and as Oldham continued to press Warburton sliced a penalty chance wide after a scrum infringement by the tourists. Next,

Oldham produced the best move of the game so far when John Donovan, Murphy and Davies combined well to put Bob Irving on a run through the heart of the Aussie defence. Hughes and Ken Wilson made further in-roads which set up position for WARBURTON to land his second drop goal, which just squeezed over the bar. The Roughyeds were really "up for it" now and after Trevor Buckley cleared up a kick through by Kelly to put Murphy away, the full-back beat two men on a clever run. Irving was also proving a handful with his forceful bursts up the middle.

As the game moved into the final quarter the persistent rain and heavy conditions began to take their toll on the stamina of both teams. Only five points still separated the sides and Oldham had put in a mighty effort but the Kangaroos did have that extra bit of pace and class that swung the game their way. It was somewhat ironic that, after all Warburton's efforts, an unarguable man-of-the-match, it was his opposite number Johnny GLEESON who was on hand to finish the move which finally took the match out of Oldham's reach. McDONALD added the extra points. In the closing minutes, though they tried, Oldham never seriously looked like breaching the Aussie line and the game ended with the final score: Oldham 8 Australia 18.

OLDHAM:
M. Murphy; T. Buckley, J. McCormack, J. Donovan, J. Collins; T. Warburton, T. Davies;
K. Wilson, K. Taylor, I. Howarth, R. Irving, M. Mooney, A. Hughes.
Subs: B. Curry, C. Smith.

AUSTRALIA:
L. Johns; J. King, R. Saddler, J. McDonald, K. Irvine; J. Gleeson, K. Junee;
N. Gallagher, N. Kelly, J. Sattler, E. Rasmussen, K. Goldspink, R. Coote.
SUBS: J. Greaves, A. Thompson.

Attendance: 3,329   Referee: Mr E. Lawrinson - Warrington

---

*Full-back, **Les Johns** (2) is met by a trio of defenders with **Kevin Junee** in support. Oldham players left to right: **Ian Howarth, Mick Mooney, Bob Irving, Martin Murphy** and **Joe Collins**.*

The 1967 Kangaroos perform their "war-cry" at Watersheddings. This was the last tour that the Australians carried out this ritual.

1967 Australian Tour			
Opponents	Result	Score	Attendance
Warrington	Won	16 - 7	11,642
Yorkshire	Lost	14 - 15	19,370
Hull Kingston Rovers	Lost	15 - 27	11,252
Lancashire	Won	14 - 2	9,369
Wigan	Lost	6 - 12	22,770
Rochdale Hornets	Won	25 - 2	2,676
GREAT BRITAIN	Lost	11 - 16	22,293
at Headingley, Leeds			
St. Helens	Lost	4 - 8	17,275
Wakefield Trinity	Won	33 - 7	10,056
GREAT BRITAIN	Won	17 - 11	17,445
at White City Stadium, London			
Castleford	Lost	3 - 22	6,137
Oldham	Won	18 - 8	3,174
Widnes	Won	33 - 11	9,828
Barrow	Drew	10 - 10	8,418
Cumberland	Lost	15 - 17	7,545
Swinton	Won	12 - 9	5,640
Leeds	Won	7 - 4	5,522
Halifax	Won	22 - 2	5,285
Bradford Northern	Won	7 - 3	14,173
GREAT BRITAIN	Won	11 - 3	13,515
at Station Road, Swinton			

Played 20 - won 12, lost 7 with one match drawn but the Ashes were secured! Skipper Reg Gasnier suffered a fractured leg in the first Test defeat at Headingley which ended his Test career, but Australia recovered to win the second and third.

Graeme Langlands top scored with 36 goals and three tries with Ken Irvine and Johnny King at the head of the try list with eight each. Langlands also made most appearances with 14.

The tourists were accorded the usual welcome at Oldham Town Hall. I remember being amongst the autograph hunters on the Town Hall steps when they arrived. After the game they were amongst the first guests to be ushered into the new social club which was opened just two days earlier.

OLDHAM

V.

AUSTRALIA

SATURDAY, 11th NOVEMBER, 1967

Souvenir Programme 1/-

Johnny Raper; *The legendary Australian international loose-forward. In the absence of the injured Reg Gasnier, it was Raper who led the Kangaroos in the Ashes-deciding third Test victory at Swinton.*

His son Stuart had a great season for the Roughyeds in 1986-87.

172

1971 1971
1971 1971

OLDHAM R.L.F.C

October 27th 1971.
OLDHAM 13 NEW ZEALAND 24

KIWIS WIN THE HARD WAY

13

...ls in England and ...weather had been ...a cold northerly ...le long was up ...e against this on

...minutes but er ...ning and Dennis ...first fest. Tatana ...he broke and fed ...istances like this. ...ough and Great ...l in front took the ...sion and penalty ...d it was. Tatana ...core wide out and

Another Oldham penalty goal and then Moore... the first of ...wo scintillating tries ...rchard was broke...

OLDHAM
Rugby League
Football Club

Kiwi crackers
ease the agony

Since they had last played Oldham - early during the 1965 tour - Bill Snowden's Kiwis – one of the less glamorous of New Zealand touring sides – had, nevertheless given the Lions a tough time in the Test series. Great Britain had won the first and second Tests 7-2 at Swinton and 15-9 at Bradford before the New Zealanders then forced a 9-9 draw at Wigan.

There had since been two tours down under. The Lions won both of the two Tests played against New Zealand in 1966 (Oldham committeeman Jack Errock was Assistant Manager) and then followed this up by making it three out of three against the Kiwis in 1970. Oldham's powerful second-row forward Bob Irving played in the first Test - won 19-15, was a non-playing substitute in the second Test, won 23-9, and played again in the third and final match, won 33-16 by the Brits. The 1970 British touring side had turned out to be one of the most powerful for years. The Australians had won the Ashes in 1963 and held on to them in 1966, but Frank Myler's men brought them back to these shores by winning the second and third Tests.

The World Cup had been played for twice. Firstly, down-under in 1968, won by Australia, and then again here in the UK in 1970, when the Aussies retained the trophy.

At the end of the 1969-70 season Oldham had finished next to bottom of the rugby league pile but a new committee, new back-room staff and the introduction of key players such as Cliff Hill and Frank Foster had produced the desired effect. Roy Christian's 1971 Kiwis had played fine football during the tour and despite winning only ten of their twenty matches won the Test series by 2-1.

The 1970s weren't a good period for rugby league. Only a combined total of 18,776 spectators turned up for the three Tests and just 1,872 at Watersheddings.

Bob Irving: Star second row forward, Great Britain international and a most consistent performer for Oldham during the indifferent period of the late 1960s and early 1970s.

OLDHAM R.L.F.C

October 27th 1971.
OLDHAM 13   NEW ZEALAND 24

A cold autumn night awaited the 1971 Kiwis when they arrived at a sparsely attended Watersheddings. However, it must have been a somewhat happy touring party due to the fact that the series against Great Britain was already in the bag by two Tests to nil.

Oldham got off to a good start when Phil LARDER slotted home a penalty after only two minutes. The tackling was keen on both sides but after a quarter of an hour the class of the New Zealanders began to shine through. The seventeen year old half-back sensation, Dennis WILLIAMS side-stepped through the Roughyeds' defence for a try near the posts, only for prop Henry Tatana to miss the easy conversion. A few minutes later it was Williams again who tormented the home side. He broke through the Oldham ranks and with plenty of support put Phil ORCHARD in for the second Kiwi try. Once more the conversion attempt was wide of the target.

Phil Larder

The Roughyeds responded well and when Larder broke through Bob IRVING was on hand to take the centre's pass and go over for the score which LARDER converted. The tourists were incurring the wrath of the referee and a further LARDER goal gave Oldham a three point advantage. One of the big successes of the tour was the goal-kicking prop-forward TATANA and it was he who took a short pass on the blind-side to score wide out. Strangely, in the light of his earlier failures, this time the big prop made no mistake with the conversion from a difficult angle. Yet another penalty goal for LARDER put Oldham back level but the last word of the half went to Maurice "Mocky" BRERETON after he feigned a pass to Orchard before going in for the last try of the half. TATANA converted to give the Kiwis a five point lead.

*Kiwi prop **Don Mann** is gripped firmly by an Oldham defender while he is watched by fellow front-rowers **Bill Burgoyne** and **Henry Tatana**.*
*The Oldham players from left: **Tommy Davies**, **Bob Irving** (grounded), **Frank Walker**, **Dick Bonser** and (No 5) **Norman Hodgkinson**.*

Half-time: Oldham 11 New Zealand 16.

For the second half the New Zealanders replaced John Greengrass with Bill Deacon. LARDER resumed in the second period like he had started the first with an early penalty. Still, it seemed that the Kiwis could step up a gear at will and BRERETON again showed his pace and skill to sweep in for his second try. Unfortunately, he injured his ankle in the process and was replaced by O'Sullivan. Oldham again fought back and spent quite some time in the visitors' half, but to no avail. Full-back Whittaker was playing a sound defensive game and linked well when coming into the attacking line. Also, winger Robert McGuinn did well to take a couple of high kicks under the glare of the floodlights. The game was finally made safe for the tourists when Deacon broke through and handed on to second-row forward Gary SMITH who finished off in style, a popular score for the "workhorse" of the Kiwi pack. TATANA kicked the goal. The half-back partnership of Williams with Gary Woollard, worked well for the visitors and they were well served by Smith, Tatana and sub Deacon in the forwards. For Oldham, Ray Clark figured well, as did the ever consistent Irving. Larder's goals were a major factor in keeping the Roughyeds in the hunt for so long, as was Kevin Taylor's victory in the possession battle from the scrum.

Final score: Oldham 13 New Zealand 24.

OLDHAM:
A. Scahill; M. Elliott, P. Larder, T. Davies, N. Hodgkinson; C. Hill, M. Murphy;
K. Wilson, K. Taylor, F. Walker, R. Bonser, R. Irving, R. Clark.
SUBS: J. Blair, B. Cornwell.

NEW ZEALAND:
J. Whittaker; P. Orchard, R. Christian, M. Brereton, R. McGuinn; D. Williams,
G. Woollard; H. Tatana, W. Burgoyne, D. Mann, G. Smith, J. Greengrass, A. Kriletich.
SUBS: J. O'Sullivan, W. Deacon.

Attendance: 1,872   Referee: Mr. R Wood - Barrow

Two "Newspaper" images from the 1971 Oldham v New Zealand match.

*Left: Oldham full-back **Tony Scahill** is too late to stop Kiwi second row forward **Gary Smith** going over for the closing try of the match.*
*Right: **Ray Clark** and **Cliff Hill** combine to bring down a New Zealand player as **Maurice Brereton** comes across in support.*

Kiwi Rugby League Touring Team
GREAT BRITAIN and FRANCE 1971

W. G. Burgoyne, K. L. Stirling, R. C. McGuinn, G. J. Woollard, R. F. Williams, D. A. Williams.

M. P. Brereton, M. J. McLennan, B. R. Lowther, J. H. Fisher, R. Orchard, P. Orchard, J. C. O'Sullivan.

J. Greengrass, H. Tatana, W. G. Deacon, J. A. Whittaker, G. M. J. Smith, M. K. Eade

D. T. Gailey, W. L. O'Callaghan(manager), F. R. Christian, D. L. Blanchard (coach), A. P. Kriletich, J R .Williams (manager), D. K. Mann

D. S. Dowsett, G. R. Cooksley, D. Sorensen.

The twenty-match itinerary for the 1971 Kiwis produced ten victories and ten defeats for the tourists under the captaincy of F.R. (Fletcher Roy) Christian. However, two of those successes were registered in the first two Tests to give New Zealand their first series victory against Great Britain in England since their first visit back in 1907-8. Loose-forward and vice-captain Tony Kriletich, along with the tall utility-back John Whittaker, played in most games with 16 appearances each. Speedy wingman Phillip Orchard topped the try list with twenty touch-downs, but the real headline grabbing story of the tour was the form of prop-forward Henry Tatana. The burly Maori kicked 46 goals which, combined with his four tries, made him the top points scorer with 104.

1971 New Zealand Tour			
Opponents	Result	Score	Attendance
Rochdale Hornets	won	23 - 8	2,374
St. Helens	lost	8 -18	8,169
Hull Kingston Rovers	lost	10 - 12	5,746
Widnes	won	18 - 15	5,787
Castleford	lost	8 - 25	5,889
Warrington	lost	2 - 13	6,295
GREAT BRITAIN	won	18 - 13	3,764
at The Willows, Salford			
Barrow	won	25 - 15	4,839
Whitehaven	won	21 - 8	3,105
Swinton	lost	15 - 26	3,280
Wigan	won	24 - 10	12,187
GREAT BRITAIN	won	17 - 14	3,925
at Wheldon Road, Castleford			
Huddersfield	lost	10 - 11	3,495
Leigh	lost	5 - 10	4,012
Salford	lost	30 - 31	7,127
Wakefield Trinity	won	23 - 12	5,367
Oldham	won	24 - 13	2,172
Bradford Northern	won	30 - 23	6,362
York	lost	5 - 11	2,803
GREAT BRITAIN	lost	3 - 13	5,479
at Headingley, Leeds			

Above: The official 1971 New Zealand tour pin-badge.

These were being sold by the players themselves and I remember purchasing mine in the pavilion after the match.

OLDHAM Rugby League Football Club
v **NEW ZEALAND**
On Wednesday, 27th October, 1971
kick-off 7-30 p.m.
OFFICIAL PROGRAMME - 4p

*Above: **F.R. (Roy Christian)** skipper of the victorious 1971 Kiwis.*
Left: The 1971 tour programme was the regular club issue.

1973 **1973**
1973 **1973**

OLDHAM FOOTBALL CLUB

OLDHAM R.L.F.C

AUSTRALIA RUGBY LEAGUE TOUR

NEW ZEALAND RUGBY LEAGUE

Oct 19th 1973.
OLDHAM 10 AUSTRALIA 44

OLDHAM CRUSHED BY MIGHTY AUSSIES

OLDHAM .. 2 2—10, AUSTRALIANS . 7 10—44

THE Australian tourists turned to football — powerful pacy football — to score ten tries and sweep a very poor Oldham team aside as they notched their biggest win of the tour so far at Watersheddings last night. It would be easy to run into raptures about the Australian performance, but praise must be tempered for the knowledge that Oldham's approach show was woefully weak.

The home side made the fatal fundamental mistake of sitting back in defence and allowing the Aussies room to get into their stride. Then they made matters worse...

Oldham always seemed to ... their opponents with the sort ... reserved for supermen— ... one reason why so many ... were dropped when players ... under immediate pressure.

... Peter Astbury and substitute ... Blair, seemingly possessed ... confidence backed by certain ... members of the side, to go ... the home side's two tries in ... patch of seven minutes ... through the second half.

OLDHAM

V

AUSTRALIA

GEOFF STARLING

CENTRE
BALMAIN

PHOTOGRAPHS BY RUGBY LEAGUE WEEK

But half-backs Tim Pickup and Dennis Ward were every bit as adept at pulling out of the home tackles, as Oldham produced a totally abject performance on defence. In truth, the fast-raiding Aussies merely proved what had become so obvious in recent weeks —that Oldham fall down lamentably in the basic art of container and on the run and putting him down with a minimum amount of fuss.

In the second half, the Aussies romped in for six of their tries, it was difficult to pick out any Oldham forward, with the possible exception of Fred Hall, who stuck manfully to the job in hand.

In the first half, Hall had an ally in his second-row partner Bill McCracken, the Cumbrian debutant. The pair fought hard to steam the tide, as did Kevin Taylor, but McCracken, half a stone overweight and playing his first game for nearly three weeks, faded from the picture

Surprise

Scrum-half Astbury short-kicked from acting half back and hampered through the last remnants of the Aussie defence to touch down for the first.

Outside-half Blair, introduced for Bob Gaitley after 50 minutes, provided the other moment of excitement from the home side in the whole 80 minutes.

Taking the pass direct from the scrum base at half way, Blair niftily sidestepped Pickup and broke away to chase half the length of the field for a diving try.

Who was the more surprised at Blair's "cheek"—the Aussies or the supporters—is arguable, but it was noticeable; in the minutes immediately following how much more adventurous Oldham became.

Blair, it seemed, had surprised even his own colleagues and one felt

... show ... detract from Blair's moment ... tory.

Sadly, even accents ... lists greater ... skill ... enthu... ... of vi...

... happy ... vided ... spruce... from t... individ... Geoff ... second-r... Ken Ma...

In see... Starling ... the fast... today. ... his eye fo... were mar... almost un... certain to ... the centre

O'Reilly, ... from Oldham couldn't hold, had a hand in several of the tries, and the speed and strength on the break of McCarthy and Maddison were a joy to behold.

Two goals by Cronin completed Oldham's scoring while Starling (4) Maddison Goodwin, McCarthy, Salt and Cronin crossed for the Australian tries with Cronin landing seven goals.

OLDHAM: Murphy, Munro, Elliott, Wainwright, O'Brien, Gaitley, Astbury, Clawson, Taylor, Wilson, Hall, McCracken, Reynolds, Blair and Daly for Gaitley and Wilson after 50 minutes.

AUSTRALIANS: Langlands; Goodwin, Starling, Cronin, Branighan; Pickup, Ward; Beetson, Walters, O'Reilly, Maddison, McCarthy, Salt. Referee: Mr. Lawrinson (Warrington).

Attendance 7770

By the time the 1973-74 season opened the inspirational pair of Frank Foster and Cliff Hill had left the club along with coaches Graham Starkey and Alan Kellett. Great Britain prop-forward Terry Clawson had been recruited and Griff Jenkins rejoined the club as coach. After the first match of the season Great Britain second-rower Bob Irving was transferred to Wigan where he linked-up again with Graham Starkey.

The Roughyeds had played twelve matches before Graeme Langlands' World Cup holders arrived mid-October and had won only two. The Kangaroos would regain the Ashes by winning two of the three Tests and lose only one club game. It wasn't the one at Watersheddings. Once again, as in 1952, it would be St Helens who would be the only club side to lower the Australian colours.

On this tour, Test match rugby league, at the insistence of the Australian R.L., returned to London with the first Test being played at Wembley. Although the poor crowd of just under 10,000 was lost in the vastness of the national stadium those who did turn up were treated to a wonderful encounter. A full blooded Test match played, as one would expect, with no quarter asked or given. Oldham prop Terry Clawson kicked four goals and turned in a "top drawer" performance.

Still it was the Kangaroos who went on to regain the Ashes they had lost on home soil in 1970 when Frank Myler's Lions came back from a first Test mauling in Brisbane to silence the crowds of over 60,000 (twice) in Sydney.

Terry Clawson:
The Oldham prop-forward seen here in action in the Wembley Test.

His four goals went a long way towards the Lions securing victory over the 1973 Kangaroos in the first match of the series at the famous London venue.

October 19th 1973.
OLDHAM 10   AUSTRALIA 44

Never was an Oldham side more mismatched against touring opposition than on the 1973 tour. Going into the game the Roughyeds had won only two matches out of twelve played in all competitions. The Kangaroos on the other hand had been victorious in all five of their previous fixtures.

In truth the tourists were just too fast, too powerful and too smart for an Oldham side lacking in confidence. Strong men in the form of prop-forwards Arthur Beetson and Bob O'Reilly, backed up by loose-forward Paul Sait, really set about the Roughyeds in the tackling stakes whereas second-row men Bob McCarthy and Ken Maddison ran the Oldham defence ragged whenever the "Green and Golds" had possession. Yet, in spite of all the forward dominance, the major match plaudits undoubtedly went to the right centre Geoff Starling whose pace and elusive running earned him four tries.

Chris O'Brien loses his balance as *Ted Goodwin* moves in to tackle with *Bob O'Reilly* in support. *Bob Gaitley* of Oldham looks on (right) as does *Elwyn Walters* (left).

Overall, Oldham simply had no answer to such a well-drilled and multi-skilled outfit. That said, there were one or two heroes for the home side on the night. Cumbrian forward Bill McCracken was impressive until he ran out of steam midway through the second half. Scrum-half Peter Astbury out-foxed the Aussie defence when he short kicked at a play-the-ball and re-gathered to score the first Oldham try. However, it was two local lads who made the best impression. Fred Hall gave his usual one hundred per cent effort in both attack and defence and he, more than any of his team mates, seemed to relish the challenge of the visitors. The biggest cheer of the night came when John Blair, on as a fiftieth minute substitute for stand-off Bob Gaitley, dodged past his opposite number Tim Pickup and then showed a clean pair of heels to the rest of his international opponents. I can remember it clearly. Blair took a pass from Astbury at a scrum just inside the Oldham half, side-stepped Pickup and set off for the pavilion corner. Graham Langlands came across and he hit the Oldham man just short of the try line but the momentum took Blair over much to the delight of the Oldham faithful.

Nevertheless, these were just isolated annoyances for the tourists whose points came via tries from STARLING (4), MADDISON (2), Ted GOODWIN, McCARTHY, SAIT and Mick CRONIN with the latter also adding seven goals. For Oldham the tries from ASTBURY and BLAIR were complemented by two goals from Terry CLAWSON. This was also the final senior appearance for prop-forward Ken Wilson; his 321 appearances for Oldham included every tour match between 1963 and 1973.
The final score: Oldham 10 Australia 44.

OLDHAM:
M. Murphy; G. Munro, M. Elliott, A. Wainwright, C. O'Brien; R. Gaitley, P. Astbury; T. Clawson, K. Taylor, K. Wilson, F. Hall, W. McCracken, J. Reynolds.
SUBS: J. Blair, A. Daley.

AUSTRALIA:
G. Langlands; E. Goodwin, G. Starling, M. Cronin, R. Branighan; T. Pickup, D. Ward; A. Beetson, E. Walters, R. O'Reilly, R. McCarthy, K. Maddison, P. Sait.
SUBS: G. Eadie, G. Pierce.

Attendance: 2,770   Referee: Mr. E. Lawrinson - Warrington

Above:
(left) **Fred Hall** - local Oldham player who relished the challenge against the Kangaroos.
(right) **Ken Wilson** - brought the curtain down on an illustrious career for the Roughyeds in the tour match.

OLDHAM

v

AUSTRALIA

Friday, 19th October 1973 K.O. 7.30

Souvenir Programme 6p

1973 Australian Tour	Result	Score	Attendance
Salford	Won	15 - 12	11,064
Wakefield Trinity	Won	13 - 9	5,863
Dewsbury	Won	17 - 3	5,865
Castleford	Won	18 - 10	2,419
Widnes	Won	25 - 10	5,185
Oldham	Won	44 - 10	2,895
Cumbria	Won	28 - 2	3,666
Bradford Northern	Won	50 - 14	5,567
GREAT BRITAIN	Lost	12 - 21	9,875
at Wembley Stadium, London			
Hull Kingston Rovers	Won	25 - 9	5,150
Huddersfield	Won	32 - 2	1,333
Leigh	Won	31 - 4	2,607
St. Helens	Lost	7 - 11	10,013
Featherstone Rovers	Won	18 - 13	5,659
GREAT BRITAIN	Won	14 - 6	16,674
at Headingley, Leeds			
GREAT BRITAIN	Won	15 - 5	10,019
at Wilderspool, Warrington			

*Above: Balmain centre **Geoff Starling** who scored a record four tries by a tourist against Oldham.*

WRITING ON THE WALL!

The table above shows that only Great Britain in the first Test and St Helens managed to register a victory over the 1973 Kangaroos. Bobby Fulton topped the try list with 16 and skipper Graeme Langlands finished with most goals (27) and most points (66). The revered hard man Artie Beetson made most appearances, playing in 13 out of the 16 games.

The Australians actually declined the invitation to a civic reception in Oldham stating that their timetable wouldn't permit. Times had indeed changed.

Below:
Roger Halstead of the *Oldham Evening Chronicle* tells it pretty much "like it was" in the match report the following day.

OLDHAM EVENING CHRONICLE, Saturday, October 20, 1973

OLDHAM CRUSHED BY MIGHTY AUSSIES

OLDHAM .. 2 2—10,   AUSTRALIANS . 7 10—44

THE Australian tourists turned to football — powerful, pacy football — to score ten tries and sweep a very poor Oldham team aside as they notched their biggest win of the tour so far at Watersheddings last night. It would be easy to go into raptures about the Australian performance, but praise must be tempered in the knowledge that Oldham's all-round show was woefully weak.

The home side made the fatal, fundamental mistake of standing

by ROGER HALSTEAD

should not detract from Blair's moment of glory.

Sadly, even accepting the tour-

1975 1975 1975 1975

AUSTRALIA RUGBY LEAGUE TOUR

OLDHAM FOOTBALL CLUB — SAPERE AUDE
OLDHAM R.L.F.C

NEW ZEALAND RUGBY LEAGUE

November 4th 1975.
OLDHAM 10 AUSTRALIA 20

AUSSIE FLIERS MEET BARRIER

t their
ed and
ss tell
the end

OLDHAM ... 10, AUSTRALIANS .. 20

OLDHAM, battling every inch of the way, gave the Australians a fright or two in another memorable performance at Watersheddings last night. And faster and more penetrative though the Kangaroos were, particularly in the first 20 minutes, the score did scant justice to an Oldham side that earned the praises of the tourists' management and players.

Twice Oldham swept in for tries to keep within striking distance of the internationals — ten points up inside 22 minutes — and with ten minutes to go, and trailing only 10—15, there was still the outside chance of a draw to shake the Kangaroos-rigid.

But Oldham surely missed the boat, and the chance of glory, with the decision to go for goal, midway through the second half, when the Aussies led only 10—5 and Oldham were at their best.

Wing Allan McMahon was penalised on the intervention of the touch judge for an offence on Chris

What they said about the match

REPORT BY
ROGER HALSTEAD
PICTURES BY
MARTIN SMITH

GRAEME LANGLANDS, the Aussie

RUGBY LEAGUE 1975
World Championship

The 1974 Lions lost an exciting series against the Australians when the Kangaroos won the third and deciding Test in Sydney 22-18 in front of a 55,000 crowd but fared better against New Zealand. They restored the balance by winning the tournament two Tests to one. Oldham prop Terry Clawson had played in two of the Test matches against the Aussies and then in the first and third Test against the Kiwis.

The match played against the Aussies at Watersheddings in 1975 was little more than a warm-up for the Kangaroos who were here to play England in the World Championships after already beating France 41-2 in Perpignan and Wales 18-6 at Swansea. The competition was contested by Australia, New Zealand, France, England and Wales with matches being played on both sides of the world. Australia eventually topped the table winning six out of their eight matches to lift the trophy. Oldham's half-back David Treasure played in four matches for Wales, including the 12-7 defeat of England.

The Roughyeds were back in the first division having secured promotion from third spot the previous season. Experienced campaigner Terry Ramshaw had been signed from Hull KR to add guile to the pack whilst fellow forward Barry Kear also arrived from Humberside after completing successful trials, with a proportion of the fee paid to Hull having first been raised by a 'pillowcase' collection arranged by the Oldham supporters!

WALES

Colours:
Red Jerseys, Red Shorts

1.	BILL FRANCIS (Wigan)	Full Back
2.	CLIVE SULLIVAN (Hull K.R.)	Right Wing
3.	DAVID WATKINS (Salford)	Right Centre
4.	FRANK WILSON (St. Helens)	Left Centre
5.	JOHN BEVAN (Warrington)	Left Wing
6.	DAVID TREASURE (Oldham)	Stand Off
7.	PETER BANNER (Halifax)	Scrum Half
8	JOHN MANTLE (St. Helens)	Front Row Forward
9.	TONY FISHER (Leeds)	Hooker
10	MEL JAMES (St. Helens)	Front Row Forward
11.	EDDIE CUNNINGHAM (St. Helens)	Second Row Forward
12.	BRIAN GREGORY (Wigan)	Second Row Forward
13.	KEL COSLETT (St. Helens)	Loose Forward
14.	GLYN TURNER (Hull K.R.)	Substitute Back
15	PETER ROWE (Blackpool B.)	Substitute Forward

RUGBY LEAGUE   1975

World Championship

WALES V ENGLAND

Wilderspool, Warrington.
Sat. Sept. 20th

Official Programme 15p

David Treasure scores a try against St Helens, pursued by Kel Coslett.

Both would appear together for Wales in the 1975 World Championship competition.

November 4th 1975.
OLDHAM 10   AUSTRALIA 20

The match in November 1975 was not part of an official tour but was organised to be the beginning of twelve months of celebrations that would culminate the following year at the centenary of the club. The Australians were over in England for the European leg of the 1975 World Championship competition. It would be exactly another eleven years before the Kangaroos would visit Watersheddings again.

Oldham were displaying indifferent form going into the match and their record of four wins out of eight first division games played would not improve, percentage wise, by the season's end. Nonetheless, the Tuesday evening crowd were no doubt encouraged by a home win over Dewsbury the previous Sunday.

The first quarter of the match saw the visitors take control with the 20 year-old Steve Rogers the most impressive player on view. Winger Allan McMahon and loose-forward Jim Porter, himself usually a wingman, were also giving Oldham a torrid time. However, it was the young centre ROGERS who was the first to score, scything through the home defence for a try converted by Graham EADIE. Three minutes later Porter again showed a clean pair of heels to the Oldham left flank to put McMAHON over. EADIE added the goal.

Lew Platz avoids the challenge of *Barry Kear* and prepares to take on the waiting *Stuart Bottom (4)* and *Chris O'Brien (5)* as *Tony Peters*, *Kevin Taylor* and half a dozen Kangaroos watch on.

So, after twenty-two minutes the visitors were ten points to the good and looking likely to pull away. Oldham eventually settled and half-backs Blair and Patterson were giving as good as they got from their international opponents Raudonikis and Mayes. However, the Kangaroos were monopolising the possession on the back of Mayes employing some dubious tactics as he released the ball into the scrum.

Oldham refused to succumb to the pressure and when Patterson latched on to a slick pass in the tackle from Fred Hall, he managed to draw in full-back Eadie to give Martin MURPHY a run to the posts. BLAIR added the conversion and all of a sudden the Aussies knew they had a game on their hands. Half-time: Oldham 5 Australia 10.

In the second half Kevin Taylor turned the tables in the scrum department and now, with a decent amount of possession the Roughyeds looked capable of producing a shock. It was deadlock until the hour mark and then came the incident that realistically took the match away from Oldham. Kear, Peters, Larder and Elliott had combined well to take play up to the Australian twenty-five yard line. Then, on the intervention of the touch judge, McMahon was penalised for an offence on O'Brien. Home captain, Martin Murphy, called up John Blair to go for goal when many in the crowd thought it might be best to continue to apply pressure on the Aussie line. Blair swung the kick wide where it was collected by Eadie. The full-back pulled out of two tackles and released the speedy ROGERS who raced sixty yards to touch down. EADIE converted to give the Kangaroos some breathing space.

Still Oldham came back and after Blair again broke through, Larder got with him to carry on the move, only to over-hit his grubber kick which rolled out of play. More pressure did produce the desired result when the ever alert Dickie BROWN capitalised on an Australian handling error to score under the posts. BLAIR slotted over the easy conversion and it was all to play for once more. It is fair to say that lady luck was not favouring the Roughyeds this day and the score that finally sealed the match was filled with controversy. Raudonikis hoisted a high kick from about thirty yards out. In the scramble to regain the ball McMahon got there just ahead of Kear and Barton but seemed to fumble the ball forward. In the melee that followed RAUDONIKIS reacted first to the awkward bounce of the ball to touch down. Despite the Oldham protests Mr Hunt awarded the score. EADIE converted and the Aussies were at last home and dry. Oldham 10 Australia 20.

Two-try **Steve Rogers**

OLDHAM:
M. Murphy; M. Elliott, P. Larder, S. Bottom, C. O'Brien; J. Blair, J. Patterson;
R. Hicks, K. Taylor, R. Welding, F. Hall, B. Kear, A. Peters.
Subs: E. Barton, R. Brown.

AUSTRALIA:
G. Eadie; A. McMahon, S. Rogers, J. Brass, J. Rhodes; T. Raudonikis, J. Mayes;
G. Veivers, J. Lang, I. Mackay, L. Platz, D. Fitzgerald, J. Porter.
Subs: M. Cronin, R. Higgs.

Attendance: 3,675   Mr. H. Hunt - Prestbury

GAME BREAKER!

The incident that took the game away from the Roughyeds started with the image above: **Tom Raudonikis,** under pressure from **Johnny Blair**, hoists a high kick towards the Oldham try-line.

The sequence of three photos on the left captures what happened next.

Top: **Allan McMahon** appeared to have knocked the ball forward in the melee with the Oldham defenders.

Middle: **Barry Kear** and **Eddie Barton** advance on the loose ball only for **Tom Raudonikis** to dart between them..

Bottom: Everyone looks across to the referee (out of picture) who awards the try.

The Australians in Europe
for the 1975 World Championship.

Date	Opponents	Result	Score	
10.10.75	Salford	Won	44 - 6	
12.10.75	St Helens	Won	32 - 7	
19.10.75	Wales	Won	18 - 6	*Swansea*
26.10.75	France	Won	41 - 2	*Perpignan*
01.11.75	**England**	Lost	13 - 16	*Wigan*
04.11.75	**Oldham**	Won	20 - 10	
09.11.75	York	Won	45 - 4	
12.11.75	England*	Won	25 - 0	*Leeds*

*Challenge match - not a recognised international.

OLDHAM

v

AUSTRALIA

Tuesday 4th November 1975

KO 7-30 pm   Programme 10p

*The rather unconventional match programme carried a photo of Australian prop-forward **Artie Beetson,** in his club colours, on the cover.*

Graham Eadie: *Full-back and goal kicker for the 1975 Australians, he later enjoyed a successful spell at Halifax.*

The Oldham points scorers against the 1975 Australians:
left: **Martin Murphy** - middle: **John Blair** - right: **Dickie Brown**

1986 1986 1986 1986

AUSTRALIA RUGBY LEAGUE TOUR

OLDHAM FOOTBALL CLUB

OLDHAM R.L.F.C

NEW ZEALAND RUGBY LEAGUE

November 4th 1986.
OLDHAM 16 AUSTRALIA 22

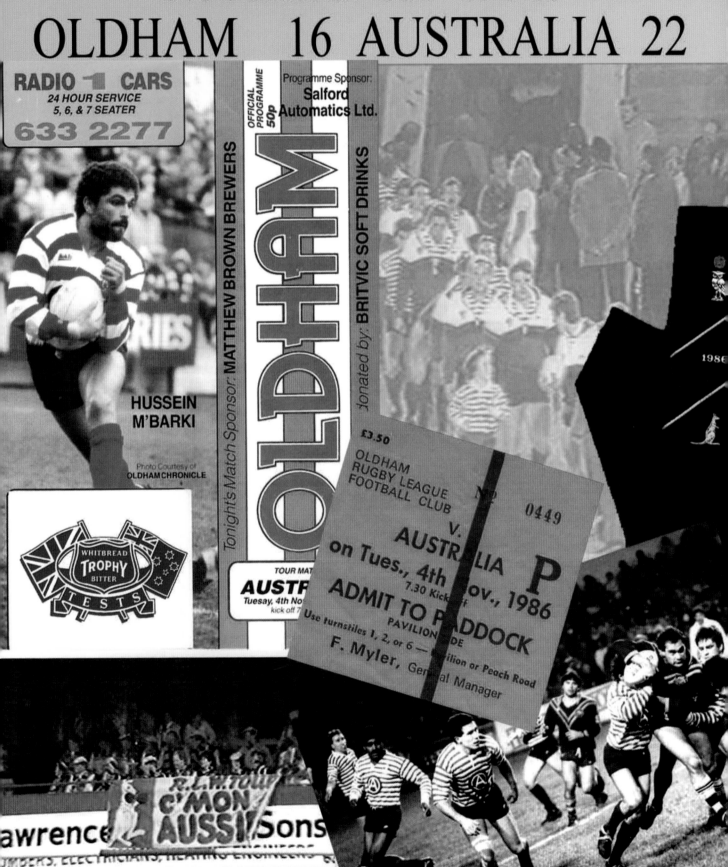

RADIO 1 CARS
24 HOUR SERVICE
5, 6, & 7 SEATER
633 2277

OFFICIAL PROGRAMME 50p

Programme Sponsor:
Salford
Automatics Ltd.

Tonight's Match Sponsor: MATTHEW BROWN BREWERS

Donated by: BRITVIC SOFT DRINKS

OLDHAM

HUSSEIN M'BARKI

Photo Courtesy of
OLDHAM CHRONICLE

WHITBREAD
TROPHY
BITTER
TESTS

TOUR MAT
AUSTR
Tuesay, 4th Nov
kick off 7

£3.50

OLDHAM
RUGBY LEAGUE
FOOTBALL CLUB

No 0449

v.
AUSTRALIA P

on Tues., 4th Nov., 1986
7.30 Kick off

ADMIT TO PADDOCK
PAVILION SIDE
Use turnstiles 1, 2, or 6 — avilion or Peach Road
F. Myler, General Manager

C'MON
AUSSI Sons
awrence

It was 11 years since an international side had last visited Watersheddings and 15 from the last time an out-and-out touring side had graced our turf. Since then things had changed dramatically in the world of rugby league tours.

The previous year the Kiwis had visited these shores and on top of playing three Test matches had played the Lancashire, Cumbria and Yorkshire county sides, Great Britain U21s and just six matches against club sides –the Roughyeds had not been included. A total of just 13 fixtures compared to the 37 played by the 1907 trailblazing New Zealanders.

The Australians had toured here in 1978 and played ten matches against club sides. York and Blackpool had been awarded slots but not Oldham. They were here again in 1982, this time playing through a 15 match itinerary with Hull, Hull KR, Wigan, Barrow, St Helens, Leeds, Leigh, Bradford Northern, Fulham and Widnes nailing down the club fixtures whilst, ironically, the Roughyeds were enjoying the most successful season in the top flight for over 20 years.

The Oldham side to play the 1986 Australians included three-quarter Des Foy, scrum-half Ray Ashton, hooker Terry Flanagan and second-row forward Mick Worrall, all of whom had represented the Oldham club during the 1984 tour down-under. That Frank Myler-led squad had also included David Hobbs- then a Featherstone player – who had since been signed by Oldham to replace the departed Andy Goodway and he would partner Worrall in the second-row in this match against the so far unbeaten green and golds.

The Kangaroos had already overpowered the Great Britain side 38-16 at Old Trafford and were facing Oldham just four days before the second Test to be played at Elland Rd., Leeds.

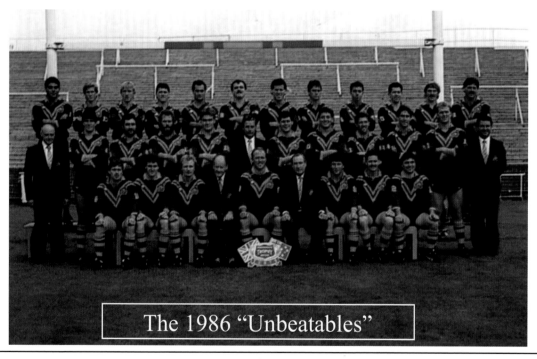

The 1986 "Unbeatables"

Back row:
Meninga, Hasler, Jack, Kiss, Shearer, Bella, Langmack, Mortimer, Alexander, Folkes, Kenny, Miles.
Middle row:
Monaghan, Davidson, Niebling, Cleal, Dunn, Furner, Lindner, Roach, Dowling, Daley, Sironen, Brittan
Front row:
Lamb, O'Connor, Sterling, Treichel, Lewis, Fleming, Simmons, Belcher, Elias.

November 4th 1986.
OLDHAM 16   AUSTRALIA 22

Much is made, and quite rightly so, of Max Krilich's 1982 Kangaroos - They were the "Invincibles", the first team to go through an entire tour unbeaten - but the 1986 tourists were without doubt the best team I have ever seen. The Test series, keenly fought by the British squad, saw the Ashes retained by the green and golds. The three to nil series defeat was widely predicted, although the score-lines, especially the second Test drubbing at Headingley, did little to reflect the effort of the Lions.

The club matches? The Aussies destroyed the best we had to offer. 40 - 0 at Leeds. 48 - 0 at Hull. 38 - 0 at Bradford. Only Wigan got anywhere near in the opening match of the tour before finally falling to a 26 - 18 defeat before over 30,000 at Central Park. That is, except for Oldham! On a bitterly cold November evening at Watersheddings the Roughyeds gave the Kangaroos the fright of their lives.

The crowd of over 5,500 greeted the teams as they entered the arena for what was to be the final tour game at Watersheddings. "Waltzing Matilda" was played for the visitors, followed by "God Save The Queen". Ray Ashton took the kick-off towards the Hutchins stand where it was fielded by Mal Meninga. Straight away one got the impression that the Roughyeds were up for the task when the Aussies were forced into losing possession on the first play of the game and there was only two minutes on the clock when David HOBBS slotted home a simple penalty after the tourists were caught offside. The game erupted on seven minutes as the first scrum broke up in a free-for-all. Several players were involved

Photo courtesy of Harry Edgar.

Greg Alexander *pounces on a loose ball as* **Des Foy**, **Hussein M'Barki** *and* **Mal Meninga** *close in.*

193

with fists flying everywhere. The end result saw four players in the bin, Martin Bella and Steve Folkes for the Kangaroos were joined by Paul Sherman and, after much deliberation, Mick Worrall from Oldham.

Ashton made a good break but not surprisingly, it was the Australians who began to make the most of the extra space available with four players off the field. Des Foy did well to defuse a kick ahead by Dale Shearer and came to the rescue again with a good tackle on Terry Lamb. To add to Oldham's worries, Hobbs had to retire to be replaced by Colin Hawkyard with only eleven minutes gone. Michael O'CONNOR levelled the scores with a penalty after a high tackle by Neil Clawson. As the game moved into the second quarter the visitors showed some of their real class as the ball passed through six pairs of hands before O'Connor's inside pass sent LAMB speeding towards the posts. Four minutes later Gary Belcher gathered up a clearance kick and galloped up the right wing. Shearer got with him and a last gasp pass, as the Oldham cover pounced, was enough for LAMB to squeeze in at the corner. O'CONNOR converted both tries to leave the tourists looking comfortable with a twelve point lead after 25 minutes.

Still Oldham refused to capitulate and first Foy and then David Topliss tested the Australian defence with good breaks. Bruce "Bruiser" Clark was enjoying playing against

Colin Hawkyard *steps out of a despairing tackle to score Oldham's first try.*

his fellow countrymen and the Oldham pack, in general, were giving as good as they got. They got their reward just before the interval. After Clark had once again battered his way into the heart of the green and golds, quick hands from Ashton and Topliss put Worrall away. The G.B. international beat several players before handing on to Ashton who took the ball out to the left where Gary Warnecke backed up and managed to release a despairing pass in the tackle which HAWKYARD did well to take and scamper over for the try.

WORRALL converted to leave the half-time score: Oldham 8 Australia 14.

The second half saw two early penalty misses, one for each side. First O'Connor was off target after Oldham were pulled up for holding down in the tackle and Worrall was also unsuccessful after an Australian obstruction. In between Hussein M'Barki did well to clear his line after a kick through. O'Connor failed with two more goal attempts but WORRALL put one over after thirteen minutes. The Roughyeds reshuffled the back line moving M'Barki to full-back and Jeff Edwards to the wing. Almost immediately it paid dividends as the Moroccan again fielded a deep kick from the tourists and beat the first wave of chasers to take play back into the Australian half. He eventually kicked ahead only for Greg Alexander to win the race for the ball.

Dale Shearer falls to a three man Roughyeds' tackle while to the left of the action, **Colin Hawkyard,** **Tom Nadiola, Des Foy, Terry Flanagan** *and* **Ben Elias** *watch with interest.*

There was some furious tackling by both teams and, after Bella was penalised for a foul on Ashton, WORRALL kicked the resulting penalty and Oldham were, incredibly, only two points behind going into the last quarter of the match. The game then turned Australia's way after a great run by Belcher took play up towards the Oldham line. A couple of plays later Ben ELIAS caught the tiring Roughyeds napping to go over direct from acting half-back. O'Connor missed the extras but the tourists now seemed to be back in control.

Another break by man-of-the-match Elias was carried on by Les Davidson to once again take play up towards the Oldham line. However, it was a reflection on how the visitors were somewhat worried about the score when there was a failed drop goal attempt from Paul Langmack. Oldham were not done yet and after they had introduced Tom Nadiola to replace Clawson a smart inside pass from Clark put Warnecke away, but the next pass to Stuart Raper went astray as he was met by Alexander. There was a lengthy delay for an injury to Shearer at which point Paul Sironen came on to replace Bella, after which O'Connor missed another goal after Oldham were penalised for holding down.

The game was made safe for the tourists when, after a fumble by Edwards, ALEXANDER went over direct from the resulting scrum, exploiting the fact that Raper was receiving attention for an injury at the time. Oldham did manage to raise themselves for one last effort. The industrious Terry Flanagan forced a knock on from Sironen and from the resulting possession Topliss put Raper clear with an inside pass. The Australian then punished his compatriots with a precision kick that was scooped up by FOY who plunged in at the corner for the last ever tour match score at Watersheddings. The conversion was missed and, much to the tourists' relief, the final whistle followed with the score: Oldham 16 Australia 22

OLDHAM: J Edwards; P Sherman, D Foy, G Warnecke, H M'Barki; D Topliss, R Ashton; B Clark, T Flanagan, N Clawson, M Worrall, D Hobbs, S Raper.
Subs: C Hawkyard, T Nadiola

AUSTRALIA: G Belcher; D Shearer, C Mortimer, M Meninga, M O'Connor; T Lamb, G Alexander; P Daley, B Elias, M Bella, S Folkes, L Davidson, P Langmack.
Subs: G Jack (not used), P Sironen.

Attendance: 5,678   Referee: Mr. K. Allatt - Southport

> *Below: The last try against a touring team at Watersheddings -* **Des Foy** *evades* **Michael O'Connor** *to score to the delight of* **Hussein M'Barki** *and* **Paul Sherman** *whilst* **Terry Lamb** *can only watch.*

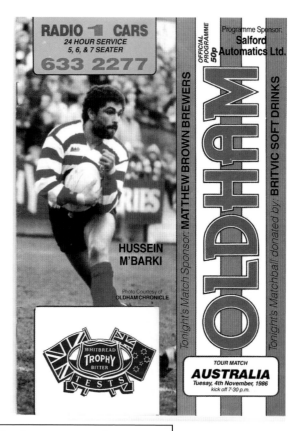

"C'Mon Aussie"
Some of the travelling Australian supporters in the top tier of the Hutchins stand.

Yours truly was seated to their right and banter was exchanged!

As I recall they were a vociferous and good-humoured crew but following this team they could well afford to be.

Match programme featuring Moroccan full-back
Hussein M'Barki.

Benny Elias: (right) Star of the match, captain on the night and an inspiration to his team-mates.

1986 Australian Tour	Result	Score	Attendance
Wigan	Won	26 - 18	30,622
Hull Kingston Rovers	Won	46 - 10	6.868
Leeds	Won	40 - 0	10.974
Cumbria (at Barrow)	Won	48 - 12	4.233
Great Britain at Old Trafford, Manchester	Won	38 - 16	50,583
Halifax	Won	36 - 2	8,000
St. Helens	Won	32 - 8	21,700
Oldham	Won	22 - 16	5,678
Great Britain at Elland Road, Leeds	Won	34 - 4	30,808
Widnes	Won	20 - 4	7,500
Hull	Won	48 - 0	8,213
Bradford Northern	Won	38 -0	8,000
Great Britain at Central Park, Wigan	Won	24 - 15	20,169

Bruce Clark:
Turned in an impressive performance against his fellow countrymen.

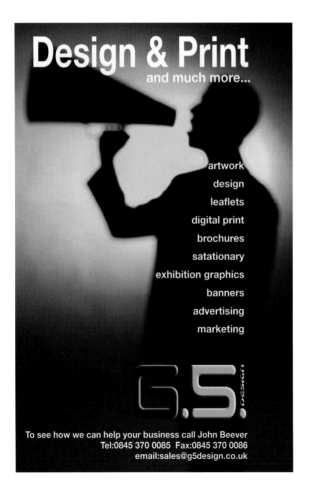

OLDHAM

1934
1934

FRANCE

1997
1997

Entente Cordiale at Watershedding

THE FRENCH

The supporters of the French national side, hosts of the 2007 Rugby Union World Cup, got a rude awakening when the Argentineans lowered the Tricolour in the tournament's opening fixture. There would have been thousands of Frenchmen who wouldn't have been able to blame their red eyes on the garlic and onions should the improbable have happened and the Irish finally guillotined France's chances. But some older members of a tight-knit rugby league community nestled in the foothills of the Pyrenees would have been only too pleased to wave two fingers.

Rugby Union was introduced to France by English expatriates in the 1870s. Its stronghold has always been in the south of the country, particularly the lands of Basques and Catalans. In 1931 the national rugby union side, which played the sport with both flair and brutality - and which 'beat' England in Paris - was kicked out of the Five Nations by the International Rugby Board for violent play. So too was its governing body, the *Francaise Federation De Rugby,* for failing to control a number of its clubs which allegedly were making illegal payments to players within a 'strictly' amateur code.

Taking advantage of the kick in union's proverbials, one Jean Galia, a union forward already suspended by the Federation, became a prime mover in both introducing and establishing semi-professional rugby league into France. In the late summer of 1934, in order to promote publicity for this fledgling venture, Galia - under the Villeneuve club banner - undertook a short tour of Lancashire & Yorkshire, during which they played Oldham at Watersheddings – losing by the narrowest of margins.

The tour paid off, with the Rugby Football League making a big effort to establish *le rugby a X111* in the republic, and in early 1935 a triangular tournament was set up to be contested by England, Wales and France, with two of the matches to be played in Paris and Bordeaux. Oldham forward Lewis Rees played for Wales against France in the match in Bordeaux which the French won 18-11. After forcing a draw against England, France shared the inaugural series. The tournament continued to be played each season until the outbreak of the Second World War, with France winning the trophy during the 1938-39 campaign.

The 1934-35 season opened in France with 14 clubs playing semi-professional rugby league. By the end of 1938 there were over 190. In addition a number of the country's big union clubs had switched codes. And the new code was growing fast. In the years running up to the Second World War it seemed certain that league would become the dominant code in France. In 1930 the French Rugby Union had almost 800 members but by 1939 this had fallen to around 470.

Then came one of the most treacherous acts in the history of sport. By the middle of 1940 the Germans had both invaded and conquered France, and the Nazi- supporting Franco – German Vichy regime had been installed to rule those parts of France and its colonies unoccupied by Germany. It would appear that just weeks after its formation one of its Ministers, Jean Ybarnegaray, came under pressure from senior officials of the *Federation Francaise de Rugby* – resulting in an announcement that the fate of rugby league was clear. Its life was over and it would be expunged from French sport.

Four months later, in December 1940, the head of the Vichy government, Marshal Phillippe Petain, signed a decree ordering rugby league to merge with rugby union - assuring that league could be played at amateur level. But it was a never- to- be- kept promise. The 13 man code was dead in the water with its assets seized, and evidently, in many cases, given to union clubs. This was seen as part of a wider tactic by the Vichy regime - to end professionalism in French sport – but stronger bodies such as football, boxing and cycling never did conform.

Rugby League in France is still waiting for an apology and has never been compensated.

After the war the sport tried valiantly to reinvent itself with characters such as former Resistance leader Paul Barriere to the fore. Again the RFL came to its aid and the triangular international tournament was reintroduced, bolstered by a number of promotional tours to this country. During season 1945 -46 Oldham's forwards Tommy Rostron and Doug Phillips played for England and Wales respectively and both the Roughyeds' centres Ernie Large and Norman Harris played for a British RL X111 against Racing Club de Paris (in Paris) with Harris scoring a try in the 36-19 British victory. French clubs were urged to make the trip here and on the Easter Monday of 1950 a combined Bordeaux and Villeneuve side played against Oldham. Bolstered by the support of the ARL, tours down-under were made by France in 1951, 1955 and 1960 and the country hosted the World Cup in 1954.

Whilst rugby league never again reached the heights that it had achieved pre-war, and there have been more than just one or two games between our two countries which can only at best be described as running brawls (causing the future of Anglo-French internationals to be questioned), the 13- man game clung on and survived. Those efforts were eventually rewarded with Catalan Dragons winning a place in the 2007 Challenge Cup final at the new Wembley Stadium.

So, a toast then to Jean Galia and all those who've played a part in keeping this great game of ours alive and kicking on the Continent.

Mind you, there will be more than just a few Oldham supporters who just might wish it hadn't when in 1997 defeat by a French club side signalled the beginning of the end for one of the most famous rugby league clubs in the world!

VINCENNES : Villeneuve XIII-Paris XIII (32-13). — Max Rousié, tenant délicatement le ballon dans la main, file vers les buts adverses après avoir feinté un adversaire. Remarquez qu'il court sans chaussures !

*Rugby League comes to the front covers of French sports magazines in February 1935. Villeneuve half-back, **Max Rousié**, very much the "golden boy" in the early days of "Rugby à treize", pictured in action in the match against a Paris Xlll.*

September 17th 1934: Oldham 26 Villeneuve 25

The first French team to play at Oldham took part in what seems to have been the most exciting of games. The Chronicle report positively gushed about the artistry and flair of the Frenchmen and stated "... *the French idea seems to be l'audace, encore l'audace et toujours l'audace"* – which they translated as "*boldness, again boldness and without end boldness"*.

In truth, Oldham started the game well and early tries from Steve Ray and Tom Egan gave the Roughyeds a six point lead in as many minutes. Max Rousié, a half-back with silky ball-handling skills, scored a try which he converted himself to bring the French back into the game. Further tries by Sam Bardsley and Fred Ashworth, combined with one conversion from Tommy Rees, gave Oldham a fourteen points to five advantage at the interval.

Contrary to the start of the first period, it was the visitors who dominated the early part of the second half. Tries from Camo, Saffagiue and Rousié, all converted by the latter put the Frenchmen 20 – 14 in front. Oldham hit back with a try from Norman Pugh, converted by Rees, but a try from left wing Sanz, again converted by Rousié, restored the six point difference. Even when Alex Givvons went over for a try to which Rees added the goal in the closing minute it still appeared as if the visitors would register the first victory

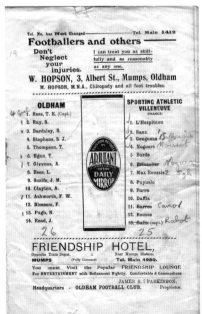

Max Rousié: outstanding player for the French.

of their mini-tour of England, but it wasn't to be. As the match moved into injury time a reckless clearance kick was fielded by Rees near the touch line. He advanced to just inside the French half and "on the run" let fly with a towering drop kick that broke the gallant Frenchmen's hearts as it soared between the posts to give Oldham a one point victory.

OLDHAM:
T. Rees; S. Ray, S. Bardsley, J. Stephens, T. Thompson; T. Egan, A. Givvons; L. Rees, J. Scaife, A. Clayton, F. Ashworth, F. Blossom, N. Pugh.

VILLENEUEVE:
L'Eespitauo; Saffagiue, Moisset, E. Cougnenc, H. Sanz; F. Nogueres, M. Rousié; A. Puyelo, J. Porra, J. Daffis, E Camo, A. Rousse, J. Rabot.
Attendance: 3,000   Referee: Mr. A.E. Harding - Broughton

Before the match the French team and officials had been received by the Mayor at the Town Hall and when the game was over they were guests at Oldham greyhound stadium where they enjoyed such a good time it took some persuading for them to go on to the dinner which was prepared at the Greenacres Cooperative (Hill Stores) function room. All the usual dignitaries were in attendance, as was the Australian tour manager Harry Sunderland. The Mayor (Alderman Shannon) presented the visiting party with souvenir cigarette lighters. These were inscribed with the wording: "Oldham F.C. 1934."

The team page from the match programme.

April 4th 1950: Oldham 14 Bordeaux & Villeneuve 3

The match against the "select" of Bordeaux & Villeneuve played on Easter Monday 1950 was, to a great degree, spoiled by the weather. It was reported that as the home captain, Bryn Goldswain, made the toss before the game, hailstones were swept across the pitch by a cold, driving wind.

Open play was at a premium and what there was of it tended to come from Oldham in the first half when they played "with the weather". Tries from Frank Daley, Jack Keith, Trevor Williams and Wilson Spencer, who also converted the Willams effort, gave the Roughyeds a 14 points to nil half-time lead. By the time the French had the benefit of the elements in the second half they were a spent force. Peyral in the forwards and the Artigalus brothers in the backs showed up well but all they had to show for their efforts was a try from left wing, Vigouroux.

OLDHAM:
L. Platt; J. Warham, T. Williams, W. Mitchell, R. Batten; F. Daley, W. Spencer;
H. Ogden, J. Keith, L. Anthony, A. Fearnley, J. Sugden, B. Goldswain.

BORDEAUX & VILLENEUVE:
E.D. Artigalus; Contrastin, Audignon, Gay, Vigouroux; Estrada, Y. Artigalus;
Palats, Inza, Treboutat, Duple, Peyral, Calixte.

Attendance: 4,901   Mr F Smith – Barrow

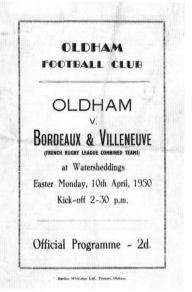

Above: The teams line up before the match and the match programme.

Left: Chronicle cartoon of the action and conditions.

September 22nd 1982: Oldham 11 French Xlll 15

This was an odd sort of fixture with the "Sélection Française" taking on what was an inexperienced, young Oldham team boosted by the appearance of just a few regular first teamers. The French were in England in preparation for the forthcoming Test series against Australia.

Unlike the goodwill that had accompanied previous encounters against French opposition, this was a bad-tempered affair which degenerated so much that by the end of the game some people were of the opinion that the referee abandoned the game in the final seconds when a Frenchman refused to walk after being sent off! However, Mr. Beaumont of Huddersfield, although admitting the game was becoming "very rough", denied he took such drastic action.

A disjointed match full of penalties saw Oldham first on the score sheet after seven minutes with a Brian Caffery penalty. Two minutes later

Guy Delauney capitalised on a teasing kick ahead by stand-off Michel Laville to score a try converted by full-back, André Perez. The same player added a penalty goal ten minutes later and about the same time Caffery was withdrawn with concussion and replaced by Mick O'Rourke with Dennis O'Neil moving to full-back. Paddy Kirwan was having a storming game for the Roughyeds and galloped though a massive gap at the play-the-ball to dive over for a try, converted by the debut-making Chris Willis, to bring Oldham level five minutes from the interval. However, it was the French who had the last say of the half with Delauney again exposing Oldham's inability to cope with the tricky kicks of Laville, to score his second try. Perez added the goal to leave the half-time score: Oldham 7 France 12.

Terry Flanagan, who was returning to first team action after injury, showed up well before being replaced after an hour by Des Foy. In fact all of the Oldham pack performed admirably with special mention given to Paul Lowndes and Bob Mordell.

The second half actually flowed better than the first and yet yielded just one more try for left-wing Didier Bernard. Either side of this Willis kicked another penalty goal to leave the final score: Oldham 11 France 15.

OLDHAM:
B. Caffery; G. Munro, C. Hawkyard, D. O'Neill, S. Dobb; C. Willis, P. Kirwan;
M. Coombes, P. Lowndes, L. Chadwick, G. Walczak, R. Mordell, T. Flanagan.
Subs: D. Foy, M. O'Rourke.

FRENCH Xlll:
A. Perez; P. Solal, G. Delauney, F. Laforgue, D. Bernard; M. Laville, I. Greseque;
M. Chantal, C. Macalli, C. Zalduendo, G. Laforgue, J-J. Cologni, R. Puech.
Subs: J. Imbert, M. Caravaca.

Attendance: 1,165   Referee: Mr. T. Beaumont – Huddersfield

In August 1991, Oldham undertook a pre-season mini-tour of France, under coach Peter Tunks, incorporating games against Pia August 18th, Carcassonne August 21st and Villeneuve August 23rd. The Pia match was won (28 – 26) but the other two were lost including the infamous "battle of Carcassonne." During the three matches the following players represented Oldham.

D. Platt, R. Blackman, S. Warburton, A. Phillip, I. Bates, P. Mitchell, J. Green, A. Donegan, R. Russell, T. Street, S. Allen, S. Longstaff, D. Bradbury, R. Pachniuk, P. Round, D. Pitts, K. Newton, N. Flanagan, B. McDermott, A. Barrow, K. Atkinson, C. Joynt and R. Irving.

SUPER LEAGUE 1996: April 8th 1996 - Paris St. Germain 24 Oldham 24

Oldham went to the Charlety Stadium on Easter Monday 1996 to take on the still relatively unknown quantity that was Paris St Germain. They returned with a share of the spoils from a match that, to all intents and purposes, they should have won.

Twice fourteen points to the good, Oldham succumbed to a last gasp equalising, converted score from Pascal Bomati. The proverbial game of two halves was dominated by the Oldham scrum-half Martin Crompton in the first, and his opposite number Patrick Entat in the second. Tries in the first period from Matt Munro and Darren Abram with three goals from Francis Maloney put Oldham in control with the only French reply coming from a good solo effort from Laurent Lucchese.

When, early in the second half, Maloney went over for a good try round the blind-side of a scrum, the Roughyeds looked like they might be in for a big win. Didier Cabestany went over for Paris with the try improved by Patrick Torreilles but a further try from Andrew Patmore restored Oldham's advantage. Still Paris refused to give up and after Entat went in under the posts the scene was set for Bomati's dramatic last minute try.

PARIS ST. GERMAIN:
L. Lucchese; P. Bomati, P. Chamorin, D. Adams, Ramandu;
F. Devecchi, P. Entat; J. Sands, P. Torreilles, G. Kacala, V. Bloomfield, D. Cabestany, J. Pech. Subs: M. Piskunov, V. Wulf, R. Pastre-Courtine, K. Utoikamanu.
Goals: Torreilles,4. - Tries: Lucchese, Cabestany, Entat, Bomati.

OLDHAM:
P. Atcheson; A. Leuila, A. Patmore, D. Abram, A. Belle;
F. Maloney, M. Crompton; I. Gildart, J. Clarke, J. Temu, G. Lord, M. Munro, H. Hill.
Subs: D. Bradbury, J. Faimalo, P. Topping, P. Davidson.
Goals: Maloney,4. - Tries: Munro, Abram, Maloney, Patmore.

Attendance: 6,327   Referee: Mr. J. Connolly – Wigan

June 28th 1996 - Oldham 24 Paris St. Germain 6

Although Watersheddings was still in use the return match against Paris was played at Boundary Park where a competent Oldham performance saw the French team, lacking in confidence after ten straight defeats, completely outplayed.

Once again Martin Crompton was instrumental in setting up the Oldham victory and it was he who went over for the first try. Paris responded and, after Frederic Banquet had a try ruled out for incorrect grounding, hooker Vincent Wulf got the verdict from the big screen to open the French account. Sadly for Paris, and despite another impressive display from the all-action Patrick Entat, the conversion from Banquet saw an end to their tally for the day. The Oldham forwards bossed the show with Jason Temu and substitute Joe Faimalo to the fore. Further tries from Adie Belle, Joe Faimalo (2), and John Clarke saw the Roughyeds comfortably home.

OLDHAM: J. Cowan; A. Belle, A. Patmore, P. Topping, R. Myler; F. Maloney,
M. Crompton; I. Gildart, J. Clarke, J. Temu, G. Lord, M. Munro, D. Bradbury,
Subs: H. Hill, P. Crook, R. Guy, J. Faimalo
Goals: Maloney,2. – Tries: Faimalo,2. Crompton. Belle. Clarke.

PARIS ST. GERMAIN: L. Lucchese; P. Bomati, D. Bird, E. Virgniol, F. Banquet;
T. Brown, P. Entat; P. Shead, V. Wulf, J. Sands, J. Parru, J. Pech, P. Chamorin.
Subs: D. Smith, G. Wilson, J. Boslem, V. Bloomfield.
Goal: Banquet. - Try: Wulf.

Attendance: 2,548   Referee: Mr. R. Connolly - Wigan

*Left: Match programme for the first visit of Paris St Germain to Boundary Park featuring **David Bradbury**.*
*Below: **John Clarke** attracts the attention of the PSG defence, including **Patrick Entat** on the left.*

SUPER LEAGUE 1997: April 13th 1997. Oldham 19 Paris St. Germain 18

Oldham came into this match desperate for victory after having lost the first five games of the season. The desired result was duly delivered but only thanks to a last minute drop goal from substitute, Francis Maloney.

A scrappy game was decided by the late one-pointer after Oldham had fought back from an early eight points to nil deficit. Martin Crompton once again played a captain's role to keep Oldham in the hunt. Gary Lord, Mike Neal and Paul Davidson were the try scorers with goals from Maloney (2) and Luke Goodwin.

OLDHAM: P. Atcheson; S. Ranson, D. Abram, M. Neal, R. Myler; L. Goodwin, M. Crompton; I. Gildart, J. Clarke, B. Goldspink, G. Lord, J. Faimalo, M. Munro.
Subs: P. Davidson, D. Bradbury, D. Stephenson, F. Maloney.
Goals: Goodwin. Maloney,2.- Drop Goal: Maloney. - Tries: Lord, Neal, Davidson.

PARIS ST.GERMAIN: D. Bird; F. Devecchi, J. Olejnik, P. Evans, A. Wall; J. Robinson, P. Bergman; J. Sands, D. O'Donnell, A. Priddle, W. Sing, Hogue, P. Chamorin.
Subs: A. Peters, A. Bellamy, D. Lomax, M. O'Connor
Goals: Robinson,3. - Tries: Lomax, Wall, Olejnik.

Attendance: 3,396   Referee: Mr. R. Smith – Castleford

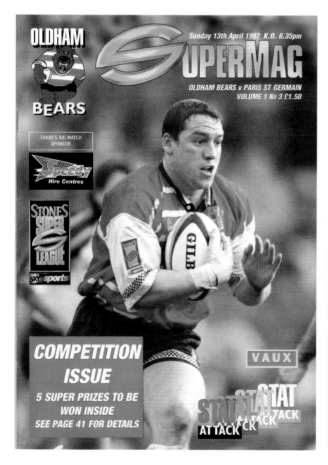

Above left: Once again it's **David Bradbury** *on the cover for the Paris programme in 1997.*
Above right: Match winner, **Francis Maloney***.*

August 26th 1997 - Paris St. Germain 23 Oldham 12

A day that will live in infamy for all Roughyeds supporters. This defeat condemned Oldham to relegation and sealed the plight of the old club. A brief look at the Paris line-up gives evidence of how much the Rugby League authorities wanted the French dream to remain alive with the consequence of an Oldham nightmare.

Eighteen-nil down at half-time, much to the dismay of their travelling supporters, Oldham did not seem up for the fight. Paris knew what was at stake and there only looked to be one winner from early in the game. A second half rally produced tries for Luke Goodwin and Paul Davidson but it was too little, too late and Oldham were, well and truly, DOWN and OUT.
Vive le kangaroo!

Howard Hill releases a pass in the tackle. Notice the empty seats. The Parisians obviously not interested in watching a team of Australians struggle in Super League.

PARIS ST. GERMAIN:
D. Bird; Mahoney, P. Evans, J. Eade, P. Bergman; M. O'Connor, Martin;
Taylor, D. O'Donnell, W. Sing, Hancock, A. Peters, D. Lomax.
Subs: A. Priddle, P. Chamorin, A. Bellamy, Hogue.
Goals: O'Connor,3. - Drop Goal: O'Connor. - Tries: Evans,2, O'Donnell, Eade.

OLDHAM: P. Atcheson; S. Ranson, H. Hill, P. Topping, D. Jones; F. Maloney,
L. Goodwin;.I. Gildart, D. Stephenson, J. Temu, P. Davidson, J. Faimalo, C. McKinney.
Subs: G. Lord, I. Russell, J. Cowan, A. Nuttall.
Goals: Maloney, Goodwin. – Tries: Goodwin, Davidson.

Attendance: 2,000   Referee: Mr. S. Cummins - Widnes.

Keeping the faith until the end.

The loyal Roughyeds supporters proudly display the colours in the Charlety stadium.

1997

World Club Championship

Come along and see

THE BEARS

SMASH THE AUSSIES!!

OLDHAM R.L.F.C

At Boundary Park

Friday 18th July - North Queensland Cowboys
Friday 25th July - Adelaide Rams

Visa Super League World Club Championship.

Whilst delayed a year because of the dispute between the Australian RL and Super League, a global rugby league club competition was played for the first time in the sport's 102 year history, when, in 1997, twelve European Super League and ten Australian / New Zealand Super League clubs competed against each other for the Visa Super League World Club Championship in Great Britain, France, Australia and New Zealand.

The tournament was financed to the tune of £6m by Rupert Murdoch's News Corporation with credit card company Visa persuaded to part-sponsor only days before it kicked-off. This was perhaps as well, too, because gate receipts - which were kept by the home club - were well below that of the level expected and travel expenses phenomenal.

The first phase of the tournament was played between the 6th and 23rd of June and the second between the 18th of July and the 4th of August. The quarter and semi-finals were staged early in October with the final played in New Zealand on the 17th of that month – the winners picking up a cool one million Australian dollars (about £470,000).

Competing clubs were separated into two groups decided upon by league positions attained during the previous season's campaigns:

A - St Helens, Wigan Warriors, Bradford Bulls, London Broncos, Warrington Wolves, Halifax Blue Sox, Brisbane Broncos, Cronulla Sharks, Canberra Raiders, Auckland Warriors, Canterbury Bulldogs and Penrith Panthers.

B - Sheffield Eagles, Oldham Bears, Castleford Tigers, Leeds Rhinos, Paris St Germain, Salford Reds (who replaced relegated Workington Town), Adelaide Rams, Perth Reds, North Queensland Cowboys and Hunter Mariners.

William Hills placed Brisbane Broncos as 7-4 favourites with Oldham Bears, Castleford Tigers, Paris St Germain, Sheffield Eagles and Warrington Wolves joint 1000-1 outsiders.

The Aussies dominated the tournament to a greater degree than was first feared with many British clubs getting hammered (Warrington Wolves, for instance, suffered two consecutive record home defeats when they lost 22-52 to Penrith Panthers and then 28-56 to Auckland Warriors, Brisbane Broncos scored a club record win when they beat Halifax Blue Sox 76-0, Auckland Warriors beat their record score four times when they scored 56 points against Warrington, 62 and then 64 both against Bradford Bulls and 70 against St Helens, Canberra Raiders ran up their highest ever score when beating Halifax Blue Sox 70-0).

Clubs in Group 'A' each played six matches, three in Europe and three in either Australia or New Zealand. The British clubs in Group 'B' played only four matches. Oldham, for example, played Adelaide Rams and North Queensland Cowboys out in Australia during the first phase of the competition with the return matches held in Oldham during the second. Whilst the quarter-finals were seeded to ensure that a European side featured in each of the four matches only eight of the 60 group matches were won by European sides - one of those eight being Oldham's 20-16 defeat of North Queensland Cowboys at Boundary Park. The frailty of the quarter-final seeding is best highlighted by the fact that two participating British clubs Bradford Bulls and St Helens didn't win one of their six qualifying matches whilst Australian

side Penrith Panthers lost out despite winning all six of theirs!
Each of the quarter finals was won by the Australian and New Zealand clubs. Auckland Warriors (home) murdered Bradford Bulls 62-14, Hunter Mariners (away) beat Wigan Warriors 22-18, Brisbane Broncos (home) dismantled St Helens 66-12 and finally Cronulla Sharks (away) defeated London Broncos 40-16. With organisers confident that at least one of the European teams would reach the last four, one of the semi-finals was scheduled to be played in Britain, but this had to be hurriedly re-scheduled to be played in Australia.

The bookies got it spot-on when an Allan Langer-led Brisbane Broncos overcame Hunter Mariners 36-12 at the Ericsson Stadium in Auckland to lift the trophy. Five of the Brisbane players were later selected for the Australian squad which would face Great Britain in the British Gas Test series.

Attendances, as was said earlier, had been disappointing. The 30 European home games averaged 6,888 and the 30 matches in Australia / New Zealand 9,160. The final attracted only 12,000. Just seven days after Oldham Bears defeated North Queensland Cowboys in a magnificent game only a meagre 3,513 crowd turned out on a fine July evening to watch them play Adelaide Rams at Boundary Park!

WORLDS APART
(above) It's kick-off time at the Stockland stadium as Oldham take on the North Queensland Cowboys. (below) One month later and Luke Goodwin sets the return game in motion at Boundary Park when Oldham gained a dramatic late victory. Probably the "Bears" greatest moment.

North Queensland Cowboys 54   Oldham Bears 16:   June 14th 1997

It's 1997 and the once-thought unbelievable has happened. Oldham are playing rugby league against Australian opposition AWAY! Not too many years before, this was something that one would joke about and yet at the Stockland Stadium in Townsville, Queensland, this incredible landmark came to pass.

The match went the way many thought it would. The young, enthusiastic Cowboys, whose line-up was packed with pace and sprinkled with superb ball handlers, were too much for an Oldham team that battled bravely but found themselves swept away by the eager Queensland outfit. Andrew Dunemann started the rout when he scythed through the Oldham defence for a fabulous try. Soon after Luke Phillips repeated the dose and converted the score to put the Cowboys ten points up. A frustrating opening period for the Bears culminated with the sin-binning of captain Martin Crompton half way through the first period. The Cowboys added a further 12 points while he was off the field and the match was as good as finished as a serious contest. The referee was doing Oldham few favours and a David Jones try, made by Crompton and Francis Maloney, just before the interval was all theY had to show for their endeavours in a torrid first half for the Bears.

After the break it was much the same, although further tries from Afi Leuila, again fashioned by Crompton, and John Clarke, both improved by Luke Goodwin, left the score not looking too bad at 38 - 16 with a quarter of an hour left. However, the try-hungry Australians, for whom Ian Dunemann was outstanding, rattled up a further 16 points, as Oldham tired, to run out very comfortable winners.

NORTH QUEENSLAND COWBOYS:
R. Cressbrook; L. Phillips, M. Shipway, S. Mahon, S. Vincent; I. Dunemann, A. Dunemann; G. Murphy, S.Walters, M. Locke, O. Cunningham, P. Jones, K. Warren.
Subs: J. Doyle, B. Tabuai, R. Mercy, L. Scott.
Tries: Walters,2. Cressbrook,2. Vincent,2. Murphy. Shipway. A. Dunemann. Phillips.
Goals: Phillips,7.

OLDHAM BEARS:
P. Atcheson; A. Leuila, H. Hill, V. Fawcett, D. Jones; F. Maloney, M. Crompton; I. Gildart, D. Stephenson, B. Goldspink, P. Davidson, M. Munro, L. Goodwin.
Subs: G. Lord, J. Faimalo, J. Clarke, P. Topping.
Tries: Jones. Leuila. Clarke.
Goals: Goodwin,2.

Attendance: 12,631   Referee: Mr. G. Annesley - Sydney

Left:
***Luke Goodwin** and **Mark Shipway** beg to differ but it's referee, **Graham Annesley** who decides.*

Right:
***Matt Munro** brings down **Steve Walters**.*

Adelaide Rams 42   Oldham Bears 14:   June 20th 1997

This was much better from Oldham, with the score reflecting harshly on a vastly improved performance than that up in Queensland the previous week. Indeed, a lot of impressive attacking play was often thwarted by the Bears own poor finishing as much as the Rams defence.

Oldham had a dream start when, after only three minutes, Paul Topping capitalised on an Adelaide error to touch down. Stand-off Luke Williamson replied for the Rams and close range efforts from Steve Stone and Brett Galea, all converted by Williamson, put the home side 18 - 6 up at the break. However, things would have been so different if first Francis Maloney and then Joe Faimalo had not put down potential try- scoring passes with the line wide open.

Still, when Faimalo made amends to score the first try of the second half, the Rams were worried enough to reintroduce star player Kerrod Walters to steady the ship. This had the desired effect for Adelaide, as he and Alan Cann began to dominate the play from there on in until the end of the game. Rod Maybon, Kurt Wrigley, Wayne Simonds and Andrew Hick added tries for Adelaide, which were all converted. Howard Hill had a try disallowed via the "big screen" before Francis Maloney went over following a kick ahead by Luke Goodwin. Maloney's solitary goal in the first half was in stark contrast to the efforts of the Rams kickers, Williamson and Wrigley, who didn't miss a goal attempt throughout the match.

Joe Faimalo is well and truly "collared" by the Rams defence at the Adelaide Oval.

Martin Crompton was again in good form for Oldham and was ably supported by full-back Paul Atcheson and Paul Topping, who had a storming game in the second row.

ADELAIDE RAMS:
R. Maybon; W. Simonds, C. Quinn, S. Kiri, M. McGuire; L. Williamson, D. Schifilliti; A. Cann, S. Stone, M. Corvo, D. Broughton, B. Galea, E. Paiyo.
Subs: B. Mamando. A. Hick. K. Walters, K. Wrigley.
Tries: Williamson. Stone. Galea. Maybon. Wrigley. Simonds. Hick.
Goals: Williamson,6. Wrigley.

OLDHAM BEARS:
P.Atcheson; A. Leuila, D. Abram, R. Myler, D. Jones; F. Maloney, M. Crompton; I. Gildart, J. Clarke, G. Lord, P. Topping, J. Faimalo. M. Munro.
L.Goodwin, H. Hill, J. Temu, D. Stephenson.
Tries: Topping. Faimalo. Maloney.
Goal: Goodwin.

Attendance: 13,852   Referee: Mr. G. Annesley - Sydney

Oldham Bears 20   North Queensland Cowboys 16 : July 18th 1997

Oh what a difference a month makes. Residing at the bottom of the Super League table one might have expected the Bears to cave in after the mauling they took in Queensland four weeks before - not a bit of it! This was a performance full of passion, concentration and sheer enthusiasm that put the Cowboys in their place.

Two- try Paul Davidson grabbed the headlines but there were 17 heroes who went some way towards redeeming the reputation of British rugby league in general and the Oldham club in particular on a wonderful night at Boundary Park. This time everything was different. The tackling was intense enough to restrict the Cowboys to three tries wide out. The handling was a vast improvement on the previous encounter and the goal kicking honours also went to the Bears with Luke Goodwin landing four shots to Luke Phillips' two. That said, Andrew Dunemann had a splendid game in the middle of the park, directing operations for the visitors, but the Goodwin / Martin Crompton partnership was also up to the task. The Oldham captain released Davidson with a peach of a pass for his first try.

The Cumbrian forward's two tries in the 26th and 76th minute were sandwiched around an effort from Brett Goldspink that was only allowed after lengthy consultation between the referee and in- goal touch judge. Meanwhile tries from Ray Mercy, Phillips and Paul Bowman, combined with the two goals from Phillips, left the scores level at 16 points each as the match moved into the last five minutes. Oldham gained possession in the Cowboys' half and most people both on the pitch and in the stands must have thought the Bears would keep it tight in the middle and then go for the drop goal. Not on this night. David Stephenson noticed that North Queensland were short on numbers on the narrow side and when Davidson called for the ball he duly sent it wide to the big second row forward. The Cumbrian still had much to do but he wasn't to be denied and crashed through two Australian defenders to score the match winner in the corner.

*Oldham winger **David Jones** is tied down by the Cowboys.*

OLDHAM:
P. Atcheson; A. Leuila, J. Cowan,
H. Hill, D Jones; L. Goodwin, M. Crompton;
B. Goldspink, J. Clarke, I. Gildart, P. Davidson, J. Faimalo, I. Russell.
Subs: D. Stephenson, P Topping, M Munro, G Lord.
Tries: Davidson,2. Goldspink.   **Goals:** Goodwin,4.

NORTH QUEENSLAND COWBOYS:
R. Cressbrook; J. Loomans, P. Bowman, R. Mercy, L. Phillips; J. Doyle, A. Dunemann;
J. Lomax, S.Walters, I. Roberts, P. Jones, O. Cunningham, L. Scott.
Subs: J. Death, J. Skarden, K. Warren, M. Shipway
Tries: Mercy, Phillips, Bowman.   **Goals:** Phillips,2.

Attendance: 2,961   Referee: Mr. R. Connolly - Wigan

Oldham Bears 2   Adelaide Rams 18:   July 25th 1997

Hopes were high for the Oldham faithful after the heroics of the previous week, but there was to be no repeat this time. Even though the Rams had to suffer a four- hour, trans-Pennine journey due to traffic problems, which delayed the kick-off by one hour, nothing was going to divert them from their task.

Oldham opened brightly and a Luke Goodwin penalty gave them an early lead. Adelaide responded and after fifteen minutes Bruce Mamando carved out an opening which culminated in Danny Grimley crossing in the corner. The Rams' game-plan was tough and uncompromising and Oldham met them with equal measure. Paul Atcheson caused Mamando to drop the ball over the Bears' line with a crunching tackle and there were other try-saving efforts from Goodwin and Paul Topping.

So, going into the second half trailing by just six points to two, there was still everything to play for. However, the game began to drift away from Oldham following a controversial incident. All evening the Rams had been impeding the Oldham players as they followed kicks downfield and after one such incident Howard Hill and Solomon Kiri were left trading punches. What happened next was that Oldham stopped and Adelaide didn't with the result that Steve Stone touched down for the Rams. After a lengthy consultation the try was allowed to stand, much to the astonishment of the Oldham players and supporters alike. Oldham tried to rally and after a superb break by David Jones, Topping put Paul Davidson clear only to fumble the return pass with the try-line open. The Bears had a try ruled out after Matt Munro followed a Martin Crompton "up-and-under" before the Rams wrapped up the match with a try by Wayne Simonds after a break by Jason Donnelly.

One must give great credit to the way Adelaide stuck to their task for this was a good Bears' performance by a team that put in as much effort and determination as the week before. I would say in all my years of watching rugby league I have never witnessed a more clinical "shut-out" of an Oldham team as that of the Adelaide Rams on that summer night.

OLDHAM BEARS:
P. Atcheson; A. Leuila, H. Hill, L. Goodwin, D. Jones; F. Maloney, M. Crompton;
B. Goldspink, J. Clarke, I. Gildart, J. Faimalo, P. Davidson, I. Russell.
Subs: P. Topping, G. Lord, M. Munro, D. Stephenson.
Goal: Goodwin.

ADELAIDE RAMS:
K. Wrigley; W. Simonds, S. Kiri, D. Grimley; L. Williamson, S. Topper;
A. Cann, S. Stone, K. Campion, A. Hick, B. Mamando, D. Broughton.
Subs: D. Schifilliti, E. Paiyo, B. Galea, C. Blair .
Tries: Grimley. Stone. Simonds.
Goals: Williamson,3.

Attendance: 3,513   Referee: Mr J Connolly - Wigan

An Australian flag greets the Adelaide Rams as they emerge from the Boundary Park tunnel.
Soon to be followed by ***Martin Crompton***, *leading out the Oldham Bears.*

Cowboys gunned dow
by Paul's two-try bla

PAUL Davidson, two-try hero of Oldham's inspiring defeat of the Cowboys, was motivated to smash the Australian team's defence by the need to repay a personal debt to the Bears management.

Chairman Jim Quinn and coach Bob Lindner stood by the 27-year-old Cumbrian (pictured right with Ian Gildart as the victory celebrations began) when he landed himself in trouble on the Bears trip to Australia in the first phase of the World Club Championship.

The chairman flew with him from Adelaide to Sydney and defended Davidson on a biting charge at a disciplinary hearing which found him guilty and banned him for three games.

Later, when the player was arrested and subsequently convicted of assault in an Adelaide court, the club closed ranks, dealt with the matter internally and restored Davidson to the team as soon as his ban was over.

And after his second consecutive two-try performance at Boundary Park on Friday, the man of the moment told how he would always be grateful to the men who stood by him in his darkest hours.

GREAT FEELING

"There was nothing intentional in the biting incident," he said, "and I pleaded guilty to the assault charge only because I would have been stuck in Australia for weeks had I contested it.

"The club stuck with me. I owed the club something tonight and I owed Bob Lindner something.

"I had a point to prove after what happened in Townsville. It was a great feeling to score our first try, but it was even sweeter to score the winner."

The Cowboys feared a Davidson backlash — and they got it.

He I
Crom!
but it
into r
ing he
With
groun
Bears
a field

SEVENTEEN Oldham Bears players did a remarkable PR job for club and country at Boundary Park on Friday night.

Fewer than 3,000 fans watched their epic 20—16 defeat of North Queensland Cowboys in the World Club Championship, but the stay-at-homes missed a treat.

With the Bears in Super League's bottom spot, a deafening silence on new-ground proposals and rumours that the club's Super League spot was in jeopardy anyway — since denied by the League — fans were demoralised last week.

But the loyalists who roared on the Bears from start to finish on a hot, steamy and memorable Boundary Park night were treated to a magnificent reward which

A NIGHT OF GREAT EMOTION TO LIFT THE SPIRITS OF LOYAL FANS

half Andrew Dunemann bossed the entire Cowboys performance with an impressive and influential display of creativity in midfield.

But the
until thei
their Aus
wide, all
Oldham
English-ty
scoring h

Davidson's tries in the 26th and 76th minutes further enhanced the growing reputation of the speedy Cumbrian as one of Super League's most improved players.

platform for David
lesser degree, Joe Fa
hard with the spe
running.

As for new-boy In
hour in his first gar
than a year and di
show that he is not
who believes he sho

Se
the
su
Cr

BEARS
and ski
ton hop
forman
boys w
season
Super
zone.
"We h
said Li
don't pa
our pe
Cowboy
throug
There i
can't."
Crom,
the turi
had t
Lindner
The
"Everyt
us last
insisted
our mi
"We k

THE SUN

Bite claim
NQ rampage

By DAVID POTTER

the way', midway through the first half.

It was one of a number of spiteful incidents in the first half of a game which again highlighted the world of difference between the Australian and European club teams.

Despite the 10 tries to three shellacking, Sheens, his opposite Bob Lindner and NQ captain Steve Walters were adamant the concept must remain.

"It's obviously not perfect, but definitely worth sticking with," Walters said.

"The games are not that far apart - honestly," said Lindner, who added that he expected the matches in England to be much closer.

Newspaper advertis

COWBOY
POM BA

From John Camplin
in Townsville

NORTH Queensland Cowboys coach Tim Sheens yesterday launched a double-barrelled blast against firstly some of his players and then the

SEE
NORTH QUEENSLAND
TACKLE SOME
POM POM GIRLS

Rams on track for finals

But victory does not come cheap

By WARREN PARTLAND

The Adelaide Rams last night took another crucial step towards a World Club Challenge finals spot with a 42-14 victory over Oldham at Adelaide Oval.

The triumph was the Rams' third successive hefty win after try-scoring feasts against Salford and Leeds and the side will now head to England next month to confront the same sides in return bouts.

Adelaide has amassed 126 points in the WWC and conceded 30 to have a healthy for-and-against record, the likely decider in which Australian side from Pool B goes through to the major round.

Victory last night, however, did not come cheaply with in-form winger Michael Maguire expected to be sidelined for up to five weeks with knee damage.

Adelaide grabbed seven tries but was forced to shrug off a spirited opponent, which defied the lengthy odds offered by bookmakers to test the home side with its own brand of attacking skill.

Oldham, despite coming to Adelaide a less credentialled side than either of the Rams' previous two English prey, refused to buckle under the Adelaide pressure and produced more than its share of flair and imagination with the ball to finish with three tries.

The Rams have conceded just three

forward Alan Cann takes some stopping last night at Adelaide Oval as he charges at the Oldham   Picture: PHIL HILLYARD.

finished with six goals from as many attempts in a superb display.

Adelaide's attack was frustrated in the second half by referee Graham Annesley's poor interpretation of the

Simonds and Leuila were both given 10 minutes in the sin-bin.

Oldham coach Bob Lindner, while lamenting missed opportunities in the first half, attributed much of the

game. Although we did improve about 60 per cent from last week's loss to North Queensland when I thought we looked a bit nervous.

"You can talk about this problem

"Oldham were by far the best team we have faced in the Challenge. They came at us very hard and threw everything at us."

Reddy accepted blame for a tactical error in the opening seconds of the game when the Rams, after receiving the kick-off, kicked the ball on the

respo
just f
five-c
fully.
Wil
for th
first g
has be

tion, Oldham
p their inten-
spected their
victory in any

(4); tries, Davidson
s— goals, Phillips

Ticket stub:
ERAM780
15MAY97
t# 1668
an415560

ADELAIDE OVAL
SUPER LEAGUE
CENTRELINE
RAMS V OLDHAM

ADULT
CENT1
B /102

FRI 20 JUN 1997 8:00PM
Section Row Seat
CENT1   B   102

EVENING CHRONICLE, OLDHAM, MONDAY, JUNE 23, 1997

Adelaide ram home a lesson in finishing

But battling Bears emerge with credit

ADELAIDE RAMS 42, OLDHAM BEARS 14

OLDHAM lifted the spirits of their travelling fans with a vastly-improved performance at the Adelaide Oval.

The score didn't reflect either the competitive manner in which the Bears took on their task, or the number of scoring chances they created with good rugby, only to finish poorly.

Goalkicking alone proved a major difference. The Rams landed seven goals from seven shots, including two by Luke Williamson and Kurt Wrigley off the touchline.

In stark contrast, Francis Maloney and Luke Goodwin both missed a relatively easy goal chance for the Bears to dim memories of similar failings up to Townsville.

"Goalkicking made a big difference to the score, if not the result," summed up Adelaide coach Rod Reddy.

So wasn't the only loss in the crowd of nearly 14,600 who were taken by surprise at the way in which Oldham tackled tenaciously on defence and moved the ball wide at every opportunity through the hands of Martin Crompton and slithery.

by ROGER HALSTEAD

side when Andrew Hick scored under the posts from a rebound.

"We were sure Hick picked up in an offside position," said Bears winger David Jones, "But the referee insisted he was played on-side because the kick hit an Oldham player in flight."

At best, there was a major element of luck about it and that was something else the Bears were not blessed with, particularly when they lost Matt Munro with a knee injury just before the inter-val.

Local journalists, home fans and the Rams themselves all agreed that the Bears did a far better job than either Salford or Leeds.

Said Reddy: "They came at hard early in the game and we had answered their first challenge they came at us again.

"We defended as well as at any other time this season and had to. And you have to give Oldham a lot of credit for that.

"Crompton showed a lot of skill and creativity. I was most impressed with him."

The Rams thought Oldham controlled the ball well. They did — to a point.

But after doing all the hard work to get a position in the home quarter they tended to get over-excited and put the ball to ground with try chances going begging.

SUPREMACY

DAMAGE

A PAIN in the neck for Joe Pairaito as the Bears man is stopped in his tracks by Rams tacklers.

orman has ugh start
Page 119

Socceroos thump Tahiti
Page 122

ent angers Sheens

S FEAR KLASH

ADELAIDE RAMS

WBOYS

Oldham RLFC (1997) Ltd

The Roughyeds

Oldham RLFC
(1997) Ltd
SEASON 2003

Tourists grab
last-gasp win

OLDHAM R.L.F.C.

NEY

NOVEMBER 2000

Australian leagues' representative sides visit Boundary Park

Whilst Wigan Warriors, St Helens, Bradford Bulls and Leeds Rhinos were lording it at the top end of Super League, Oldham's new coach Mike Ford had inherited a side that had ended the 1999 campaign next to bottom of the Northern Ford Premiership, but after strengthening the side with a whole raft of new signings the club ended the 2000 season in sixth position claiming a major semi-final play-off spot.

In November of 2000, as part of their preparations for the 2001 season, Oldham entertained a South Sydney league's representative side over here to champion the cause of the most famous and successful Australian club side in the history of the game - South Sydney Rabbitohs.

The club, in 1908, became founder members of the first Australian rugby league body - the New South Wales RL. They would be crowned Premiers on no less than a record 20 occasions – Champions to us Pommies – and produce 61 Australian internationals (five of whom skippered their country). Regardless of their illustrious past, twelve months earlier, they had been unceremoniously kicked out of the National Rugby League Championship, late victims of the Super League War

In December 1997 eleven clubs from the Australian Rugby League (ARL), including South Sydney, amalgamated with eight clubs from the recently- formed Super League and along with one new club, Melbourne, they formed a twenty club National Rugby League Championship. The league was gradually to be slimmed down to 14 clubs and on the 15th of October 1999 it was announced that Souths would be one of the last three clubs to be axed.

Despite them being clear of debt, and taking no consideration of their proud, proud record, Souths were dumped out of the league. Legal action was taken against the NRL and its two owners, albeit Souths failed to get a breakthrough. But persistence did pay off. Persistent protests, lobbying and further legal action ensured that, four years later, the Rabbitohs would take their rightful place in the 2003 NRL Premiership.

In November 2003, it was the turn of a side billing themselves as Manly Warringah to provide the opposition at Boundary Park. The NRL side Manly Warringah Sea Eagles had suffered a disastrous season, propped up in the league only by South Sydney! The touring side was made up primarily of younger players who had played the previous season in the Manly district and junior leagues was here in England, for no other reason than to further their playing experience.

At this time former Great Britain forward Steve Molloy was at the helm for the Roughyeds as player-coach, replacing Mike Ford, who had left to join the Ireland RU coaching team. The Premiership had been split into two divisions for the 2003 season with Oldham ending the campaign in fifth position, losing 38-24 away to Hull KR in the play-offs.

OLDHAM RLFC
v
MANLY WARRINGAH
Wednesday 19th November 2003
7.45 Kick-off

OLDHAM		MANLY
Gavin Dodd	1	Sam Foster
Nick Johnson	2	John Wilson
John Goddard	3	Matt Hill
Ian Marsh	4	Rob Toshack
Will Cowell	5	Neil Nacinovic
Simon Svabic	6	Nathan Smith
Neil Roden	7	Richie Plummer
Steve Molloy	8	Ricky Parker
Keith Brennan	9	Greg Armstrong
Martin McLoughlin	10	Steve Watene
Martin Elswood	11	Lee Phillips
Dave Newton	12	Jim Curtis
John Hough	13	Martin Cook (Capt)
Adam Clayton	14	Troy Osbourne
Gareth Barber	15	Paul Thackery
Gavin Johnson	16	Nathan Shatte
Dane Morgan	17	Zoey Hart
Adam Sharples	18	Ben Munro
James Lomax	19	Andrew White
Paul Bennett	20	Eugene Latimer
		Coach: Phil Foster

OFFICIALS
Referee: Phil Bentham
Touch Judges: Shaun Knowles, Bob Smithies

Since the Roughyeds reformed late in 1997, they have played two matches against Australian opposition. These were both played at Boundary Park. The first was on November 19th, 2000, when a team representing South Sydney took on Oldham and played out a 14-14 draw.

The playing conditions were awful, but a competitive match prevailed, with tries from Neil Roden and Gareth Barber along with three goals from Pat Rich producing Oldham's points.

Joe McNicholas gets gripped!
Action from the match against South Sydney in 2000.

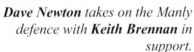

Dave Newton takes on the Manly defence with Keith Brennan in support.

Exactly three years later on November 19th, 2003 it was a side from the Manly district who again produced an exciting spectacle in another tight encounter.

It looked like once more the scores would finish level but a last minute drop goal from Nathan Smith gave the Aussies a 27 - 26 victory. Iain Marsh (2), Martin McLoughlin and Keith Brennan scored tries for Oldham, with three goals from Simon Svabic and two from Gareth Barber completing their scoring.

Portrait of Clive Churchill
by Robert Burns

Adam Sharples falls to a two-man tackle in the match against Manly in 2003.

"Quotes"

1908 – DALLY MESSENGER – RL08

"At Oldham, where we lost 11-5, we kicked-off all right. Then it started to snow. We couldn't feel any of our extremities. When we tried to pass the ball it was just like chucking a block of wood. To hit the ground sometimes was like landing on spiked granite. That's the famous day I played with 13 boils on my knee - I had to as we were starving to death as far as gates were concerned. Placards everywhere announced "Messenger will be playing". So it was up to Dally, with 13 boils on his knee, to do the martyr act. The public was a little disappointed with my game. But none of us had much of a chance after the snow came on."
'The Truth' newspaper, Sydney, undated newspaper cutting (courtesy of Sean Fagan / RL1908.com).

1921 – BILLY HALL – Press interview.
"When they scored the first try everyone stopped. We were sure we heard a whistle. It must have been in the crowd or from outside."

1929 – FRED ASHWORTH – quote from Benefit programme in 1938.
"The hardest game I ever played in was against the Australians in season 1928-9. We lost, but what a game. I went home after the club dinner and slept from 8 pm to 8 pm the next day."

1951 – FRANK STIRRUP –
Speaking on "Hall of Fame" CD and in June 2006:
"My second try was just like the first. Frank Daley said we should give the "dummy" move another go and it worked like a charm. As we walked back Daley said… 'I told you! These two will fall for the five card trick…' I think that game against the Kiwis in 1951 gave the club a tremendous lift and the success that followed was born out of that match."

1952 – JOE WARHAM – Speaking in May 2006:
" I remember the Australians kicking off and the ball being fielded by Arthur Tomlinson who was met by an enthusiastic and vigorous welcoming committee from the tourists. On rising to play the ball he found himself surrounded by approximately six Australians and immediately pointed out that they were all sons of convicts (or words to that effect) and would take them all on if they so desired." Joe also remembers Clive Churchill audibly barracking his own team manager during the after dinner speeches.

"Quotes"

1956 – SID LITTLE – Speaking in May 2006:
"I only remember that there was never an easy game against any team from Australia, New Zealand and South Africa in either code. The results in the games I played suggest Oldham had a fine side in the 1950s."

1956 – JOHN ETTY – Speaking in July 2006:
"After good attacking play by Derek Turner, I supported Frank Stirrup who gave me a perfect scoring pass after being held up in a tackle. Our forwards laid the foundation for the win. They dominated the opposite six."

1959 – VINCE NESTOR – Speaking in May 2006:
"The Fight! I think there were only me and Brian Pendlebury who weren't involved."

1961 – ALAN KELLETT – Speaking in June 2006:
"The idea that I was holding back for the county game is nonsense. When you step on the rugby field you are not just playing for yourself but for the team. Also, anything less than full effort could sometimes lead to injury."

1963 – DAVE PARKER – Speaking in June 2006:
"That game was my first experience of Australians in a sports context. There was never any doubt that they were physically hard, mean-minded and definitely there to win. I was pleased with my own game and the way I coped with Johnny Raper who had received some good reviews on the tour."

1963 – VINCE NESTOR – Speaking in May 2006:
"It was a tough match. I remember getting a hospital pass from Jackie Pycroft just as Harrison the Aussie stand-off was going to tackle."

1965 – DAVE PARKER – Speaking in June 2006:
"We thought going into the last quarter that one big effort would give us the win. Unfortunately, it wasn't to be but I thought we had been as good as them on the day. Our front-row of Bott, Taylor and Wilson played really well. A well-knit unit and three good tacklers as well."

"Quotes"

1965 – TREVOR WELLSMORE (tour manager)
Press interview Aug 31st 1965

"I know we were orthodox and the backs were rarely brought into the game. Nevertheless, with a young side out we were pleased at the way things went."

1967 – JOE COLLINS – Speaking in May 2006:
"As usual for "Sheddings" it was a cold, wet and windy Saturday on which the ball hardly reached Trevor Buckley and I on the wings. Our pack did all the graft and did it well."

1967 – JOHN DONOVAN – Speaking in July 2006:
"What I remember most about the match in 1967 was all the wives of the Oldham players ogling Reg Gasnier, and he wasn't even playing!"

1973 – JOHN BLAIR – Speaking in June 2006:
"I remember stepping inside Tim Pickup and setting off for the line. Graeme Langlands covered across but I just managed to get the ball down as he tackled me. Also, there was the confrontation between Terry Clawson and the Aussie props Artie Beetson and Bob O'Reilly. They were all no-nonsense lads and it carried on into the Test matches."

1975 - JOHN BLAIR – Speaking in June 2006:
"This was another tough encounter. I was up against Tom Raudonikis and found him to be a very strong and powerful player. When Johnny Patterson put Martin Murphy clear for his try Graham Eadie came in and 'cleaned him out' just as he passed the ball. This caused a bit of a melee, as they used to say."

1975 - GRAEME LANGLANDS - Press interview Nov 4th 1975:
"Oldham came back superbly to trim our lead and until the Raudonikis try, I believed they might snatch a draw. We murdered Salford and St Helens and without doubt Oldham were by far the best and toughest club side we have encountered."

"Quotes"

1975 - ARTIE BEETSON (non-playing captain) -
Press interview Nov 4th 1975:

"We under-estimated the strength of the opposition. I always felt we were in control but credit Oldham with a terrific show for a club side."

1986 – MARTIN BELLA –
Touchline interview during the match:

"The first scrum was a set-up. The call went out and they really got into us."

1986 - TERRY FLANAGAN -
Press interview November 4th 1986:

"We treated it like a Test match. As far as we were concerned we were representing Britain. There was some old fashioned English grit and courage."

1986 - STUART RAPER -
Press interview November 4th 1986:

"To set up that late try for Des Foy on such an occasion was the biggest thrill of my life. We promised we would give them a game … and I think we did."

1986 - DAVID TOPLISS -   Press interview November 1986:

"We played really well against the Australians. Our tackling, commitment and effort was fantastic and made the rest of the league sit up and take notice."

224